to Hellas and back

Lana Penrose was born, bred and raised in western Sydney, Australia. Her various incarnations include record company promotions manager, music journalist, television producer and personal assistant to the pop elite.

At the time of writing, Lana alternates between Athens and Sydney and doesn't really know where she belongs in the world any more. But she is still known to arrive home late at night and dance wildly to KISS in front of the mirror.

For more information, go to www.myspace.com/firewoman111

PENGUIN BOOKS

Lana Penrose

to **Hellas** and **back**

PENGUIN BOOKS

Published by the Penguin Group
Penguin Group (Australia)
250 Camberwell Road, Camberwell, Victoria 3124, Australia
(a division of Pearson Australia Group Pty Ltd)
Penguin Group (USA) Inc.
375 Hudson Street, New York, New York 10014, USA
Penguin Group (Canada)
90 Eglinton Avenue East, Suite 700, Toronto, Canada ON M4P 2Y3
(a division of Pearson Penguin Canada Inc.)
Penguin Books Ltd
80 Strand, London WC2R 0RL, England
Penguin Ireland
25 St Stephen's Green, Dublin 2, Ireland
(a division of Penguin Books Ltd)
Penguin Books India Pvt Ltd
11 Community Centre, Panchsheel Park, New Delhi – 110 017, India
Penguin Group (NZ)
67 Apollo Drive, Rosedale, North Shore 0632, New Zealand
(a division of Pearson New Zealand Ltd)
Penguin Books (South Africa) (Pty) Ltd
24 Sturdee Avenue, Rosebank, Johannesburg 2196, South Africa

Penguin Books Ltd, Registered Offices: 80 Strand, London, WC2R 0RL, England

First published by Penguin Group (Australia), 2007
This edition published by Penguin Group (Australia), 2008

10 9 8 7 6 5 4 3 2 1

Cover design by Kirby Stalgis © Penguin Group (Australia)
Text design by Elizabeth Dias and Kirby Stalgis © Penguin Group (Australia)
Front cover photograph of author by Steven Chee, background photo by Getty Images
'Gorecki' lyrics on pp. 159–60 copyright © Alfred Publishing, reprinted with kind permission
Typeset in 12/16.5 pt Fairfield by Post Pre-press Group, Brisbane, Queensland
Printed and bound in Australia by McPherson's Printing Group, Maryborough, Victoria

National Library of Australia
Cataloguing-in-Publication data:

Penrose, Lana.
To hellas and back.
ISBN 9780143007715 (pbk).
Penrose, Lana.
Australians – Greece – Biography.
Journalists – Australia – Biography.
Greece – Social life and customs.

949.5076

penguin.com.au

For Geoffrey

Prologue

Barely acknowledging the azure Aegean that laps close to my doorstep, I tape another cardboard box. The sound of ripping packing tape reverberates off concrete walls and marble floors, drowning out the sound of choking sobs. I'm not entirely sure why I'm crying, whether they're tears of relief or sadness or both.

I'm distracted by a shadow that looms large across the red tiled, sun-streaked verandah outside. The shadow belongs to one of my closest companions: an enormous, filthy grey and white dreadlocked cat that appears to have emerged from the depths of hell itself. Grateful for the diversion, I take a moment to step outside and make another feeble attempt to stroke his mottled fur. Fixing me with a ferocious gaze that threatens my very existence, he assumes pounce position, his dull yellow eyes locked on mine, daring me to step closer. I notice his whiskers are knitted together by blackened cobwebs and that a burr protrudes stupidly from a grey bottom lip. Although in many ways frightening, he looks quite ridiculous. I feel a vague sense of affection for him, even sympathy, yet on some level I'm also a little offended by him. It's a familiar feeling. It's similar to the way I feel about Greece.

Looking back over my time in Athens I'm unsure whether I can best describe my experience as a comedy or a tragedy. When my boyfriend, Dion, was offered work in the birthplace of modern civilisation, we considered it a marvellous opportunity. We were young and in love and happily threw caution to the wind for a chance to experience life from a different angle. But just how obtuse that angle would turn out to be, we hadn't a clue, and for that we dearly paid.

Now, sitting on dirty tiles next to a cat that would rather puncture a lung than have me near, I know I have a story to tell; the story of a quasi-normal Australian couple whose mettle was put to the test against one of the world's most alluring backdrops.

Many have fallen in love with the majesty of this region and felt moved to express themselves through heartfelt prose, poetry and sporadic bursts of interpretive dance. My story, however, is a little different. It's a story written from a culturally electrified perspective, by a girl who may as well have crash-landed from another planet. An ignorant girl who the Dark Mistress of the Aegean deemed fit to wrestle until one of us screamed, 'Theo!' It is also written by a girl not to be defeated.

I reflect upon Greece as a type of mystery woman who's at times sophisticated, beautiful, warm and kind, but at other times, through distorted vision, one hell of a bitch! On this day in particular, I see her only as talon-clawed and cruel – *everything* is her fault.

I give up on the great mistake of the animal kingdom at my ankles, and resume taping up boxes with gusto and determination. The bitch hasn't quite won yet.

Act 1

But go away, do not anger me, that you may return safer.
Homer, *The Iliad*

I was made for lovin' you

I remember the night of the phone call. I was sitting cross-legged on the floor in front of the television, absent-mindedly inhaling a bowl of bolognaise, when the phone rudely interrupted an edge-of-your-seat episode of *Sale of the Century*. I had no intention of answering it. I was far too engrossed in Glenn Ridge's suit as spaghetti lashed against my cheeks and disappeared with a wriggle down my oesophagus. My eternally patient Greek-Australian boy-friend, Dion, was therefore forced to hopscotch over two plates of food and pirouette between an array of condiments laid out on the floor of our tiny rented Sydney apartment to take the call. Evening floor picnics had somehow become a peculiar nightly ritual, and, as far as I was aware, we were the only couple receiving carpet burns as a result of consuming our evening meals.

I distinctly recall becoming more and more agitated that night as Dion's phone conversation unfolded. I mean, how in blaze's name could I possibly concentrate on *Sale* above all that racket? My boyfriend hung up, hovered dumbfounded, and waited politely for an ad break.

'I think I've just been offered a job!' he finally blurted.

'*What?* Where? Doing what?'

'Would you believe me if I said in another country?'

Dion went on to explain that there was a position going for a radio station manager in the Greek capital of Athens.

'What do you make of that? Fancy living in sunny Greece for a while?' he invited cheerfully.

I do believe my initial, well thought-out response to this life-altering proposal was, and I quote:

'Greece, huh? Sure! Why not!'

I paused. Dion blinked at me, doe-like, slightly confused by my flippancy. His expression begged for elaboration. So I complied.

'I mean, I don't know about you, but I'm pretty adaptable.' I paused again, my mind setting sail on a tangent, as it is wont to do. 'Hey, remember in the movie *Grease* when Olivia Newton-John *vomited* after Frenchy pierced her ear?' I chuckled and then threw in a succession of 'Born to Hand Jive' moves that I'd learned from the movie.

Dion half-laughed, but the questioning look upon his face remained.

When I think back to this moment, it's so much more than all the hand-jiving that nauseates me. It's the words 'I'm adaptable' that rattle most menacingly. Throughout the years, I've replayed them often with a view to taunting myself half to death. Each time, they've echoed, dream-sequence style, through the corridors of my mind as though I'm trapped in a cheesy daytime television drama.

'I'm adaptable, adaptable, *adaptable* . . .'

Pffffft. Give me a friggin' break! *Sure* I was adaptable! Why, I'd lived in London for a whole minute back in those heady, backpacking days. Athens couldn't be much different, right? I'd even been to Athens on the way to the alcohol-soaked party island of Ios. *Twice.* In fact, I'd been to a whole *host* of Greek islands during my years of wanderlust. What could possibly be so difficult about moving to Athens? I already had it nailed. I returned my finger to its imaginary buzzer and resumed my *Sale of the Century* game playing.

You see, around this time I'd been working hard days and nights producing MTV News. A typical 'record' day would see me shocked awake by a screaming alarm clock at 5 a.m. I'd snap out of bed, tie my dirty hair back, punch a wall in aggravation over my lack of time and personal hygiene, and zip off to the studios to finalise the day's news scripts. Many hours later, a presenter would surface, yawn, go into hair and make-up and fall one step short of having my hand shoved up her arse as I puppeteered as required.

On top of this, I was also the talent and relations manager. This meant that I was the lucky soul who got to liaise with record companies and various MTV department heads to determine who should and shouldn't be interviewed by the network. In between such important deliberations, my fellow producers, production assistants and I spent much of our time turning up the volume on television monitors to drown out assaults from a loud stereo, edit suites and each other. We'd also entertain ourselves with show reels from on-air hopefuls, try and fail to keep track of office romances, throw missiles over cubicle walls, swear a lot and send covert emails to one another that often inexplicably featured Rottweilers. Over the years within this asylum I'd undoubtedly had the most fun I'd ever had during my working life. My colleagues had fast become more than people I worked with; they were like family.

At radio station Triple M, Dion was having the time of his life too, doling out complimentary icy-cold cans of Coke and nonstop blocks of rock like an unmercifully sponsored rock'n'roll Santa. However, at the ripe old age of thirty, my boyfriend was definitely one of the most ambitious guys in Australian radio. He loved his job, but aimed high, his aim no doubt fuelled by the fact that he was a

Capricorn and that his girlfriend was on a higher salary. Fortunately for Dion, by the time he'd received the Great Grecian 2000 Job Offer, despite all the MTV frivolities, I was growing work weary. I'd begun fantasising about what it might be like to spend quality time alone rather than on the phone with the German Embassy to discern the correct pronunciation of the band name Rammstein, and I was tired of posing inane questions to the illustrious and not-so-illustrious of the rock and pop world as they stared back at me like I was a fuckwit. Even bang in the middle of shielding myself from the blinding whiteness of Jon Bon Jovi's teeth, I caught myself dreaming of a less hectic lifestyle.

So not long after Dion's intriguing phone call, I could be seen prancing about our living room with George Michael's 'Freedom' on high rotation in my mind. I'd just learned that I wasn't permitted to work legally in Greece, and Dion had happily volunteered himself as breadwinner. At thirty-two years of age, I was being granted the opportunity to put short-term retirement plans into action. And I was freakin' *chuffed*!

If I'd had any sense, however, I would have put a finger to my cheek and cast my mind back four years, to a time before Dion and I were united as a fabulous couple. In those days, Dion was music director at radio station 104.7 in Canberra and I was a promotions manager at Sony Music in Sydney. It was my job to cajole him into adding Sony tracks to his play-list, mostly achieved by way of paying multiple unwarranted compliments and laughing hysterically at jokes devoid of humour.

One day, I'd called him to arrange flights to a Sony Music hip-hip-hooray fest and he'd confided a secret.

'My surname isn't actually "Summers". That's my *radio* name. See, my *real* surname's too difficult for radio. For the sake of the booking, you should know that it's actually . . . Giamoreyos.'

'Huh?'

'Giamoreyos.'

'Gamma-Ray-Us? What?'

'*Giamoreyos.*'

'Are you a Trekkie?'

'No.'

'How do you spell it?'

'G. I. A. M. O. R. E. Y. O. S.'

'Oh!' I exclaimed. 'Is that . . . Italian?'

'Italian? No! What? No, it's *Greek*. My parents are Greek.'

Soon after, he revealed that his parents had migrated to Australia from the mysterious Greek island of Lesbos in the 1950s. And not long after that, he also revealed that his *full* name was in fact *Dionysios* Giamoreyos. If I'd been aware of this precious, little-known fact from the start, I'd of course have laughed childishly, and constantly said things like, 'What was that, *DIONYSIOS*? Did you say something, *DIONYSIOS*? Ha ha ha! Your name sounds funny!' I would have laughed even harder had I known he was named after a one-legged, club-footed uncle who had fallen down a hole to meet his maker on Lesbos circa 1962.

So, if I'd thought about the repercussions of moving to Greece a little more, I'd have realised that with a secret name like Dionysios Giamoreyos, a cultural understanding of Greece and a dormant knowledge of the Greek language, Dion had a distinct head start when it came to integrating comfortably into a Hellenic lifestyle.

Pre-romance – when Dionysios Giamoreyos was simply 'Dion Summers' and we'd shared a strictly professional relationship – he'd had a penchant for scabbing as much free promotional material from Sony Music via yours truly as possible. Despite his unrestrained kleptomania, we forged an immediate kinship. We had both grown up in Sydney's west, a part of the urban sprawl that is a cocktail of race, religion, under-age drinking and sporadic violence. The fact that we were both from parts of the city that were looked down upon by the elite gave us an environmental common denominator that bonded us as westies and friends.

Such humble beginnings made Dion down to earth, on top of being charming, affable and kind-hearted. He was the opposite of worldly in his naivety and possessed a certain irresistible innocence. To top it all off, he also happened to be tall, dark and handsome. With the brooding good looks typical to many of European extraction, he was difficult to resist. But resist I did. Never mind his sparkling brown eyes, olive skin and milky-white perfect smile. It took months before I caved and finally accepted one of his constant pleas to go out with him on a date. At the time we were both in our mid-twenties, or maybe *I* was closer to my late twenties, but who was counting?

It was soon the eve of our first night out and Dion rocked up right on time wearing attire that scared the living shit out of me. There he stood at my front door unashamedly resplendent in a black silk vest worn over a dress shirt. He was also armed with a bunch of blood-red roses, which he enthusiastically thrust in my face, the act seeming like an overture preceding a serenade on bended knee. I stared at the vest.

'You ready, gorgeous?' he sang merrily as his glistening eyes danced.

I coughed as a diversion. Through our various work-related rock'n'roll encounters, I'd grown accustomed to seeing Dion in fitted T-shirts and jeans, and rather preferred things stayed that way. As we ate dinner that night in the inner-city suburb of Balmain, he tried desperately to come across as full of life and hilarious.

'Do you like Thai? I *wear* ties, you know.'

I stared uncomfortably at the menu, taking refuge in the fact that he had a steamy, velvet-soft radio voice that purred from his breath. Unfortunately, his nervous attempts at humour proved overwhelming, and the night ended with serious reservations on my part. But as I would soon learn, Dion wasn't one to give up easily. Not long after, a pair of tickets to see KISS perform at the Sydney Entertainment Centre slid onto my desk at Sony with a note scrawled in convulsive, infantile writing:

'You. Me. KISS.'

Call me fickle but in an instant the guy had completely redeemed himself. KISS just so happened to be my all-time favourite rock band and had been since I was twelve. A lifelong member of the KISS Army, I had to stop myself daily from applying KISS make-up, ingesting blood capsules and stomping about in stack-heeled boots. From that moment forward, Dion could do no wrong. At the concert, we sang every word to every song in between vomit-like chortles over Paul Stanley's camp theatrics and Gene Simmons' demonic blood-spluttering. I sure knew something – I was beginning to fall for this guy.

Nightly, Dion whispered down a Canberra to Sydney telephone line and I drank in his rich, hot-chocolate tones. 'You know I was sent to look after you, don't you?'

'Oh, my God! That's so beautiful!'

I had no idea what the guy was on about. But I did know that he was thoroughly romantic and I was being gently swept off my feet and wrapped in love's silken tendrils. Like an angel, Dion showered me with warmth and reassurance. And so steadfast was his belief that I was 'The One', the light he relentlessly shone eventually burst through the clouds. This felt like something more than falling in love. It felt like destiny.

Soon divine intervention played its part and Dion was offered a job at Triple M in Sydney. We promptly moved in with one another, our hearts opened cavernously and we fell deliciously in love.

Four years later, after experiencing many close encounters of the Greek kind, I still felt worlds apart from Dion's parents. We didn't really know one another; or rather than *know*, a better word might be *get*. They were in their mid-sixties and, despite half a century in Australia, they still conformed to a strict Greek way of life amidst the multiculturalism of western Sydney. When it came to their own flesh and blood they were amazingly giving, hardworking and dedicated. They particularly enjoyed becoming involved in family matters, which was all well and good, unless it got all weird, which it often did.

Dion's mother, Katerina, was a handsome, talkative woman, full of life and obsessed with domesticity and all things Greek Orthodox. She possessed a classical Greek beauty, and her dark, flashing eyes conveyed a kind of 'wary friendliness' whenever we united at the kitchen sink. I rarely saw her without a gold crucifix around her neck or a cooking utensil in her hand. I, on the other hand, wasn't exactly known for my religious dedication or adept tomato-cutting skills. I was therefore regarded with grave suspicion. So I tried to make it all better. I tried to make myself at least interesting, if not lovable, revealing insights into my life that were always politely ignored. Conversations would be effortlessly steered back to cooking, ironing sprays or factory outlet bargains, without anyone noticing – except me. It seemed that talk of African adventures or celebrity eccentricities didn't factor into a world that revolved around sons, wives, grandchildren, extended family, fruit, vegetables, cleaning, gardening and bulk-bought poultry. Sometimes I felt that I didn't exactly factor into that world either.

Dion's father, Kostas, was a quiet, rotund man with flushed

cheeks and an enduring twinkle in his eye rivalled only by his son's. He always had a ready smile and was extremely friendly. Unlike Katerina, he spoke very little English, but certainly knew his place as the family patriarch. He served his family well, and in return his wife served *him* well with unwavering subservience. When it came to *me* and subservience though, forget it! I was careful to keep up appearances around Katerina and produce the odd hankie as required. But I let Dion know from Day One that when it came to me licking his shoes clean, he'd have more chance of receiving council approval to knock down the Sydney Opera House and replace it with a Paddle-Pop-stick replica of the Parthenon. Katerina sensed my aversion to domestic slavery and resented it.

'Men no clean, the gerlls a-clean! But I no say *notheeng*,' she'd often croak.

I gathered early on in the piece that, in her eyes, my upkeep of her son was all wrong. And lazy. And typically Australian.

At Giamoreyos family gatherings, of which there were plenty, I could usually be found shirking in a corner somewhere as Greek music filtered through cheap 1980s tape decks.

'Has anyone seen Lana?' Dion would enquire of one of a dozen cousins loitering on the fringes of an exclusively male assembly protected by a testosterone force-field.

'Nah, but what *I* wanna know is this: Why doesn't Triple M play The Floyd's "Dogs"? Classic, mate! I don't give a rat's arse if it's twenty minutes long. You're the music director, right? You can do whatever you want.'

Dion would look around distractedly, only half-listening.

'And don't get me started on Vangelis again, man,' the cousin would continue. 'He's one of our finest. Christ, we've been down this road before. He's progressive *rock*. Your station *plays* rock. Why. Don't. Youse. Play. Vangelis?'

As his cousin searched desperately for someone to back him up, Dion would take this as his cue to extract himself from the conversation. That's when he'd usually find me pressed up against the side of the garage, hiding. His face would visibly soften.

'There you are!'

He'd gently wrap his large protective hands around my waist and give me a soft kiss. I'd then relax and remember why I was there in the first place: because I was in love with a kind-hearted prince who I was certain would give his life for me.

'What are you doing back here, babe? Why aren't you in the kitchen where you belong?' he'd tease.

Simply put, Dion got me and I got him, and we had a remarkable ability to laugh off things that weren't really all that funny. Our stolen kisses would usually be interrupted by hoarse calls from Katerina that heralded . . . 'The Circle'. And this was when I'd become *really* uneasy as Dion led me by the hand towards his extended family. Flapping madly from outside the human circumference, Katerina would beckon her three sons to join 'The Circle' as music wailed via tinny speakers and attendees danced ring-a-ring-a-rosy style, connected by tightly clutched handkerchiefs. With white knuckles aimed skyward, crazy legs would scissor below. I'd remain on the outside, forcing myself to tap a foot and clap.

This scenario – played out in open garages, yards and driveways across suburbia – left me feeling awkward, like an interloper, possibly because I was. Being half Maltese and half Australian, the only 'Greek' I had in me was Dion. I'd never seen anything even close to this before, and nor had the passing neighbours who slowed to a snail's pace to more closely inspect the unannounced cultural exhibition taking place in their street.

Dion would usually do a little dance to meet expectations and then reposition himself close by my side, which I found greatly reassuring. Never before had I had a boyfriend who cared so deeply about my comfort levels. And Dion wasn't into all this traditional Greek stuff anyway. His outlook was Australian, to the point where he was usually more preoccupied with whether he'd added enough Australian content to his radio station's play-list. As *bouzoukia* squealed in the background, Dion could only hear in his mind guitar riffs from The Angels, AC/DC, Midnight Oil and Cold Chisel.

The longer we went out, the more that nights like these began to dominate our social calendar. Before then, a typical night out for us had involved seeing bands, bumping into friends, going to bars, and spurting streams of alcohol and obscenity into the face of my beloved MTV boss before dropping a glass and breakdancing with colleagues on an alcohol-soaked dance floor. The chasm between these crazy rock'n'roll nights and Greek family festivities might help explain why I'd taken to sneaking around corners and pressing myself up against garages at family get-togethers.

In between dancing up a storm in 'The Circle', Katerina would ricochet off the walls like the silver ball in a pinball machine. She'd prepare food in three kitchens simultaneously for up to ten hours at a time. I repeat – *three* kitchens for up to *ten* hours. I'm not even exaggerating. And on many occasions I'd witness an Oedipal relationship play out before my very eyes, where Dion would be lifted to demigod status as his dear mother fell just short of chewing up, swallowing and regurgitating food into his mouth for ease of consumption. I found all of this highly disturbing, to say the least. But Dion didn't seem to mind it at all.

By comparison, family get togethers at my parents' house were much more subdued. We'd usually visit Mum and Dad on a Sunday and, along with my three younger brothers, salivate like starving hyenas over the smell of roasting lamb as we got stuck into Dad's cheap wine. Food preparation was more of a communal affair where we each contributed in our own special way: Mum would do the roasting, I'd do the peeling, a brother would set the table, another would carve the meat (and sample half the carcass) while another would slip peas into our drinks after Dad had poured the wine. To varying degrees, we'd then all help clear up.

Like Dion, I came from a loving, supportive family, but in my case our clan was presided over by a beer-guzzling Aussie battler with an unparalleled passion for the outdoor barbecue and rugby league. My beautiful olive-skinned mother was a strong-willed woman who cried tears when she laughed. She had emigrated from Malta to Australia when she was four.

I can safely say that both Mum and Dad adored Dion. Sometimes Dion would become so overwhelmed by emotion, he'd sweep me up in a bear-hug embrace and squeeze the air from my lungs right in the middle of their kitchen. He'd then let out a small shriek, which I'd reciprocate – respiration permitting. He and my mother would exchange warm smiles. Mum's smiles would become laughs, and then the inevitable downpour would follow, her face streaked with happy tears. She knew I was in good hands, as did my father.

My folks had brought up my brothers and me with a 'give it a go' attitude and I suppose it's for this reason that I grew to be a rather adventurous adult. In my twenties I'd traversed the globe several times, lived in countless different apartments, and changed jobs whenever the mood suited. I guess that's why I hand-jived at the prospect of moving to Greece in the first place.

2

Should I stay or should I go?

As I deliberated over what would be my third stint living abroad – having lived in London on two earlier occasions – I made a solo visit to my parents. Mum went quiet in preparation for yet another disappearing act by her wayward daughter, her deep brown eyes turning sad and glassy, while I sought the wise counsel of my father. With dedicated expertise, he was turning marinated meat on the barbecue with one hand and bringing a beer to pursed lips with the other. I posed my question to him as though he was an oracle whose insights were induced courtesy of Victoria Bitter. I watched and waited. He swiftly set the can down beside the grill with impressive dexterity.

'Struth, nearly lost that chop. I dunno, Lana. Do you really wanna do this?'

He looked at me quizzically, his uncombed grey hair bowing to the right as he absent-mindedly rubbed marinade all over his favourite, filthy red jersey. He'd been modelling this particular item of clothing for quite some time. Paint streaks still adorned it from when he'd redecorated my bedroom in 1974.

'I don't know. I want to go, but I don't as well. Know what I mean? What do you think I should do?'

'Is it serious enough with Dion?'

Dad looked at me expectantly, ocean-blue eyes intense, tongs in one hand, beer can back where it belonged in the other.

'It's been four years, Dad! Yes! Of course it's serious.'

'Well, might as well then, I s'pose. He's a great bloke. What have you got to lose?'

Dad looked at me. I nodded. And that was that.

Mr and Mrs Giamoreyos, on the other hand, took a different approach. Despite being as Greek as could be, they were against the idea of us moving to Greece to the point of utter mortification.

There were tears.

'You no LEAVE!'

There were long-winded debates.

'YOU no leave!'

There were actual *fights*.

'You NO leave!'

My parents weren't exactly tickled pink either, but let's just say they were a little less 'expressive'. As far as Katerina and Kostas were concerned, sure they adored Greece, but why we'd opt to live in a place they remembered as poor, if not volatile, was beyond their comprehension. To my surprise, they put an incredible amount of pressure on Dion to stay in Sydney. It was made very clear they didn't want their youngest son living on the other side of the world. Further, they didn't want their baby boy left in the care of a Skippy girl who couldn't effectively dice an onion – well, Katerina didn't anyway.

Family opinions aside, Dion and I came to a final decision all by ourselves by drawing up a list of pros and cons. I, of course, guffawed at the irony of the column headed 'con'. But finally we thought *Screw it, why the hell not?* This was an amazing opportunity for Dion and by this stage we would have followed one another to the ends of the earth.

So, four weeks before departure, we got down to the task of packing and completely rearranging our lives. I passed the days merrily, fuelled by the prospect of an extended holiday and thinking more about sunbathing beneath a vivid Athenian sun than anything practical. At the same time, Dion's adrenalin positively pumped with anticipation and ambition. In a good way, we were both pretty much tripping out.

Although it took only three seconds to write the word 'pack' on our 'To Do' list, it felt as though we were destined to devote the rest of our lives to crossing it off. Forever sidetracked by the discovery of a yo-yo or an amazingly bouncy rubber ball that ricocheted off bathroom surfaces, the days flew by.

Another job on the list was telling everyone we knew of our decision. Reactions fell roughly into three categories: Happy (articulated by those who called us 'lucky bastards'); Disinterested (via those who changed the subject to bullying in the workplace); and Sad (delivered by those prone to imitating babies' voices).

Day and night, the packing continued. Dion arranged the necessary permits to live and work in Greece through the Greek Consulate, all the while convincing himself that the vague yet complex instructions provided by its consular representatives were in no way indicative of Greece's bureaucratic practices.

In the meantime, I hit the World Wide Web to research the country we would soon inhabit. This thorough exploration resulted in a suppressed shriek that marked the discovery that in Athens, chucking paper into a toilet bowl was *not* a given. In some instances, *bins* were used to allow for fragile plumbing, which led to the obvious conclusion that the city did not possess the basic infrastructure for human survival. I made an urgent dash to the supermarket to stock up on all of life's necessities, inexplicably including a dozen or so coat hangers and enough Cherry Ripes to inspire Veruca Salt to renounce her allegiance to chocolate forever.

While I ruthlessly scoured the confectionery section, Dion did a further Internet search and found basic Greek words which he burned onto a CD for my listening pleasure. Once home, I sat and listened, intrigued by a heavily accented voiceover on top of a *baglamas* sound bed that sounded like a baby bouzouki in the throes of strangulation. As I listened, my mind drifted. I visualised my 'teacher' as a fat, balding, moustached man riding a donkey side-saddle as he strummed, plucked and tutored. Not only did this idea amuse me, I also quickly learned how to say 'hello' and 'pencil'.

After three frantic weeks, all was almost in order. Wistfully, we looked out of our tenth-floor Vaucluse apartment window to soak up a view that in just one week would no longer be ours: dramatic cliff faces and crashing waves, a view typical of Sydney's eastern suburbs. Holding hands, we stared out to sea for a very long time that day, as though trapped in a poignant Michael Bolton video clip.

Despite my initial flippancy, as our departure date loomed, grave doubts began to surface that extended beyond plumbing concerns. Rather than drifting about assured that things would magically fall into place, I actually became nervous. How would I function in this new civilisation? How would I cope with leaving everything I knew and loved behind? *How would I fucking speak?* It became a case of 'bye bye, friends, family and job, and hello gaping vortex of uncertainty burping with whiffs of souvlaki'. I felt flutters in my belly, like I'd been pushed way too hard on a swing.

What in God's name are we doing?

Dion simply floated about in a state of perpetual optimism,

stopping every now and then to wrestle me to the ground and tickle me half to death. Once the laughter and pleas 'for the love of God *stop!*' had subsided, I suggested we pay a visit to Sydney's Powerhouse Museum to check out an Olympic Games exhibit. Thematically, there was a strong Greek component and I hoped it would somehow offer inspiration, perhaps even an answer.

While browsing the displays, our arms placed reverently behind our backs as is compulsory when viewing boring exhibits, we happened upon a giant wall-mounted aerial shot of Athens. It depicted a sprawling white mess that looked as though a flock of seagulls had excreted en masse over a series of undulating hills. To me it seemed horrifying, a scene that even Alfred Hitchcock couldn't have envisaged during production of *The Birds*. In that instant, the enormity of being thrust into alien territory punched me square in the jaw and I promptly burst into tears. Although onlookers gave me a wide berth, Dion didn't notice – he was too engrossed in a plaque commemorating a fragment of Greek history. I pulled myself together before he realised anything was amiss, glad that he was the only bugger in the place not to witness my outburst. I didn't want to freak him out. I *had* to remain positive.

In the car later, I recounted all the plusses associated with our impending move, for my sake if nobody else's. I cleared my throat.

'You know, Dion, I've always been a massive fan of change, and we're about to embark upon one hell of a crazy adventure, hey?'

'We sure are, babe. It's unbelievable!'

'And we'll have the Greek islands at our disposal. How magic is *that*?'

'Can you believe it?'

'We're about to live in *Europe*, too. We're so bloody lucky, right?'

'Aren't we ever!'

I began to feel more at ease.

'And what about your job! This is going to be so great for your career!'

'Yes, yes it is. And soon it shall all be mine!' Dion threw back his head and let out the exaggerated, sinister laugh of a villain hell bent on world domination. I was soon drowning out his laughter with villainous mirth of my own.

Once again we went over our plan. Dion would gain further experience in the radio world. I'd rest, then re-emerge rejuvenated like a fire-breathing phoenix ready to conquer the next phase of my career. Dion would play working man and guardian angel. I'd play the 'behind every great man, there has to be a great woman' role. I looked upon the upcoming year as a sabbatical licked with the promise of adventure, safe in the knowledge that Australia was a mere twenty-four hours away.

It was Y2K and as athletes demonstrated incredible sporting prowess at the Sydney 2000 Olympic Games, our only race was against time. Australian patriotism had reached alarming heights. Grown men were publicly weeping over beer commercials that celebrated the meat pie and the Hill's Hoist rotary clothesline. And that was just the tip of the iceberg. We were also wallowing in the praise of the world press for our exceptional organisational skills. Everybody loved everything and everyone 'Austray-yan'. Our Olympic athletes became deities. Ian Thorpe, aka 'The Thorpedo', was unstoppable in the swimming pool. The whole city was partying, and while it was in full swing it seemed Dion and I had a curfew.

Amidst all the revelry we found ourselves wandering Kingsford Smith Airport, surrounded by stuffed wombats and all manner of kitsch Australiana. As luck would have it, a slow, gut-wrenching rendition of Peter Allen's 'I Still Call Australia Home' was being piped through the airport audio system as we proceeded to immigration – a subliminal effort to ensure the safe return of all Australian nationals. We marched slowly, as though approaching the gallows. Reality had finally sunk in. This was it. We were blindly jetting off into the unknown. Dion and I looked at each other and held hands tightly. Dion's palms began to sweat and the roller-coaster feeling returned to my stomach. There was no turning back. Our future was a blank canvas. And I prayed like mad that it wouldn't be painted multiple shades of brown.

At our request, none of our friends or family came to see us off. We were worried that some might cause a scene. And by 'some', I of course refer to Katerina. Nevertheless, just before boarding our flight, Dion put in a frantic call to his mother for a final goodbye and a quick refresher course on how to count to ten in Greek.

'YOU NO LEAVE!'

It was to be Dion's first trip overseas.

There was plenty of time to come to terms with the decision we'd made during the thirty hours it took us to get to Greece. Dion and I busied ourselves with earphones and volume controls, never once mentioning our destination country. We'd become lost in our own cerebral holding patterns. We sat staring at our glowing screens, dehydrated, swollen and delirious. We hardly spoke a word.

By the time we finally touched down in Athens, I'd completely lost the plot, barely aware of who I was, where I was, or what year it was. I began to ponder the important things in life, like why people so willingly embrace the Chicken Dance during celebratory moments. We disembarked feeling like chewed-up and spat-out pieces of meat that had been hidden behind sofa cushions for several years.

The egos had landed.

3

Greece is the word

The airport terminal was old, run-down and stiflingly hot. Moustached men sat chain-smoking and staring expressionlessly into a far-off void, their smoke swirling across streams of afternoon sunshine. With its orange plastic seats lining the walls, the terminal looked more like a school canteen in which somebody had activated a smoke machine.

Dazed and confused, Dion and I trudged to the baggage reclaim area where a prewar conveyer belt spat out suitcases and clumsily taped cardboard boxes with big, black foreign words scrawled across them in uneven handwriting. After thirty minutes, everything had been collected bar a lone unlabelled plastic shopping bag knotted at the top and doing an encore circuit. The terminal was all but empty. Dion stood with his suitcase by his side looking tired and lost. I stood by Dion's side, looking tired, my *suitcase* lost. Wearily we looked at one another.

Now what?

We found what we guessed was a lost-luggage counter attended by a young and attractive woman. A half-empty frappe sat on the counter before her, the top half of the receptacle murky with streaks of dirty brown foam. This was to be our first face-to-face contact with an Athenian on Greek soil. Unfortunately, however, there was no trace of her ever having supped upon the milk of human kindness, although she'd apparently had more than her fair share of frappes.

I got the impression that she didn't like us, or any member of our race. And by race I of course mean *human*. I smelt stale coffee and cigarettes on her breath. When I explained that my luggage had been lost, her face contorted in revulsion. A piece of paper was thrust at me depicting sketches of luggage of various sizes and designs. In harshly accented English, I was told to circle the picture that best represented my bag. I did so and gingerly handed it back.

'Thees ees *not* you bag! Thees ees military bag! *WHUT. EES. YOU. BAG!*'

The final sentence was delivered in shotgun bursts, her eyes dark and icy. Dion intervened, taking advantage of his first opportunity to speak Greek in his family's ancestral land. As a Hellenic sentence tumbled out, I wanted to burst into applause, even if it sounded fictitious, like a barrage of bullshit spilling from the mouth of a child pretending to speak another language. Although Dion instantly seemed like a stranger, I decided he'd also make a rather fine ally. And he looked more than a little pleased with himself, too. Our plan was already working! I looked smugly at the clerk. She remained diffident. In Greek she barked back to Dion what sounded to me like a command. He in return took a pen and paper and wrote something that undoubtedly looked to her like the scrawl of a four-year-old. She looked at it, disgusted.

'*THEES EES NO ADDRESS!*'

But it was. It was the address of our new home. I left the airport somewhat perturbed.

'What the fuck was *her* problem?' I asked Dion.

He reached for my hand. 'Search me. Maybe she was having a bad day. Or maybe I didn't attend Greek school as often as I should have. But don't worry about it. Let's find a cab and check out the apartment!'

We dropped Dion's suitcase into the boot of a shiny yellow taxi and hopped in. Brown wooden beads adorned the rear-view mirror from which the driver's dark eyes peered back at us. It was a lazy sunny day, the sky a blinding, clear blue.

'Labrou Katsoni, Voula, deka-exi parakalo,' Dion directed, his voice sounding deeper and raspier. I looked at him suspiciously to ensure he was the same person I'd boarded the aircraft with in Australia. It was Dion all right, but I suspected he was channelling the spirit of a Greek fisherman.

Bumping up and down on the back seat, we drove along dusty roads, most of them littered with parked cars that transformed them into one-ways. Right of way was determined only by who arrived first, a car or two speeding towards us brazenly challenging us to a head-on. Everything looked parched, including the emaciated dogs that lay panting in the street, tongues flapping against sunken cheeks. There was a notable absence of greenery and a bit more concrete and marble than we were accustomed to. We passed some agreeable apartment buildings, several abandoned shopping trolleys and a procession of run-over cats lining the rudimentary gutters.

A Greek hairdresser in Sydney had told me that the suburb we were moving to – Voula – was quite affluent. I was as amused by the word 'affluent' as I was by the name 'Voula'. Con the Fruiterer, an interesting Greek character from the 1980s Australian TV show *The Comedy Company*, often mentioned his daughter Voula at the end of his skits. I was amused by the word 'affluent' only owing to its proximity to the word 'effluent'.

So there we were, speeding towards affluent Voula, me inter-changing the words affluent and effluent as appropriate, and noting the unfinished nature of many man-made structures. We passed a 'park' that to my eyes more closely resembled a dump than it did an area in which I'd ever choose to frolic. This park, as I was about to learn, was adjacent to our new home.

'Labrou Katsoni, Voula,' the driver announced gravely.

'Is that a *park*?' I asked Dion, not understanding the driver's sober proclamation.

'Sure is. Hey! Check out our new building!'

It was brand new, and looked as though it had just been lac-quered with its final coat of gun-metal grey. With its enormous balconies jutting at various angles and pristine windows winking at us from each of four levels, the building practically sparkled. It was the kind of building I never could have imagined in Athens, such were my preconceptions.

'Poli oreo,' commented the melancholic cabbie, clearly hoping for a tip.

'Ne,' agreed Dion with a satisfied smile.

'What?' I asked, confused.

As Dion and the taxi driver had apparently agreed, our new apartment building was beautiful. We entered the front garden via a large metal security door and walked along a small path with emer-ald grass sprouting on either side, the first true sign of greenery.

Inside the complex, we found ourselves in a cool, light-filled foyer that smelt of fresh paint and car exhaust fumes. We pressed the lift button and grinned inanely at one another as we waited for it to transport us to the third floor. There we were confronted by an enormous wooden door with multiple locks. As though trapped in a horror movie with a predator hot on our heels, Dion fidgeted anxiously with a set of keys. I braced myself for the worst. And then the door swung open to reveal an apartment fresh from the pages of *Vogue Living*.

Like a couple of excited children after a hit of remarkably strong red cordial, we began a frenzied exploration of our new home. The lounge room had gleaming polished floorboards and natural light streaming in upon matt-white walls. A large mahogany coffee table rested squarely on a pink Persian rug. Two comfy cream sofas were arranged in an L-shape. To our left, glass sliding doors led to a magnificent sun-drenched balcony complete with a marble table and a variety of bright flowering plants in large clay pots. The balcony overlooked the street of Labrou Katsoni, the apartment building opposite and the park that I'd mistaken for a dump.

To our right was a small open-plan kitchen separated from the lounge room by a high bench.

'WE HAVE A DISHWASHER!'

Things were looking good! Desperate to take in everything at once we ran down a hallway past the kitchen, our scurrying feet clopping along the floorboards, and reached a small bedroom. Back in the hall we opened large white cupboards at random, revealing a small, secret library and a washing machine that burst into view as though caught in a game of hide and seek.

The next room was a good-sized ultra-modern bathroom with two peach-coloured steps that led to a spacious bath by a frosted window. Sunshine poured in, promising shiny and happy ablutions. And after experimenting with a solitary sheet of toilet paper, crossing our fingers and flushing, we determined that the toilet readily accepted paper. Dion and I looked at one another, breaking into toothpaste commercial smiles.

At the end of the hallway was our bedroom. The bed, made up with crisp white linen, was minuscule, designed perhaps for those possessing a latent dwarf gene. By comparison even a short-arse like me suddenly felt elongated. We jumped up and down on it like a couple of imbeciles before noticing another, smaller balcony and an en suite with a toilet and bath. While the apartment may not have boasted the dramatic ocean views of our Sydney abode, it certainly made the grade.

We sank into our comfy new sofa and, courtesy of Greek television, tuned in to our beloved home town. Feeling proud though somewhat displaced, we witnessed the closing of the Sydney 2000 Olympic Games and were confronted by a close-up of Kylie Minogue's rear end as she entered on a surfboard, her posterior hungrily gorging on her knickers. The unintelligible Greek commentary over the footage acted as a constant reminder that we were a long way from the familiar posteriors of those we'd left behind.

The following morning, I stirred and opened my eyes to find my boyfriend gazing at me with adoration. It was Day One of our Greek adventure. We held one another and whispered proclamations of a love bigger than the whole wide world, no, *infinity*. We were a couple of triumphant pubescent runaways who'd escaped the authorities. We sprang from our tiny custom-made bed happy, dopey, sleepy . . . and *starving*. Our body clocks still on Australian time, a primordial urge spurred us to hunt and gather.

We stepped out of the apartment, and Dion pressed the lift button, turning to reveal a ridiculous face he was pulling. He'd opened his mouth and eyes as wide as possible, his eyebrows arched sky-high. I endeavoured to outdo him by returning the same expression, but with my head tilted at a right angle. Just then, a door identical to ours opened on the opposite side of the lift. Our expressions sobered.

Out stepped a tall, impeccably dressed middle-aged woman, her hair perfectly styled and her make-up flawless – the very definition of demure. She smiled at us warmly.

'Yia sas. Ti kanete?'

I looked at her blankly. Dion responded.

'Yia sas. Er . . . eimai o Dionysios kai afti eine . . . um . . . e yianeka mou, e Lana. Er . . . Menoume stin Labrou Katsoni tora!'

I looked at Dion, amazed. The woman pointed to herself.

'Eimai e Maria. Hkerete!' She extended a hand, first to Dion and then to me, looking me directly in the eyes. 'Ti kanete?'

I felt like an idiot child.

'Hello. I don't speak Greek.'

'Ah!' She half-nodded in sympathy, and turned to Dion. They began a conversation. I became redundant, lost in Dion's shadow.

The lift arrived and we entered together, Dion and Maria chatting and smiling. I could see that Dion was putting himself across as polite and charming as I simultaneously put myself across as an awkward, newly arrived refugee. Feeling a little left out, I thought about performing a tribal war cry to more strongly establish my presence. We strolled to the small outdoor car park area together – Maria and Dion laughing, me silent – and then bade our new neighbour goodbye.

'Yia sas kyria, Maria!' sang Dion.

'Bye!' I offered with a flapping wave.

'Yia sas!' she sang back, looking at Dion and throwing a dubious micro-glance my way.

Parked in the space reserved for our apartment was a gleaming black Opel Astra, Dion's very first company car.

'YES! Check it out!'

My boyfriend could hardly contain his excitement. Scrambling inside, he bounced in the driver's seat, breathing in the new-car smell. I joined him, and he pressed the magic buzzer to open a rumbling blue steel gate. He reached for my hand and gave it a squeeze, then took off on the left side of the road.

'Right! *RIGHT!* Remember, to stay on the right!' We both laughed in the face of death.

We went in search of a supermarket and found one only a couple of turns away from our flat. Dion parked on a dirt patch opposite that seemed to be a vacant block of land packed with other cars in disorderly fashion. Carefully crossing the road, we entered air-conditioned comfort. Dion jubilantly grabbed a trolley as I attempted to block out the Greek muzak that stealthily entered my subconscious.

The supermarket spanned two levels and was chock-full of fruit, vegetables, cheese, olives, bread, fish, octopus, chocolate, coat hangers and anything else we might need. It was just like any other supermarket only more like a jumbo delicatessen, with incoherent signage in every aisle and on every label. Well, incoherent to me anyway. We bought some essentials and returned to Labrou Katsoni to make ourselves a couple of enormous bread rolls full of fresh lettuce, dill, ripe tomato and, for Dion only, slabs of feta cheese. You see, I *hate* feta cheese, an idiosyncrasy that would prove rather unfortunate.

Later that afternoon, we discovered a snorkelling nook ten minutes from Labrou Katsoni and held each other's hands tightly as we swam, the sun on our backs and the warmth of love in our hearts.

Later that evening, Dion and I lay all over one another on the sofa watching Greek television, *watching* being the operative word. Neither of us really understood what anybody was saying or doing. But Dion grasped snippets and we attempted to piece together what was taking place in the world around us.

'He just said something about *grass*,' Dion offered.

'Grass? Why? Are they legalising marijuana?'

'NO! Grass as in the green stuff you walk on, not smoke. I don't know why he's talking about it. I think he's some kind of Greek minister or something.'

I was beginning to wonder just how fluent Dion's Greek really was when we were distracted by an urgent thump at our apartment door. We looked at one another.

Who on earth could that be?

'You can get it!' I offered helpfully.

Dion arose to answer it and I followed, shrinking behind him.

Before us stood a man who appeared to be some kind of Grand Wizard. He fingered an infinitely long grey beard and wore a flowing black cloak and a crazy kind of flat-topped witch's hat, grey hair poking at taunting angles from beneath.

Jesus! An acid flashback in Athens. This is all I need.

The Wizard invited himself inside, placing himself in the centre of our lounge room. He began speaking in Greek and smiling without looking at either one of us in particular. Eventually it dawned on me that this man was in fact an Orthodox priest. But why he had suddenly appeared in the middle of our lounge room remained a mystery.

Borrowing a cup of holy water perhaps?

'Um . . . Lana . . . this is a priest,' Dion advised sagely, looking from him, to me, then back again.

The priest pieced together Dion's attempted introduction, and nodded cordially. He then turned to Dion, resuming a conversation to which I was not privy. Then there was a second's silence before I was all but bowled out of the way. The priest made a beeline for our bedroom in a half sprint.

'What's going on? Did his Frisbee fly through the window and he's come to retrieve it? Or is he here to fluff our pillows?' I was incredulous.

'*Ssh!*' whispered Dion, attempting to create an air of respect. 'Okay. Not quite sure what's going on here. Just go with the flow.'

The sound of distant chanting began flooding the hallway towards us. The priest slowly exited our bedroom, splashing droplets of holy water from a small basil sprig that had materialised out of thin air. He disappeared momentarily, chants echoing off tiles as he entered the bathroom, chants muffling as he entered the spare bedroom, and chants amplifying as he re-entered the front room in which we stood. He did a circuit of the living room and returned to starting position, looking satisfied.

'I'm thinking he's just blessed the house,' said Dion out of the corner of his mouth. He turned to the priest, thanking him reverently and bowing his head.

'Efharisto para poli.'

The priest smiled and looked at us, pleased. He rocked back onto his heels and looked at us some more. We looked at him, smiling. He looked at us, smiling. Nobody spoke. He looked at each of us again in turn. We stared back at him stupidly, near-bursting with forced appreciation. He regarded us a moment more as if considering something, then eventually broke the silence with a goodbye.

'Yia sas.'

He paused yet again, glanced at us both for a few seconds, nodded, then disappeared from our apartment as quickly as he'd appeared.

We later learned that we were meant to pay him for his services, but we weren't too bothered. No, we were new to this land and separate from the rules that governed Athenian society. And our house was now pure!

Master and servant

It was my first day alone in Athens. After two days together, Dion had kissed me on the forehead on the Monday morning and dashed excitedly off to work, leaving me to unpack and arrange things in our brand-new apartment. As we had only the one suitcase, this took all of ten minutes. My suitcase wouldn't arrive for another week. I sat alone on the couch, tapping an index finger to my lips. I admired the fresh paintwork on the white wall opposite.

Hmm . . . nice wall!

The apartment was eerily silent, except for the sound of the humming refrigerator resonating from the kitchen. I sat a while longer, until my stomach growled with all the ferocity of the MGM lion after being poked in the eye with a stick. I then sprang into action, my bare feet thudding against the floorboards. As I opened the fridge, a welcome coolness exhaled over me. Stocked with the emergency provisions that Dion and I had purchased, its contents were like an artist's pallet. I prepared a plate of *mezedes,* a small selection of Greek delights that included olives, packaged octopus tentacles, a dollop of smooth pink fish-egg paste called taramasalata, a dollop of creamy, tangy tzatziki and a handful of thick, crunchy savoury biscuits the size of mini bread rolls. We were no longer talking Ryvitas topped with Vegemite and limp slices of processed cheese.

Plonking myself down in the midmorning sunshine on our outside balcony, I felt decidedly European. I watched a flock of unfamiliar black and white birds fuss and fight in a large tree in the otherwise barren park. Strangely, the tree appeared to belong to the eucalyptus family. I entertained the thought of stapling a stuffed koala to a branch to make myself feel more at home.

I turned my back to the older apartment building opposite to discreetly lick the remaining morsels from my plate as a melange of Mediterranean flavours swirled across my tastebuds. I put the plate down. The birds screeched and swooped to my left. It was then that the inevitable question arose.

NOW WHAT THE FUCK DO I DO?

The days that followed became repetitive in a *Groundhog Day* kind of way, although Bill Murray's day was slightly more varied than mine. After Dion shook me free from his ankles and headed to work each morning, I sat in the apartment bewildered, unsure of what to do or where to go. I didn't know a soul. I was about as orientated as a blindfolded Thompson's gazelle dangling from a bungee rope in the middle of the Bahamas. And I wasn't exactly viewing circumstances as a unique travel opportunity. Given that my boyfriend was hard at work, I no longer felt like an intrepid traveller. In fact, I actually felt a little bit scared. Instead of taking on the world with wide open arms à la Julie Andrews in the opening sequence of *The Sound of Music*, I felt immobilised, as timid as a house mouse. But of course I had to do *something*. The only thing I could think of was to call the Australian Embassy. I dialled the number and waited.

'Australian Embassy!'

'Oh, hello. I'm an Australian who's recently moved to Greece . . . from Sydney. I was just wondering . . . is there anything to *do* in Athens?'

There was a pause on the other end of the line.

'Have you registered with us yet?'

'No.'

'You really ought to register you know.'

'Okay, I will. But is there anything to *do*?'

'One moment please.'

I absent-mindedly looked out the window and noted clouds in the distance as I twirled the receiver cable around my finger.

'Yes, hello? One of my colleagues has told me that there's some sort of amateur archaeology group that meets every month.'

I thought for a moment.

'Archaeology? Oh. Okay. Thank you. Have a good day.'

'Don't forget to register!'

'I won't.'

I meant I wouldn't register. I hung up the phone and tried to envision myself scurrying around piles of ancient rubble. I broke into a light sweat.

NEXT!

I fired up our dial-up connection and sat online for an hour searching for potential activities and scrawling notes on a small sheet of paper.

1. Souvlaki – find it and eat it.
2. Soldiers in dresses – too good to be true.
3. Omonia Square – colourful and cultural.
4. Acropolis – look at it.

I gazed through the double glass doors, wondering if the clouds in the distance might spoil an otherwise perfect day. Much later, I would learn that it was *always* 'sunny yet cloudy' in Athens at this time of year. The foreboding grey was actually pollution, known as *nephos*, similar to a typical Los Angeles skyline. Oblivious, I stayed in our luxury apartment and consoled myself with the only activity I could think of outside of archaeology. Ironing.

Little did I know that ironing would become the focal point of my life. I strained to remember lifting an iron back in Australia, but my mind drew a blank. While I surely must have carried out the task on at least one occasion, ironing was of little consequence, much to Mrs Giamoreyos' chagrin. Back then Dion and I happily threw on jeans and crumpled T-shirts before flying out the door to tiptoe around rock star egos. But now everything had changed. Dion was wearing business shirts and I'd slipped into the role of housebound housewife, armed with a freakin' *iron*! How had *that* happened?

A few days into My Big Fat Greek Life, while sweating over the ironing board in my pyjamas at one in the afternoon, I reassured myself that this new arrangement was only temporary. In the meantime, cabin fever already stalked, hiding behind a pile of perfectly clean bed sheets that I'd deemed fit to wash for no reason other than to give myself something to do. I figured that if I was going to kill time, I might as well kill it with cleanliness.

As I contemplated ironing Dion's underpants, the table placemats, the bathroom rug and my hair, I was interrupted by the doorbell. The three-chime ring echoed throughout the apartment like the irritating sound preceding a rail announcement. Startled, I wondered who of my countless Athenian friends it could possibly be. With my cream silky dressing gown flapping behind me, I made for the door and opened it hesitantly.

Standing before me was a tall, robust woman dressed in white trousers and matching jacket. Her short copper hair framed an oval face with darting green eyes. Crooked teeth came into view as she spoke.

'Yiaaa-sas-ti-kanete-kala? Eimai e Athina, kai eisai? Esi eisai?' she asked in a harsh, hoarse voice.

From the expectant look in her eyes, I gathered she was asking me a question, but concerning what I hadn't a clue. 'Would you be interested in joining my Bible study group' perhaps? I was suddenly overcome by a sense of dread. I was about to make my first feeble attempt at speaking Greek.

'Oh. Um . . . Hello! Y-y-yia sou. How are you? Eis . . . eis . . . p-pos eis?'

As I clutched my dressing gown tightly over my chest in the afternoon sunlight, I feared my puerile Greek made little sense. Or worse, no sense at all. I laughed self-consciously. The laughter wasn't reciprocated. The smile slid from my face. I attempted to revive the conversation.

'Sorry, I don't speak Greek. Do you speak English? Who are you?'

It was the looming woman's turn to blink back at me stupidly. It seemed we'd reached a communication stalemate. Still, the look in her eyes seemed expectant. I had an idea.

'Wait a minute. I'll call my boyfriend.'

I gestured a stop signal, followed by a raised index finger and then mimed the act of speaking into a telephone receiver. The woman at the door shifted on her feet and looked back at me quizzically.

I called Dion and explained that there was a weirdo at the door and I didn't know what the fuck she wanted. He laughed patiently and asked me to put her on. The woman then spoke loudly into the receiver. I could hear Dion's voice rising and falling through the earpiece, his tone sounding friendly. The woman smiled broadly as she triumphantly thrust the telephone back into my hand.

'Sorry, babe. I forgot to tell you. Our apartment comes complete with an Albanian cleaning lady. She'll be coming to our building every Thursday. Her name's Athina.'

The concept of having my very own cleaner was completely alien to me. I couldn't *wait* to tell my mother. I knew better than to mention it to Katerina. Call it instinct. Call it self-preservation. I just knew that I'd be crucified if this was discovered by Dion's older relatives, specifically those who urinated while seated.

'She haf cleaner? She no work? She LAZY!'

I turned to the cleaner with a wide smile and welcomed her into the apartment.

'I'm Lana.' I pointed to myself, smiling broadly.

'Ti? Lama?'

'La-*na*.'

'Lunna.'

We both grinned. I'd just been rechristened. But it was close enough.

She pointed to herself.

'Eimai Athi-*na*.' There was a dramatic pronunciation of the last syllable.

'Hi A-theeee-na.'

She shook her head violently, her face growing stern.

'Ohi! A-thi-*NA*!'

I knew that if I didn't pronounce her name correctly I could very well expect a broom handle to strike me violently across the back of the head. Still, my very own cleaner! This *had* to be every housewife's dream.

Holy fuck! I'm a HOUSEWIFE!

As the hours rolled by, I learned that Athina was exceedingly thorough and an enormous fan of me making her multiple cups of coffee. She didn't do ironing – leaving me at least something to do – and didn't speak a word of English, only Greek and Albanian. If I attempted communication, I'd inevitably begin by mispronouncing her name. In return, the towering warrior-woman would offer an expression that one might extend to another possessing the IQ of a mollusc. I began relying heavily on mime artistry.

As Athina powered into her third hour of bustling around our apartment, I couldn't help but feel our arrangement was pretty much absurd. Despite her size, the Albanian was a goddamned *machine*! And there *I* sat, pretending to be engrossed in an English to Greek dictionary that I'd purchased in Sydney, while a complete stranger ten years my senior sweated and groaned around me, gesturing for me to lift my feet so she could mop beneath them. I felt guilty. I was too embarrassed even to eat in front of her. It seemed elitist. I doubted I could successfully offer her food, even if I wanted to.

Would you like smoked salmon on rye with grated lemon rind, capers, mayonnaise and wholegrain mustard, served with a parsley garnish and a glass of freshly squeezed orange juice?

I began flicking through the pages of the dictionary, searching for the Greek equivalent of the word 'salmon'. I slammed it shut and instead attempted to dream up an effective mime.

If I flap about the floor as though swimming against an upstream current . . .

That's right. Through body movement alone, I was hoping to represent a salmon sandwich for an Albanian cleaning lady rocketing through my apartment like a tornado.

I would later learn that while it wasn't uncommon to find Albanians plucking pubic hairs out of cakes of soap, or digging holes, it was uncommon to offer them lunch. You see, Albanians are the soldier ants of Greece, prepared to take on all the crap jobs for less pay. In the early 1990s, when Albanians of 'Greek heritage' were permitted to enter Greece, they had arrived by the truckload to take any jobs going, creating better lives for themselves than they could ever hope for in poor, messed-up Albania. Many Greeks quite openly regarded them as a scourge on society. I, on the other hand, saw Athina as some kind of authority figure. I was even slightly afraid of her. It may have had something to do with her forearm being twice the size of my thigh. It may have had something to do with my inability to communicate or interact with her on practically every level. Or it may have had everything to do with her being a fellow-foreigner who, unlike me, had a firm grip on a Greek way of life. There was nothing else for it. I had to get as far away from her as possible.

To put a little distance between Athina and myself, I decided to stock up on canned goods in case the Y2K bug struck a little behind schedule. The quick shop I'd done with Dion had seemed simple enough, so I left the apartment bursting with confidence.

After miming the act of pushing a shopping trolley (Athina no doubt presuming I'd soon be mowing a lawn), I strolled past buildings similar to ours. None were higher than five levels, most had white exteriors and all had large balconies confining ferocious Alsatian-crosses presumably for the term of their natural lives. Occasionally I'd pass a simple, one-level dwelling complete with an old couple sitting motionless on wooden seats in the middle of a hard-dirt yard, staring either into space or at me. The old men wore uniform brown trousers, white vests and fishing caps, the old women black dresses and tattered, comfy shoes.

The footpath was uneven, often disappearing only to reappear with a whopping olive tree sprouting from its centre. I ducked dramatically beneath branches, an olive or two inflicting temporary blindness. Forging ahead using only the sense of smell, I was overcome by the tart-spicy scent of citrus emanating from tiny oranges that had fallen from trees and been unceremoniously squashed on the road by passing cars.

I arrived at the wide road that led to the supermarket. As I walked, I passed many palatial buildings that looked thoroughly out of place amidst vacant lots of land, or lots that contained partially constructed grey concrete structures: hulk-like skeletons that brought drabness to an otherwise sunny day. There were also a few dirt lots occupied by excitable chickens zigzagging madly between docile goats that chewed on clumps of dry yellow grass.

After fifteen minutes I reached Sklavenitis, the shopping mecca that was to become a part of my weekly ritual. In light of my linguistic handicap, I made a deal with myself to avoid human contact there at all costs, which wasn't easy for as soon as I entered, a rare breed of annoying product representative moved in for the kill. They lurked in most aisles, ready to pounce with an offer of a free toilet roll or something of similar value with the purchase of product 'x'. Of course, each sales pitch fell on deaf ears, and in my case was followed by a great deal of shoe-shuffling awkwardness and my sophisticated Neanderthal response.

'Huh?'

Frightened or appalled – I wasn't sure which – most representatives quickly broke eye contact. Only one insisted on translating into broken English the advantages of bulk-purchased fabric softener, a spiel that doubled as the long-awaited cure for insomnia. I continued browsing.

Fortunately, product packaging came complete with pretty pictures. An image of a dog leaping over a fence alerted me to the fact that the item in my hands was indeed a packet of dog biscuits and not savoury bar snacks, thus neatly averting a *mezedes* disaster.

A trolley rammed into the back of my legs. I turned to the perpetrator, expecting an apology. But she looked right through me. I noticed a pattern emerging. *Most* shoppers barged into me and none apologised. But it got worse. Some appeared to be prepared to maim for the sake of a ripe tomato! As I foraged through the vegetable section with my fellow shoppers, my arm was repeatedly pushed aside as others made a grab for the most desirable produce.

I further noted that everyone seemed to be dressed for a wedding reception, while I scampered about in T-shirt and jeans. This was all too close to an alien abduction. Not long ago, I'd been in familiar surroundings, and now here I was among strange beings, praying like mad that nobody raised the subject of inserting an investigative probe.

Finally, bruised and confused, I made my way to the cash register. I was on the home stretch! I was almost there! And that's when something shit happened. I dropped the eggs.

Yes-sir-ee, ladies and gentlemen, the invisible girl has DEE-ROPPED the eggs! Why, come see for yourself. They're smeared all over the floor!

A small commotion ensued. People gravitated towards me from every direction. I didn't know what anyone was saying or doing, and strained to interpret the body language and shouts around me. Like Athina, their reactions suggested that I was missing a chromosome or two, and I couldn't help but notice that nobody was smiling reassuringly to alleviate my embarrassment. The cashier offered only an expressionless shrug. An old woman with dark rings around her eyes materialised with a mop, grunting as she cleaned.

After a minute or two, the commotion died down and people

lost interest. Desperate to get the hell out of there I handed over a fistful of drachmas in the vicinity of 30 000. Or was it 300 000?

Noting trolley swiping was common practice, I wheeled mine onto the bumpy road outside to avoid the shoddy footpaths and commenced the trudge back to the relative safety of the apartment. And *that's* when a barely domesticated Athenian canine came bounding towards me. More wolf than dog, it barked and snarled and nipped at the trolley wheels for the better part of the perilous journey home. I used my entire body weight to steer my purchases – overflowing with bulk-bought fabric softener – away from oncoming traffic and potholes.

I dragged swollen plastic bags into the apartment from the lift one at a time. A bag leaked a carton of orange juice all over Athina's freshly mopped floor. I smiled sheepishly. She released a long, mournful sigh. I'd managed to make a public spectacle of myself, dodge a wolverine *and* piss off an Albanian cleaning lady all in the space of a single afternoon. I was only five days into my Greek odyssey, and I couldn't *wait* to tell Dion how great it had been so far.

Welcome to the jungle

'May I share with you how much of a shit time I've been having?'

Dion's eyes glowed with sympathy when I regaled him with tales of hounds and broken eggs, but soon returned to their usual state, glinting with blinding exhilaration.

'That's terrible, babe. But let me tell you about *my* week! Okay, I can sense the staff are slightly wary, but they're actually looking to me for direction. Me! Can you believe it? I've started implementing programming strategies that they see as *revolutionary. And* I'm communicating most things in Greek! In *Greek!*'

He grabbed my shoulders and shook me softly to convey his euphoria. He then performed an impersonation of someone on ecstasy rave dancing to specialist dance music.

'But I want to communicate in Greek too!' I squealed like a whiney brat, matching his dance moves.

So Dion dutifully burned ten Greek language lessons off the Internet, certain that this would help to ease me into our new environment. These lessons were somewhat more intensive than those on the introductory CD voiced by my side-saddling mentor. Dion and I were convinced that my vocabulary would expand fast, catapulting far beyond the vernacular genius of 'hello' and 'pencil'.

Dion arose on the Saturday morning to find me cross-legged before the stereo enunciating harder than Eliza Doolittle in *My Fair Lady*.

'E karekla. The chair. E karekla. The chair. E karekla. The chair.'

He smiled. I pressed stop. I felt like a twat. This was our first 'real' weekend since arriving, and I wasn't about to waste time barking random nouns. I was anxious to get outside, to explore more of Athens. Of course, I could have been doing that already, but I wanted to discover it with Dion, not only as an exercise in togetherness, but because the ability to utter the words 'hello', 'chair' and 'pencil' wasn't going to get me very far. By default, Dion unofficially became my tour guide, voice box, interpreter and spokesperson.

So we set off in the company car, heading for the city. When we hit the main road, Vouliagmenis Avenue, Dion began reciting a mission statement for his radio station. I, on the other hand, recited the rosary – I wasn't too sure we'd make it to the centre alive.

'My station will be the number one station in Athens!'

'Hail Mary, full of grace, the Lord is with thee . . .'

Motoring was a kaleidoscope of dangerous overtaking, near hits and misses, speeding, tailgating, environmental disregard, relentless high beam flashing, redundant seatbelts, chronic helmet avoidance, lane blocking, auspicious indicator usage and what appeared to be a general on-road selfishness set to a looping car horn soundtrack.

In no particular order, I deduced that all of the above occurred with a view to:

a. Breaking all land-speed records;
b. Rising to the challenge of the complete fuck-knuckle;

c. Endangering the lives of others;
d. Eating auntie's *tiropita* (cheese pie) sooner rather than later; and/or
e. Co-ordinating dangerous moves with the untimely approach of watermelon trucks.

It came as no surprise to learn that Greece has one of the highest rates of road-related deaths in Europe. From the dubious safety of the passenger seat, I was convinced I could *never* get behind the wheel of a vehicle in Athens without first undergoing a frontal lobotomy. I much preferred to play the humble passenger with a quirky predisposition for imbedding fingernails into dashboard upholstery. Dion, in the meantime, had instantly taken to driving like a true Athenian. It must have been buried deeply within his DNA.

We passed what appeared to be a military airport, several wig shops, a handful of flattened cats, a phenomenal number of furniture shops, kitchen and bathroom re-fitters, various car dealerships and a baby store strangely named 'Mister Baby'. Pakistani and Kurdish hawkers took red lights to mean go, and ambushed stopped cars with bottled water, bananas, street directories and tacky flashing key rings. They smiled, raising their wares in the air as drivers and passengers stared dead ahead, ignoring them.

As we tore closer towards the centre, a grim, concrete jungle unfolded before me – the very definition of contradiction. Women fastidiously cleaned balconies amidst the grime, and bursts of brilliant fuchsia flowers relieved what seemed to be an otherwise uniform filth. An ornate, domed Orthodox Church would unexpectedly emerge from between exhaust-blackened buildings, its bells pealing a distinct glimmer of hope; or an orange tree would appear between grey concrete slabs. I officially concluded that the city of Athens was a paradox.

'What *is* this place?' I asked Dion.

'What do you mean?' he responded vaguely, listening keenly to the radio, ensuring all was as it should be.

'Why's it so, you know, weird . . . and *dirty?*'

'Dunno, babe.'

While Dion wasn't exactly heartless, he was being a bit dismissive, probably because my inarticulate line of questioning had absolutely nothing to do with Anna Vissi, who was now playing on his station. Anna Vissi, you see, is Greece's answer to Madonna, give or take a few years, unless you take her plastic surgery into account, which would make her Madonna minus twenty years. Or Madonna back in the womb, depending on how recently she's visited her surgeon. In this moment, Dion was more attuned to Vissi than he was to the city around us. And as far as I could tell, he was blissfully unaware that we were dredging our way through a place that I judged 'aesthetically displeasing'. He turned up the radio, concentrating hard on a post-Vissi talk break that was apparently running too long.

We were heading for a place that, according to the Internet, promised a 'colourful, cultural experience'. It was called Omonia Square, just beyond the city's core. Arriving, we parked and stepped out of the car only to be slapped across the face by the stench of death.

What the hell is THAT?

Looking around, we found ourselves in a carcass jungle where rows of stark maroon and red animal corpses swung gruesomely from enormous, macabre hooks. We'd unwittingly stumbled face-first into a meat market, the perfect kick-start to a Saturday morning. Holding hands and trotting in the opposite direction as though escaping a skunk explosion, we turned the corner to enter a sizable vegetable market. Admiring stall after stall of colourful fruit and veg, I decided to make the most of the experience by purchasing a token bunch of bananas.

'Bananas! Four!'

I held up four fingers, smiling hard at an old fruit seller, inviting him to join the friendly game where he guessed what I meant and then tried to teach me the equivalent in his native tongue, finishing the exchange with a ruffle of my hair and a pinch of my cheek. Instead, the fruit seller repaid a small, karmic debt for something I'd done to him and his family in a previous incarnation. He slapped seven bananas into my hands and muttered something gruffly. Dion intervened and paid him some money. This exchange wasn't quite what I'd expected. My feelings hurt, I turned to see a dirty, impoverished child with no shoes pick-pocket a passer-by.

'I think we should get out of here,' I said to Dion, deflated.

'Me too. This place sucks.'

Like me, Dion was failing to see the allure. Let's not forget he had never been outside Australia before. For us, the 'colourful, cultural experience' was turning out to be more of a grey.

Half an hour later we were back in the car, snaking up a winding, forested road. Eventually we reached a dry and rocky outdoor theatre far from the chaos below. We were partway up Lykavittos, a remarkable hill in the middle of the city which, at 295 metres, reaches even higher than the Acropolis itself. We climbed what seemed like a stairway to heaven – a thousand steps to the tiny white church of Agios Yiorgos (St George) that crowns its peak.

Just inside its entranceway, pencil-thin candles flickered invitingly. A gold-covered Bible sat nobly upon a lectern. Religious icons abounded, painted in drab colours flecked with gold and silver. Jesus stared down at us from a range of paintings, following our movements, as did a vast selection of Greek Madonnas of the non-Anna Vissi variety. In each instance, the Virgin Mary was depicted with a long, slender nose and dark, sad eyes.

We were the only two people in the chapel, yet there was not a lot of room to spare. We each bought a candle and reverently placed it in a large sand-filled tray amidst a miniature forest of dripping wax. Moved by the sanctity of the moment, I felt a wave of love for Dion sweep through my being. We smiled at one another. I sent a silent shout out to God.

Dear Christouli
Please make this time in Athens as excellent as can be. Help me to
forgive the guy with the bananas just now. And bless my beautiful
boyfriend, Dion. I love him. Thanks!
Lots of love,
Lana
PS All the best to the holy family.
Amen

As we left the church, we passed a little man selling religious trinkets from an outdoor table, then wandered over to a ledge to check out Athens far below. We stopped for a moment's embrace and I peered over Dion's shoulder. And *that's* when I began to panic – a fear that had absolutely nothing to do with vertigo. See, what happened was I got the distinct impression I'd been teleported directly from Sydney's Powerhouse Museum into this very moment. The panoramic vista before us – threatened by fast-approaching clouds – was identical to the aerial shot that had moved me to tears only a couple of weeks earlier; the infamous mounted picture of Athens that I'd rudely associated with bird excrement. Ducking, I looked nervously overhead for seagulls.

'Wow! Isn't this *spectacular?*' spluttered Dion.

I didn't quite know how to respond. *I* saw an urban sprawl that trumpeted my insignificance – one puny Australian amongst a population of 5.5 million. I pictured myself earlier in the week hidden away in one of the tiny buildings that my eyes now brushed over, shut off from the rest of humanity. I didn't say any of this, of course. I didn't want to dampen Dion's spirits. Instead I offered a non-committal response: 'Mmm.'

Still, the view offered an excellent opportunity to get orientated. We were surrounded by dry, imposing hills, and the Saronic Gulf glistened in the distance. Filling every inch of space in between was a densely populated grey and white metropolis. There were no skyscrapers, only flat-roofed buildings of several levels each. A million television antennas stood to attention on rooftops like a breed of enormous Jurassic stick insects.

Dion pointed out one of the hills in the distance as Mt Imittos, a place where most radio stations positioned their broadcast towers. Seeing that I was paying attention and liking it – perhaps a little too much – he assumed the role of orienteering guide and turned his body in a certain direction, arm and finger extended, like a human compass.

'To the north over there is Omonia, where we were just before. Remember the meat and veg markets?'

'How could I forget?'

Glancing up to ensure he hadn't lost me, he swung dramatically in the opposite direction and pointed far beyond the centre.

'Okay, so if that's north, then south is where we live.'

His finger swivelled back to the centre. 'And Plaka is around about there somewhere . . .'

He swung west and then east, commentating as he did so.

'Monastiraki's near Plaka – and Kolonaki I think is to the east.'

'What are you on about? A colonoscopy to the east? Surely it would be to the south?'

I was assured that all would be revealed over the coming months. I also got the distinct impression that my boyfriend was making things up as he went along.

Only a few kilometres away, the Acropolis stood over the city, a constant reminder that we were in the cradle of modern civilisation. I felt a little ashamed for not being more respectful. We stared at the mighty construction for a while before deciding to make a pilgrimage to it another day. Being Athens' quintessential landmark, I had a funny feeling that I would probably get to know it rather well.

Back in Labrou Katsoni, Dion fell fast asleep on the couch in front of the television. I plucked through laundry and put on a load of washing, desperate for something to do. I couldn't *wait* for my next batch of ironing. Not because I liked it. Let's get that straight. I already *hated* it. But it was my *thing*. It was what I *did*. And do you know what else I did that afternoon? Without a word of a lie, I logged onto the Internet, typed in the word 'ironing' and learnt the best method of tackling Dion's work shirts from a bored fifty-something housewife in Oregon, USA.

But as ironing savvy as I now was, I still needed something else to do. So in compliance with my new role as domestic goddess, I typed 'Greek recipes' into a search engine, found a website and read through the menu options:

Melitzanosalata (eggplant salad)
Horiatiki (Greek salad)
Spanakopita (spinach pie)
Keftedes (meat balls)

Soutzoukakia
Dolmades

There was no description for *soutzoukakia*, so I clicked on the word to get more of an idea. Beside the recipe was a photograph of what appeared to be dog-paddling turds in a bowl of soup. I quickly clicked the 'back' arrow and settled for dolmades instead.

Dolmades are the little Greek delicacies of minced meat and rice wrapped in vine leaves with a tangy lemon aftertaste. They're delicious! And it just so happened I'd bought some vine leaves from the supermarket that very week. At the time it made me feel exotic, and I was determined to be able to compare my cooking prowess with Dion's mother's.

After more than two hours of intense labour in the kitchen, my final offerings looked more like a collection of alien abortions than anything edible. Still, I locked them away in an airtight container and refrigerated them, eager to present them to my man.

He'll be so proud!

If I'd presented them to his mother, on the other hand, she'd probably have been more inclined to administer a Chinese burn. It was a good thing she was a world away.

When Dion eventually resurfaced from his afternoon nap, I raced to the fridge to retrieve the fat wilting pillows of green and brown muck, enthusiastically shoving the container in his face.

'Dolmades!' I yelped.

Thinking he was either still dreaming or in the throes of a nightmare, Dion ran a hand over his face.

'What are they, babe?'

'Dolmades!' I looked at him expectantly, puppy eyes blinking.

'Oh! *Dolmades!* Very good! Excellent. Wow! Did *you* make these? They look fantastic.'

Although deep down I knew this was the same psychology a parent might apply to a child, I accepted it as a well-earned compliment. I'd made dolmades and my culinary prowess had been acknowledged by the man of my dreams.

'We've got time to eat a few,' I said. 'Dinner's still a few hours away. Want some?'

'No thanks, babe. Maybe later.'

Dion fell asleep again, in what became a pattern for our Saturday nights. Gone were the days of meeting friends, downing a few sneaky drinks and dancing the dance of the uncoordinated. Here, we didn't know where to go and I suspected that Dion didn't really care if we left the apartment in any case. Instead, our Saturday nights now starred an exhausted version of my boyfriend and an overly energetic version of me climbing the walls and having conversations with a sock puppet I'd affixed to my right hand.

I spent the remainder of the evening ironing a stack of towels.

6

Dance little lady dance

Thankfully we weren't entirely alone in Athens. Dion had an aunt and uncle who lived in Peania, an hour's drive from Voula on a good day. His aunt's name was Nota, her husband's Nikos. We drove to meet them on our second Sunday, taking a series of narrow, single-lane roads. We passed town after town, each with a succession of shop windows displaying thalidomide mannequins modelling crooked mahogany-coloured wigs and low-class fashion. En route we found ourselves stuck behind buses, unable to overtake because we lacked the built-in death wish that was every Athenian's birth-right. There was talk of a motorway being constructed in time for the 2004 Olympic Games, but of what use was that to us? We had to come to terms with the fact that getting from A to B was always going to be a test of patience.

Peania is nestled in the foothills of Mount Imittos on the city's north-eastern outskirts, and features caves with large stalagmites and stalactites that, according to tour guides, have assumed the shape of lions, other animals and, curiously, a giant penis. The residential part of the town has a spacious, lazy feel to it, as chickens, goats and stray cats take up squatters' rights on vacant land.

Parking across the road from the home of Nota and Nikos, the first thing I noticed was that while the lower level of their home could be considered decent housing, the upper level could not. Like many houses in Greece, a skeletal concrete framework marked an upper-level space yet to be completed. A piece of string had been stretched between the walls, acting as a makeshift clothesline.

Traditional Greek folk music and delicious cooking aromas floated out of the house to greet us, as did Dion's aunt. In fact, she was so delighted to see us that she began excitedly dancing around the citrus trees and exquisite fuchsia-flecked shrubbery. Her moves involved arms shooting upwards and downwards à la Safety Dance, one leg crossing over the other, and a dipping action with her head, after which she placed the leaf of an obscure herb behind my ear. Somewhat flummoxed, I offered a curtsey.

Nota laughed, her kind, round face bobbing about on her generously proportioned body. She hugged us both warmly, our faces becoming lost in her dough-like cleavage, and then invited us inside.

'*ELA! ELA!*'

Latching onto Dion's arm to prevent any mad-dash escape, she stared into her nephew's eyes with sheer adoration as we entered a dark, modest home filled with dark, modest furniture. A large wall cabinet in the living area displayed a multitude of colour photo-copies of photographs that leaned against 1960s glassware on top of plastic-covered doilies. The shots depicted Nota, Nikos and other relatives smiling feebly before a variety of partly built sea vessels. Both Nikos and Nota were boat-builders and of this fact, they were rather proud.

Nikos emerged from a bedroom wearing a pair of black trousers and a white vest. He smiled at us, pointed at one of the boats and raised an eyebrow.

'Okay, mate?'

This, we were to learn, was the full extent of Nikos' English vernacular. It was more expansive than Nota's.

Uncle Nikos was a small man with a crazy, gap-toothed laugh and a cigarette eternally smouldering from the corner of his mouth. He patted me on the back by way of introduction and offered me a beer.

'Beera?' he rasped, and burst out laughing. He looked at Dion. 'Okay, mate?' And he laughed again, extending a hand to shake Dion's firmly.

We all laughed. I instantly liked him. I instantly liked them both.

Nota quickly shepherded us into a brown-tiled kitchen with a table as its centrepiece. The table was filled with a variety of Greek delights: we would soon be stuffed with stuffed tomatoes, stuffed zucchini flowers, stuffed peppers, lamb chops, octopus and large chunks of hard bread. Large plastic water bottles filled with local red wine stood to attention at either end of the table like sentinels. It was obvious that Dion's uncle and aunt were exceedingly accommodating.

For the remainder of the day and night, as Nota unashamedly doted on Dion – some five hours in total – I sat there, imperceptibly aging. From what I could determine, everyone discussed in Greek and at great length . . . oranges.

I went to the bathroom for a moment's respite, noting the small bin beside the toilet filled with used toilet paper, and formulated a cunning plan. Rather than being a shrugging, retortless entity, I was going to learn how to speak Greek. And I was going to be really, *really* good at it.

The fact that it was imperative that I learn the Greek language was rammed home even further the following week when I found myself in a butcher shop snorting like a pig. As I pushed up my nose with a finger in an attempt to procure a pathetic-looking pork chop, nobody was particularly amused. Instead of appearing cute, I was seen only as an imbecile. My Internet language CD wasn't really cutting it. And henceforth, Dion and I would become vegetarian unless I could purchase meat products without dialogue.

I made enquiries about language lessons from a private tutor who would make house calls. I decided I would try to learn only the most basic phrases and words. After all, we were in Athens for a good time, not a long time. However, I quickly understood that it might take an entire year to learn how to say 'thank you' in Greek, let alone 'STOP! Your yiros has a hair in it!' I learned this after only two one-hour lessons with a Greek woman named Vagelio, pronounced 'Va-gel-YO'. Correctly pronouncing her name was a lesson in itself.

Vagelio was a tall, middle-aged woman who had spent some time in Britain. She spoke the Queen's English with great aplomb and had trained as a teacher. Stern but fair, and very patient considering my level of aptitude, she also had a dirty great mole protruding from the right side of her chin with a huge black hair angrily extending from it. I could barely tear my gaze from it.

The lessons that took place in my living room were like taxidermy – complex, and at the end of the day, relatively pointless. Like the chin mole that I was faced with twice a week, I found the Greek language utterly perplexing. Nouns were divided into feminine, masculine and 'eunuch', if not hermaphrodite. My syllable output tripled as I vomited words with my own hopeless enunciation. Bizarre hieroglyphics and squiggles filled my workbook pages as I attempted to scribe a peculiar new alphabet. After a time, however, I began to develop a microscopic droplet of courage and daringly decided to bury my burgeoning paranoia and embark on a little linguistic experiment.

Phase One began with a simple telephone call to a nearby gym. My objective was to have a brief 'conversation' in Greek. It was to be my first phone call to a Greek organisation.

I dialled the number, listened to it ring and swallowed hard.

'Ne?'

And then I panicked. 'Um, yeah. Hi. Um . . . English? Do you speak it?'

CRASH! My ear rang with the sound of a slammed down receiver.

This time do it properly!

Apprehensively, I re-dialled.

'Ne?'

'Yia sas. Er . . . Milate Anglika?' (Hello, do you speak English?)

'*Ohi!*' (No!)

CRASH!

Hmm. This isn't going so well. Proceed to Phase Two.

Not to be deterred, I somewhat bravely took the experiment to the streets. And let me make it clear that for a girl like me, whose confidence was already beginning to plummet, this took an enormous amount of bravery.

Full of trepidation I walked to a nearby bistro and planned to order a bowl of penne. Being an Italian word on a menu written in English, this was obviously cheating. However, my big chance at linguistic development came when the food arrived at the table stone cold. I wanted it hot, so I called a stumpy young waiter with lovely clear skin back to the table.

'Signomie!'

Signomie, I had just learned, meant 'excuse me'.

The waiter returned to my table, a questioning look on his cherubic face.

It worked!

I proceeded to convey the dilemma of the cold penne using an interesting combination of English, sign language, the click language of the Kalahari Bushmen and, most importantly, the complete extent of my Greek vocabulary, including 'hello', 'chair', 'excuse me' (again), 'pencil' and 'do you speak English?' The waiter at first appeared confused, but gradually a cartoon light bulb illuminated above his head.

He did an about-face, leaving the bowl of penne behind and returned minutes later with a bottle of Tabasco sauce and a bowl of grated cheese.

I concluded that for our remaining days in Greece there was a rather strong likelihood that Dion would have to communicate exclusively on my behalf. Sharing this conclusion with my boyfriend that night over a crisp salad, baked eggplant with fresh tomato sauce and not-so-fresh bread, he smiled placidly as he watched my face contort.

'She hung up on me! And *he* rocked up with a bottle of Tabasco and some fucking *grated cheese!*'

Dion laughed his throaty laugh and reached across the table to take my hand.

'Don't worry about it, babe. We haven't been here long. Things will get better, and in the meantime, I'll look after you!'

I stared back adoringly and thought for a moment. I was touched that my boyfriend was so *there* for me, and that he had such confidence in the fast development of my Greek adaptation.

'But she hung up on me. *Twice!*'

Only the lonely

I awoke with a start. I was alone.

WHERE AM I? WHY'S THE ROOM ALL WHITE? IS THIS A SANATORIUM?

Oh, no, that's right. I'm in Athens, Greece.

WHERE'S DION?

Oh, that's right. He works. I don't.

Dion had left, but this morning I hadn't noticed him kiss my forehead as he'd done every day since our arrival. After hearing of my adventures the day before, perhaps he had been reluctant to rouse the sleeping beast beside him. Regardless, today was a brand-new day and fearlessly I decided to again venture into the outside world. I settled on a more thorough exploration of Voula. I didn't have any other bright ideas or the guts to go much further.

As I walked the streets, angry dogs barking wildly in every direction, I noted that our area was essentially a confined-canine haven and really quite nice. In fact, we were only a few blocks away from the ocean. I walked these blocks, heading for the water.

Having crossed the menacing highway of Poseidonos Avenue I dipped a toe in the water, then sat on a wooden bench to soak up the immense beauty that lay before me. The sea was a still, dark blue, rimmed by a slim, rocky shoreline. Shadowy islands obscured by haze jutted in the far-off distance, while a few people in swimming caps bobbed up and down in water that to me seemed a bit too cold. I felt an unfamiliar tranquillity.

Yeah, I live in Greece.

I sat with this thought, testing how it sat with me. I wondered what this adventurous year might have in store and what it would be like spending a fair whack of time in my own company.

Okay, I guess. I'm pretty cool to hang out with. But Christ, this could end up being a hell of a lot of 'me' time!

As the waves lapped before me and the traffic soared behind, I hugged my knees close to my chest. The tranquillity receded, and loneliness swept through me like a desert wind. I shuddered. Shit. I really was alone.

After several minutes, I pried myself away from the view and stifled a nagging doubt that was struggling to surface – the mental equivalent of suffocating it with an overstuffed pillow and walking away fast as though a murder hadn't just taken place. I didn't want to think about it. So I busied myself with happy thoughts, like how proud my brother was of being such a fast walker. I stepped up the pace, as if he was beside me and this was one of our usual competitions.

Along with learning to enjoy my own company, I was finding it hard to adjust to a city with so many contradictions. While afternoon traffic whizzed by in a perpetual state of emergency, many citizens were actually crashed out in their homes, observing the time-honoured siesta period. Time as I'd known it was now an entirely different phenomenon. For me, life's pace had slowed and time was no longer the competitor. Everything around me – aside from the manic driving – happened s-l-o-w-l-y.

I discovered that shops closed for long periods midafternoon and didn't open at all on Sundays. I decided that this wasn't always going to be convenient for a consumption-mad westerner accustomed to being able to pop out on a whim for a block-mounted poster of Farah Fawcett-Majors if the need arose. However, although a deviation in retail practices was never going to kill me, I would discover other idiosyncrasies that were much harder to deal with. It started in the company of produce sellers at a local *laiki* I'd stumbled across.

A usually animated and happy affair, the *laiki* is a weekly outdoor market full of fresh seasonal fruits, vegetables and fish that takes place on the streets of most Athenian localities. Stall attendees bellow sales pitches at old and middle-aged women who race by, expert eyes darting. The sweet aroma of souvlaki sometimes fills the air and lost lettuce leaves pave the way underfoot.

Despite Greece producing the best fruit and vegetables I'd ever sampled, including succulent tomatoes and oranges as big, fat and juicy as Mick Jagger's lips, I found myself intimidated by the seriousness with which those around me approached their shopping. I tried my darnedest to remain inconspicuous, marvelling over the fact that these people could actually communicate. Being that my confidence and boyfriend were nowhere to be seen, if – God forbid – someone spoke to me, I experienced it as a small trauma. Hey, call me timid but this was how I'd suddenly come to experience life. As well-dressed locals went to great lengths to explain their particular preference when it came to melon circumference, all I could do was idiotically giggle and point. And when I coughed up money, I had absolutely no idea if I were being charged double for my sins.

The greatest problem for me, however, was that nobody seemed to exude any outward signs of friendliness. *Nobody!* Was it just me? Or was I actually being disregarded? Wherever I trudged, I trudged with the anticipation of being frowned upon. And what you expect is what you get. I now know that better than most.

Without words, all I could use to comprehend the attitudes of those around me were their facial expressions, but these seemed very different from the ones I'd grown up with. Where I came from, people generally smiled more, and abruptness was usually interpreted as rudeness. In Australia, if somebody grunted, didn't return a smile or snatched money from my hand, I could safely assume they were either having a rough day or had the screaming shits with me. But here, *everybody* was doing it! So was everyone pissed off? Or just pissed off with me?

Floating through this sea of colour like a black shadow, I took to walking briskly away from vendors if I didn't like their attitude – not that anybody gave a flying fuck. But I wanted the perpetrators, filled with remorse, to chase after me, and to fawn all over me to try to rectify the situation. I wanted to introduce the interesting concept of 'good customer service'. Alas, it wasn't to be. Nobody even noticed.

By the end of my second week in Greece, I began to feel like a real stranger, which I was, but more of a lonely and resented one. Yes, I actually felt resented. I tried to look at my new circumstances as humorous or even culturally compelling. But in my heart, the seeds of alienation and sadness began to sprout, tended to most diligently by myself.

In the meantime, Dion was doing wonderfully well. He'd come home nightly with stories boasting common themes of triumph and success. On the odd occasion, he'd also confide in me his confusion over unexpected staff behaviour or strange business practices. It had become apparent that his staff worked to live and not the other way around, that in the Greek business world palms were expected to be greased, and that things tended to happen tomorrow, rather than yesterday. But still, my boy was on fire and we were both extremely happy with the multiple achievements he'd already made at the station. I felt myself drawing closer to him as my only supporter. While I experienced each confounding incident as a small travesty, Dion found a way of turning it effortlessly into a comedy routine that he acted out in the centre of our living room. He put such a positive spin on things and had such a generous spirit that I could usually laugh myself into a state of forgetting what it was that had tied me in knots in the first place.

I began to wonder about my man's mysterious daytime world. His work was obviously playing a part in him seeing the world through rose-coloured glasses while I squinted through a pair smeared with shit. I wanted to steal a sample of Dion's happiness for myself.

'Why not come to the station and see where all the magic happens firsthand, beautiful?' Dion offered. He then took an enormous bite from a basketball-sized peach I'd bought from the market, juice trailing down his forearm.

With Dion favouring 6 a.m. starts – the time of day that most Athenians returned home from a night out – I decided to make my own way to the radio station the following day. I'd grab a taxi. Simple! One approached on Poseidonos Avenue speeding towards me at 100 kilometres per hour. As it neared, it slowed, and I screamed my destination into the driver's window. A plump and sweaty driver in co-ordinated browns and blacks raised his eyes, made a clicking sound with his tongue and nodded his head. I made for the door. He sped off. That's how I learned that this nod didn't in fact mean 'yes', but quite the opposite. The repetition of this nod that meant no from another seven cabbies only served to reinforce the fact. After many attempts, I finally had a taker and shared my cab with another passenger balancing a cabbage on her knee.

The radio station was in a multistorey, modern building with a brilliant glass exterior that belied its dated interior. After taking a slow lift to the fourth floor, I noted the primitive radio equipment and discovered that Dion's office, shared with the station's financial controller, was the size of a postage stamp. A large proportion of each man's workday was spent trying to avoid outer thigh contact.

I squeezed in for a look around, tripped over a network of computer cables, and became wedged between a chair and a filing cabinet. Awaiting rescue, I peered out of a dirty window that overlooked a traffic jam on a major arterial, and the blackened exterior of a huge concrete dome that would be used during the Olympics. If I squinted hard enough, I could also just make out two cats mating on the docks of an abandoned shipyard.

For the life of me, I couldn't understand why Dion had never mentioned these less than desirable work conditions. As far as I was concerned, the prospect of running a radio station in Europe had sounded a lot more enticing over the telephone than it proved in reality. However, the truth was Dion didn't even notice that he no longer had a prestigious view of the Sydney Harbour Bridge as he'd done at Triple M. He just got on with things.

Seeing the concern on my face, my boyfriend smiled his familiar smile, raised a steaming cup of coffee that had been lovingly prepared by one of his adoring staff and, like an overly animated boy, beckoned me over to admire treasured programming equipment. I kept my observations to myself and instead enthused over technology that I didn't really understand.

Metropolis

We'd been in Athens for a little over a month. As another weekend rolled around, it was time for our weekly visit to Nota and Nikos, which had fast become a fixture. Each Sunday, Nikos and I picked up where our engaging repartee had left off the week before:

'Okay, mate?'

'Okay, mate!'

Beyond this, our activities schedule had blasted into the stratosphere with a visit to the almighty Acropolis. We didn't feel like residents, and nor were we tourists. But we felt more like tourists than we did anything else. And what did tourists do? They visited the Acropolis. So once again Dion ferried us into the centre at breakneck speed and once again I found myself overwhelmed by the city beyond Voula and the number of head-on collisions we narrowly avoided. Yet again, I was confronted by the city's in-your-face paradox: its urban decay of grey concrete, garbage and smog made bearable by a solitary kerbside olive tree, a playful stray kitten or the blinding colour of a bougainvillea creeping around a balcony railing. An ancient ruin would crop up on the perimeter of a main road and Athens would instantly redeem itself.

Again I raised the question, *what is this place?* I was guessing that after 7000 years of habitation, the residents of the Greek capital looked fondly upon their city as a tattered but comfortable pair of old jeans. I, on the other hand, looked upon it as a well-used dishrag. Once again, Dion seemed to see the city for what it was, while I fell headfirst into the looking glass after dropping bad acid. Sure my negative perceptions were in overdrive, but my feelings of entrapment were nevertheless real. I wanted to love the place. I truly did. But I didn't. I only loved Dion. And I loved everyone back home too. I began thinking about them. I began thinking about them *a lot.*

Luckily for Dion, his primary sense was aural. With his ears so keenly attuned to the radio, I wasn't sure if he even noticed the city around us and it wasn't that easy to find out, either. I learned to speak to him only midway through tortuous Greek melodies, post-talk break and after it had been established that the artist, tempo and song were appropriate for that particular time of day. I'd then, and only then, deliver a question that was nine times out of ten annoyingly pointless.

'It's kind of ugly here, hey?'

'It's not that bad. Hang on a minute, babe.' Dion would turn up the radio a fraction and an announcer would then jibber in a lexis I didn't understand, followed by a song that would have me consider extracting my own eardrums with a pair of pliers.

So this is what rocking in the cradle of European civilisation is all about, huh?

I sulkily peered out the car window.

As we neared the centre of town, the landmark we were chasing disappeared behind buildings and then re-emerged magnificent, lording over the city, a testament to the glorious wisdom, chaos and spirituality of years gone by. Meticulously designed in the fifth century BC, the Acropolis had witnessed cult worship of the goddess Athena, followed by Christian and Muslim conversion; it had been claimed by the Turks and blown up by the Venetians. Ignorant of all of this, I thought it was 'okay'. Yep. That's right, 'okay'. If anyone had asked me my opinion of one of the world's greatest and most recognisable landmarks, I would have replied, 'It's okay, I guess,' and left it at that. Sad but true.

We approached the 'okay' attraction, through narrow, hilly streets lined with parked cars sniffing each other's behinds, and crawled among the shadows of stock standard apartment buildings. They were all a little bit dirty, a little bit grey, roughly five levels high, and most had plant-filled balconies. Eventually we found a car park that belonged to a taverna restaurant. As soon as we pulled up, an attendant sauntered over, popped a hand on the car roof, a head through the window and blabbered something in Greek.

'What's he saying?'

Dion blabbered something back.

'What did you just say?'

The attendant blabbered something in return.

'What's happening?'

After Dion switched off the engine, he explained to me that we could only park in this area if we were patrons of the restaurant. This wasn't a problem. Dion told the attendant we'd be back to eat, but just in case we fell victim to natural disaster, he greased his palm with a small monetary offering. The attendant was satisfied. Little did I know how instinctively Dion was tuning into the Athenian way, where money talks and bullshit, well, is equally effective. We then began the steep climb to the Acropolis beneath the subdued early-October sun, Dion triumphantly boasting about how much his Greek had improved in the short space of a month.

'Mine too!' I was such a liar.

Our trainers suctioned the slippery stone steps leading skyward. This, however, didn't prevent Dion from gasping and wheezing like an asthmatic 93-year-old. Along with the vast majority of the Greek population, Dion was a chronic smoker.

I had always assumed that the Parthenon and Acropolis were one and the same thing. Not so. The Parthenon – the great big Doric-columned structure usually covered with scaffolding that stands proudly as the symbol of Greece – is actually the centrepiece of the Acropolis. It's the second thing you think of after John Travolta when someone shrieks the word 'Greece' in a word association game. *That's* the Parthenon. The other structures that surround it, including the Odeon of Herod Atticus, the Theatre of Dionysios, the Temple of Athena Nike and the Ionic Erechtheion (featuring columns sculpted to look like a row of fair maidens), collectively form the Acropolis.

How did we know all this? Well, we didn't. We certainly hadn't done any research. We were far too lazy for that. Instead we assumed the look of inconspicuous German tourists and hung on the fringes of an *'Acropolis for Dummies'* tour group. We learned a lot that day, discovering that each of the wonderful constructions surrounding us was built hundreds of years before Christ. We also learned about the Elgin Marbles.

As many people know, the Elgin Marbles are not a colourful set of tiny glass balls that eight-year-old boys might flick across a lounge-room floor. They are the elaborate frieze sculptures that decorated the Parthenon. At the beginning of the nineteenth century, the presumably pompous British ambassador, Lord Elgin, bought these priceless commodities from the Turks who occupied Greece at the time for the price of a dying mule. He shipped them back to the motherland and they've been stashed in the British Museum ever since – the British government obstinately refusing to return them to their rightful owners. This is something that understandably pisses the Greeks off. It kind of pissed us off too.

Mulling this over, I stumbled with Dion from the Acropolis to the Plaka, the quaint little area below the Acropolis that provides an insight into what Athens might have been like if it had been left alone to develop with a sense of dignity. Instead, much of Athens had been 'redesigned' with little architectural consideration thanks to rampant urbanisation, civil engineers doubling as architects, and a government that randomly doled out building permits to gain favour with voters in the '60s and '70s.

The Plaka, one of the oldest sections of Athens, is sensitively maintained and closed off to traffic. Its ambience tricks one into forgetting about the chaos that lies just beyond its boundaries. Outside the main tourist zone, neat, simple homes decorated in neoclassical pastels are nestled in quiet back streets. It is a place with atmosphere and is what I wished all of Athens was like.

Dion and I traversed stone-paved labyrinths, pointing delightedly at red-roofed cosy homes or unexpected Byzantine churches, until we eventually entered a hub of cafés, restaurants and tourist outlets. Our nostrils filled with the combined aroma of yiros and espresso. While many retailers offered generic tourist knickknacks, some of the classier establishments sold eye-catching art and genuine antiques. Back-to-back jewellery stores displayed a plethora of diamond-encrusted gold pieces – enough bling to make even P. Diddy blush.

We passed stores overstocked with Che Guevara T-shirts. Others offered religious icons, globes, olive oil, Spartan helmets, ashtrays, plaster statues depicting Greek gods, postcards, chessboards and sea sponges. Dion bought his first set of *komboloi*, little worry beads that we'd seen old men flick around their fingers as a way of keeping their gesticulation-prone hands busy. Feeling left out, I settled for a sponge.

We sauntered past taverna restaurants where old geezers played *tavli*, the Greek version of backgammon, at outdoor tables. Some restaurateurs beckoned us to take a table while others sat dormant on small wooden chairs, lazily watching us stroll by. We settled at a table beneath the shade of a tree and watched herds of passing tourists betray their foreignness by way of white T-shirts, money belts, beige shorts, hats and sensible sandals, a look that was way, *way* too undignified for any self-respecting Athenian.

Animated accordionists honed in on us and played until we threw money at them to make them go away, then little gypsy girls took their place offering flowers. We declined. They persisted. We pretended they weren't there. They floated away. Why we dissed the skinny little girls is anyone's guess. Our generosity or lack thereof was indiscriminate, but those wearing beige seemed much more obliging. As Dion ordered our food in Greek, I wondered what I was about to eat, quietly annoyed that I no longer had the small luxury of choosing my own food. Ignorant of my frustrations, my boyfriend innocently sipped from a glass of ouzo he'd diluted with water, turning it a murky white. Soon we were gnawing on barbecued lamb chops, liquid fat glossing our lips and chins as I kicked off a discussion on the plight of the Elgin Marbles.

'Don't you think it sucks that the Greeks don't have a significant part of their very own Parthenon? It's not fair. Why should the English hoard them?' I paused for dramatic effect. 'What would you say if I suggested we try to get them back?'

'Get who back? The Brits? What, are you a terrorist now?'

'No! I mean get the Elgin Marbles back.'

'I'd say, "Yeah, okay. Great idea . . . *fruitcake!*"'

Dion smiled as his dark fringe flopped into an eye. He raised a quizzical brow.

'Okay, hear me out. You're running a high-profile radio station, right? And aren't the people of Athens passionate about getting those Marbles back? What if you put the station behind petitioning the British government? What if you gave the people a voice? What if you ended up in the history books, heralded as a hero for altering the course of Greek history? What if —'

Dion cut me short. He could see I was getting caught up in a *Scooby Doo Mystery of the Missing Marbles*–type fantasy.

'Nice idea, but . . . AS IF!' He flicked his new silver worry beads twice to emphasise his point. I squeezed my sea sponge.

'Maybe it's not as crazy as it sounds. I'll help you. I'll figure out a way to make it work. Imagine if we did this and something actually came of it? Imagine if they were returned in time for the 2004 Olympic Games? Wouldn't that be great? Wouldn't your mum and dad flip out?'

I'd struck a nerve. I'd mentioned Dion's mother.

'I suppose so . . . I guess it wouldn't hurt to try. Maybe I'll look into it.'

The following week, I walked to a sparse, unpopulated hill that I'd been staring at pensively from our kitchen window. It was only forty minutes from our Labrou Katsoni home. Halfway up the hill I sat down and agonised over the logistics of pulling off such a feat. With pen in hand and tongue positioned firmly at the corner of my mouth, I stared at the far-off ocean for inspiration. A wild, stumpy-footed tortoise trundled past, four-wheel-driving over colourless dry shrubs and rocks. I scrawled notes onto reams of paper. Then I drew a cartoon depiction of a turtle with a big smile, winking coyly. My strategy was infallible. The Elgin Marbles would soon be returned.

A week later, Dion met with an official lobbying group. They looked at him as though he'd lost his own set of marbles. They seemed dejected. No, more than that, they seemed disinterested, as if they'd all but given up hope. It transpired we weren't the first to decide that the Greeks had been kicked in the Marbles. Prince Charles had already voiced hopes to key members of the Greek community in London that Lord Elgin's spoils would be back in Athens in time for the 2004 Olympic Games. And Bill Clinton had also made it his business to support Greece in its campaign, publicly declaring that he intended to have a nice little chat to Tony Blair about it personally. However, there was never any shift in the British government's stance. If the voices of even Prince Charles and Bill Clinton weren't heard, what hope had two little Australians lost in Athens? I soon became despondent, and my grand plan fizzled out.

After the ill-fated marble recovery project I was back to my weekday self – disorientated, intimidated and bored. I became more and more conscious that I was doing very little with my life. So I filled the void by investigating the neighbouring suburb of Glyfada. It was a stroke of genius!

I walked along Poseidonos Avenue as cars flew by at unbelievable speeds. Along the way larger-than-life billboard advertisements depicted extreme close-ups of women's g-string clad arses, women strewn across tables simulating acts of depravity, or lesbian acts feigned by women who would never be seen dead in comfy shoes and k.d. lang T-shirts. Upon closer inspection, as far as I could tell, these advertisements were targeting female consumers. I didn't quite get it. I had to remind myself that I was in *Europe*. This was what Europeans *did*.

By now preconceptions of Greece courtesy of travel programs viewed throughout the years were completely thrown out the window. Glyfada is a modern, chaotic suburb of designer clothing stores targeting the Euro-chic fashion-conscious if they can manage to squeeze past bumper-to-bumper triple-parked vehicles and into desired outlets without first falling off diminishing pavements after hurdling the odd stray dormant canine. Hemmed-in motorists leaned on car horns until a birthday came and went. Cars parked *in the middle of the road*. There was not a donkey anywhere to be seen!

After carefully observing the people who pushed past me as though I were an invisible yet intrigued anthropologist, I couldn't get past the high level of grooming. Statuesque Athenian princesses paraded by, my stumpy Maltese legs struggling to keep up. I recognised early the essentialness of matching clothing with shoes, bags, wallets, jewellery, sunglasses, eye colour, hair colour, fingernails, toenails, cars and general apartment furnishings. Men were equally co-ordinated and ne'er shied away from the manbag. I looked down at my Stussy cargo pants, Converse shoes and sloppy red T-shirt, intimidated by the designer dress code, frightened by the excessive make-up, gleaming nail polish, flashing jewellery and ultra-extravagant hair. By comparison I looked like a twelve-year-old boy. I definitely wasn't cutting it.

I established then and there that what I first required to blend naturally into the environment was a pair of seven-inch-heeled pointy shoes that could knock the testosterone out of Robbie Williams. I just wasn't sure about the seven-inch heel part. While wearers of such stilt-like foot apparel exhibited impressive gravity defiance, I knew that once I'd strapped on a pair I'd be forced to scramble along the ground on all fours. Naturally I was apprehensive. But over-the-top couture was the name of the game, even amongst the youth. Around Glyfada, signs of punk, goth, skater or indie 'individuality' were as common as a fabled yeti sighting.

There was urgent shopping to be done. Despite a usually strong sense of personal style, I knew I *had* to look just like everybody else if I wished to remain inconspicuous. As I tested the waters in one or two stores, I was delighted to note that most of the delicately coiffed beings peered at me from behind their counters as though observing a rare poisonous marine specimen washed up on a shoreline. I tried convincing myself that they were mesmerised by my exotic beauty. However, as I continued shopping, I began wondering if I was actually being mistaken for a suspected murderer. I felt that shopkeepers were either treating me with general offhandedness or utter contempt and I became more and more deflated. I was soon snapped out of my reverie.

'*Ohi!* No touch!'

I'd been chastised for picking up and inspecting folded items of clothing since it necessitated merchandise re-alignment. Loss of dignity notwithstanding, I was determined to discover the key to a pleasant shopping experience. There *had* to be a secret to it. So I came up with a tricky new approach that seemed infallible. It involved:

(a) Walking briskly past a shop window looking rushed and preoccupied;
(b) Darting a look at my watch while flashing a detached expression, as if contemplating Pythagoras' theorem; and
(c) Entering a store at random with an erect posture and feigned air of confidence.

Unfortunately, I conceived this plan around the same time as I was having trouble not only shopping but *walking* in Greece. I was so unaccustomed to Athens' irregular paved surfaces that I found myself tripping over constantly, which did very little for my diminishing self-esteem. My first grand entrance into a store was therefore foiled after I stumbled over an undetected marble step and crash-landed into a clothing rack. The store was quiet and empty, save for a lone, gorgeous-looking shop assistant I'd rudely distracted from gazing at her fingernails. She looked up, bored. There was zero recognition of my buffoonery. I wasn't sure whether to be insulted or grateful.

Gathering what was left of my pride, I began browsing, determined to win the girl's approval. I paused longer than necessary at each item of clothing and smiled emptily at piles of feathered, ornate and extravagant tops reserved for the hedonism of a *bouzoukia*, hoping to appear amiable and interested.

The sales girl sighed. After all, she'd just been forced to leave her cigarette smouldering in a colossal orange ashtray on the counter. She approached grudgingly, and in Greek queried presumably either 'Can I help you?' or 'Can I interest you in physical harm?' to which I responded with a nervous smile. She didn't smile back. I was obviously doing something wrong.

As I continued to drift about the merchandise, my sighing and unsmiling friend began tailing me, barely a pace behind, shadowing my every move. I could feel the condensation of her breath on the back of my neck. It was as though we'd become a choreographed cabaret duo renowned in Vegas. To this day I'm unsure if her attempted piggybacking was an anti-shoplifting measure, or an effort to 'assist' based on tried and tested Mafia techniques. For a split second I stood transfixed by a rack of diagonally cut skirts adorned with fur, leather and lace, then made an unexpected dash for the exit.

Back on the street, bypassing limbless beggars and pirate CD sellers, I took a seat in a fast-food restaurant where I knew I could order by pointing and saying 'hkkamburger' in English with an exaggerated Greek accent. I sat and ate alone. People dashed past, silently competing to out-dress one another despite essentially wearing the same thing. I debriefed with myself, dreaming of the day I'd merge into their world, looking exactly like them.

When I told Dion of the day's episodes, he patted me on the head, told me things could only get better and recommenced working from his laptop. As I dutifully removed a cup from the table beside him and placed it in the dishwasher, I can't say his response exactly brought any reassurance. I knew there was very little that Dion could do. And I knew that my anxious observations could become tiresome. But if I didn't vent to him, then what else could I do? Confide in a pot plant? Keep the perplexing world unfolding before me a dirty, dark secret? No, there was nothing else for it. If Greece was gonna be a bitch, I was gonna dob her in to my boyfriend. Even if there wasn't a lot he could do to rectify circumstances.

People are strange

By our second month the weather had cooled considerably. Athina's visits came and went with alarming regularity, as did my language lessons. The long hours outside of these highlights were tedious, lonely times spent ironing, studying Greek, writing emails to friends and family professing my undying love for Dion and my reservations towards Athens, and taking daylong baths. Daylong baths . . . sounds like a dream, doesn't it? Trust me. As unbelievable as it seems, the novelty soon swirls down the drain along with a slick of dead skin cells.

I always managed to squeeze in the odd excursion to Glyfada, usually dressed in an outfit that looked like it had been bought for my auntie's sixtieth birthday party in an effort to blend into the scenery. There was never any real reason to visit this area, but it got me out of the house and on this particular day I had a letter to post – a very important mission indeed. It was at the top of my list of things to do, an addition that was a significant deviation from the previous day's list:

Post letter.

Write emails.

Do Greek homework.

Tend to ironing.

Take a bath.

I closed my sanctuary door behind me and bumped into our neighbour, Maria, waiting for the lift. A hint of her perfume wafted in the air.

'Ti kanete?'

(She asked me how I was.)

'Kala.'

(I lied that I was good.)

We then stood in awkward silence, entered the lift in silence, stared ahead in silence and exited in silence.

'Yia sas,' she shouted in relief as she headed briskly for the car park.

'Bye,' I replied as I headed for the street.

I trudged along the familiar path I'd begun wearing into the earth like a goat track, stopping at a quiet street I needed to cross. As I stepped onto the road, I noticed a car rocketing towards me with no intention whatsoever of slowing down. In fact, I could have sworn that the driver actually *accelerated* upon registering there was a pedestrian in range. I was forced to throw myself back onto the sidewalk in a desperate bid to hold onto my mortality. Furious, I began channelling Satan. Not that the driver had any idea he'd caused such outrage; no, he was busy breaking the sound barrier and had possibly crossed into Macedonia even before I'd formulated the ingenious idea of screaming at the top of my lungs:

'You're a fucking *DICKHEAD!*'

Dear God! What was happening to me?

Screaming profanities out on the streets now are we? Now that's what I call class!

At that moment, my foot struck a typically uneven section of footpath and I found myself 'chucking a helicopter' to regain my balance. So there I was: arms flapping about, staggering all over the pavement, screaming 'DICKHEAD!' at nobody in particular. To the casual observer it may have appeared that there was a dickhead out on the street screaming 'dickhead'. But I wasn't about to be discouraged by attempted murder. No, I still had a letter to post, so I continued determinedly on my quest to the Glyfada post office. I was about to learn that the procedure in a Greek post office differed slightly from the one I was accustomed to.

My observations started with the queuing system. Once inside, it wasn't so much a case of forming an orderly line as it was forming a human pyramid. The queue formed upwards and outwards, with individuals climbing the torsos of complete strangers as though attending an Aerosmith concert, circa 1977. The building was packed to the rafters with a sweaty mass of hair and impatience. I waited while those around me demonstrated what seemed to be grotesquely exaggerated aspects of various personality disorders.

Never before had I witnessed such pandemonium surrounding the simple act of posting a letter. Every counter window had up to ten customers competing for service, whether or not they had an appropriately numbered ticket. There was jostling, shoving and baring of teeth. I didn't quite get the method behind the madness. Nor, I gathered, did the elderly gentleman who had begun pacing behind the throng like an agitated hyena. Without warning, I watched with horror as his annoyance erupted with greater force than the volcano that had nearly destroyed the island of Santorini in the Bronze Age. He began bellowing with evangelical vigour, and in this concrete sanctuary of acoustic perfection we all paid the price. He shouted at the top of his lungs, either about the inefficiencies of the postal service or the remarkable success of his citrus trees that season.

Amazingly, everybody continued about their business as though nothing out of the ordinary was happening. One woman was even laughing. She was sitting beside me and laughing so hard that her eyes threatened to fall out of her head and bounce off her knees. She turned to me with an invitation to join in on all the fun. Unlike her, however, I didn't get it. To foreign ears, the old man sounded terrifying. I nevertheless half-laughed, pretending I *did* get it, but after an extended period of fake hilarity, I belied my ignorance by asking, 'What's happening? What's so funny?'

Realising I spoke an unintelligible mystery language and that I'd possibly recently emerged from the depths of Atlantis, the smile of the dear woman faltered and she shifted her expression and body as though the exchange had never taken place. I chose to take it personally and made a mental note to be annoyed with her for the rest of my life. Meanwhile, the old man's protests continued while everyone remained unfazed. I would soon learn that throwing tantrums was often an effective means of communication in Greece. The Greeks are passionate and explosive. Yelling and screaming get things done. But not all the time.

Finally my number was called and I pushed my way through the mob to shout my request for a stamp at a tired postal worker with black circles around her eyes. Triumphant, I proceeded to a table to address and stamp my envelope. In the meantime, the Yelling Man left the building, marking his exit with a raised, shaking fist. Just after his timely departure I registered out of the corner of my eye a glamorous Athenian princess heading in my direction. Like many of the breed of women lurking around these parts, she was flawlessly groomed all the way down to her pink-painted nails. Her tight-fitting designer pants incorporated a faux animal print – the tiger stripe – suede tassels, diamantes along the outer seam, and the ubiquitous groin-area camel toe. Her seven-inch-heeled pointy shoes of course reached the post office table well before she did.

As I innocently licked my stamp, her shadow descended upon me. She settled at the opposite side of the table as if poised for an unexpected photo opportunity. It was not forthcoming. Spying next to me a pen that had been sticky-taped feverishly to a piece of string, she sauntered to my side. And the next thing I knew I was knocked off my feet. *Literally!* With a flick of the hips I was pushed out of the way in order for her to wrap her talons around that germ-ridden pen. I turned to her questioningly, awaiting at the very least an apologetic eyelid flutter. However, no reaction whatsoever registered on her daytime soap opera face.

I tried to contain it. I honestly did. But that special strain of Tourette's Syndrome that had visited me earlier made its grand return – bigger, better and louder than ever. I wanted to learn from Yelling Man's mistakes, but it seemed beyond my control. I felt something like Bruce Banner as he began his metamorphosis into The Hulk.

'Sorry?' I began, dumbfounded.

There was no reaction.

Don't make me angry. You wouldn't like me when I'm angry.

I looked around for backup. There was none.

'SORRY?' I said a little louder, the sleeves of my shirt beginning to rip, exposing green flesh.

Again, no reaction. Then came the explosion I'd been dreading. And what spewed forth was *not* the clever, well-thought-out quip I was hoping for:

'YOU FUCKING *BITCH!*'

Oh dear Lord! Did I really just do that?

The words echoed around the post office, confirming that Yelling Man and I had several disturbing things in common. We were both stupid enough to make public spectacles of ourselves, *extraordinarily* uncool, and *completely* ignored to the bitter end. I was starting to get all weird.

I loved my boyfriend! I truly did. So that's why I began complaining my arse off to him.

In between working hard, Dion pacified me through active listening, well-timed nods and general words of encouragement. 'It's gonna be okay' or 'you'll get the hang of it' concluded most conversations. Aside from this, there was little else he could come up with to help make my experience as pleasurable as his. However, I had an idea. I took to drafting promotional plans for his radio station, uninvited. Although my partner in crime had always respected my professional opinion, I felt Dion's appreciation for my marketing expertise was on the wane. He no longer needed to hear ingenious ideas for Coca-Cola–sponsored weekend key-ring giveaways. As Dion found his feet more and more, my suggestions became less and less welcome. Not surprisingly, none were ever implemented.

So, as an outlet for creativity, I began experimenting with my eating habits. I'd see if I could survive an entire day on only one cold baked potato, portioning out bite-sized pieces that I'd nibble on at the start of every hour. On other days, I'd eat an entire jar of Nutella and walk around the apartment with chocolate smeared across my face.

Who cares? Nobody can see me.

I'd then dance wildly around the living room.

Yes, I really did do all these things.

I then began to behave even more strangely, fixating upon certain foods that, although readily available in Australia, were now nowhere to be seen. Unavailable perishables transformed into priceless commodities more treasured than my own vital organs. By this point I would have gladly exchanged my spleen for a

packet of Tim Tam chocolate biscuits and a bunch of fresh coriander. Encountering food common in Australia, but rare in Athens,
resulted in outbursts that opened up the possibility of arrest. Back
home it certainly wasn't usual for me to clutch a plump, juicy piece
of dead animal to my chest before launching into a 1950s matinee
dance routine in celebration.

Meanwhile, some local delicacies had me pulling faces similar
to ones I might pull after wolfing down a glass-splintered grapefruit
while cradling a vicious, rudely awakened ferret. It was just my luck
that I happened to *despise* feta cheese and cucumber, and harboured
a secret resentment towards the humble olive. Believe it or not, I
was also mildly allergic to tomato. As Dion ordered and interacted
at various tavernas on my behalf, I often sat in silence wondering why the lamb tasted funny, something like a cross between
a sheep and a rare hybrid of wild mountain goat. It was slightly
different. No biggie, right? But lamb, feta, cucumber, olives *and*
tomato issues? I mean, come on! They're only the five staples of
the Greek diet. Hell, I didn't even drink coffee, the national drink
of choice. Even Greek *babies* chose coffee over mother's milk.
I could only conclude that the universe was playing some kind of
elaborate practical joke upon me and was doubled over, pissing
itself laughing at my expense.

Don't get me wrong. There is absolutely nothing wrong with
Greek cuisine. It was *me* who had the problem. Greek food is
top-notch. There are delightful salads and dips, creamy yoghurts,
grilled octopus, eggplant moussaka, baklava and spanakopita – all
delicious. And remember the striking resemblance between dog-
paddling turds and *soutzoukakia*? This dish turned out to be beyond
delicious. My new Greek diet, however, wasn't always gracefully
accepted by a palate corrupted by Australian diversity. Where were
my spicy Thai fishcakes loaded with coriander when I needed them?

Why would the Greek military be called in if a local happened upon a wok, mistaking it for a crash-landed piece of space junk? And why was the ever-accommodating Aunty Nota so insistent that I cram as much of the local stuff down my throat as possible on our weekly Sunday visits?

She would look at me, smiling, and bellow a sentence that lasted several minutes. I would glance at my watch, then ask Dion to interpret. He would oblige.

'Eat! Eat! You too *skeeeeny!*'

Nikos would add to the discourse, 'Okay, mate?' and I'd force myself to nibble on a crumble of feta.

✖ 10 ✖

I'm bored

Month Three.

God I was bored. It wasn't just about food. And it wasn't just about my own company. I got through most days eagerly awaiting Dion's return like a faithful Labrador staring at the door awaiting its master. My Greek god would come home from work, eat, and fall asleep on the couch. The guy was exhausted. I wasn't. And deep down I couldn't help but wonder if Dion saw this little worker/housewife routine of ours as simply the way things should be.

As he slept, I'd flick through television channels praying like mad for an old American cop show – *anything*, just as long as it was in English. Occasionally I'd hit the jackpot. More often than not, I didn't. However, late one evening I did stumble across free-to-air porn where English wasn't required to follow the 'plot'. That's right. *Porn*. Let's just say it was the second-last thing I was expecting and that it led to third-degree burns as a hot mug of cocoa surged into my lap after my body convulsed in shock. I'd already heard the worst uncensored profanities ever uttered in English-language movies, which I found hilarious, but this was getting ridiculous. There would be no end to Greece's surprises, of that I was certain.

In any event, by day especially, I was becoming increasingly lonely and homesick. I didn't like my life, but I didn't know how to create one that I did like. I felt empty. And I was running out of ways to fill my days. Let me walk you through what I was doing the afternoon the telephone interrupted an otherwise normal 'Day in the Life of Lana'. I was in the bathroom, focusing hard on my reflection in the mirror. I'd just shaved off my eyebrows. You see, I no longer *cared* for them. I'd decided to pencil in a new pair at a later date. I was also wearing a hot pink lipstick that came free with a bottle of hair colour and was trying to decide whether or not it suited me. It didn't. It looked rubbish. *I* looked rubbish. Still in my pyjamas, I stared intently at the browless, clown face before me and made extravagant stop signals at my own reflection.

'*Stamata!* Stop. *Stamata!* Stop. *Stamata!* Stop.'

This was a method I'd come up with to learn Greek. I felt that if I associated a word with a physical representation it would stick. God knows my study wasn't working in the conventional sense. I wasn't only saying and acting out the words either. I was varying the pitch and tone of my voice while carrying out a series of impersonations. This was all intended to keep myself entertained. At times I'd say 'Stamata! Stop!' in a high-pitched Irish accent. At other times I'd sing it in an Italian baritone. Yeah, it was just another day.

The telephone rang. I looked at myself, exaggerating a silent-movie look of horror.

'Oh, no! *Telephono!*'

I hoped it was Dion's daily phone call and not one of the occasional callers that would crash a phone down in my ear after I answered. It was neither.

'Ne?' I barked into the receiver, attempting to sound like an aggressive fishmonger's wife.

'Hello?' responded a perplexed Australian voice on the other end of the line.

'Hello? Who's this?'

It was Leonie, a friend from my former life who worked with Australian pop sensation Savage Garden. Aside from my mother, she was the first Australian to have made vocal contact with me in three months. She was calling from San Francisco. I felt ecstatic to hear her voice; so relaxed, so friendly, so familiar. She asked how I was doing.

'Oh, okay, I suppose.'

'I hope I'm not interrupting. What were you up to?'

'Um . . . Nothing much. Just going over some Greek homework. What's going on?'

'I was just thinking about you, that's all. I was thinking that with Italy practically on your doorstep, maybe you should come and meet us in Milan near the end of the European tour. I've got a big, fat hotel suite all to myself that you're more than welcome to crash in. What do you reckon? It'll be fun!'

I agreed – immediately. Dion thought it was a good idea too. Anything to stop me from stagnating. He understood I needed time out. It would also give him the opportunity to focus 100 per cent on work.

A couple of weeks later, my eyebrows making a reluctant comeback, I found myself in an Italian taxi heading for an entourage of fun-loving Australians, all working away in a business they appreciated, but that I'd left behind. In the cab, I wistfully reflected on my former career. I'd worked with and interviewed some of the world's most successful performers, contemporary and otherwise: Celine Dion, Foo Fighters, The Corrs, INXS, Christina Aguilera, Gwen Stefani, The Cardigans, Neil Diamond, Garbage, The Presidents of the USA, Sarah McLachlan, Rob Thomas, Korn, Metallica,

Max Cavelera, Ben Harper, Portishead and Australian film director extraordinaire Baz Luhrmann. In this fabled former life, I was pretty sure I'd been surrounded by people who were generally aware of my existence.

So, in Italy, the prospect of being around 'my own people' again filled me with a sense of elation. Once I'd arrived at the plush Milanese hotel to be surrounded by the Savage Garden entourage, their familiar accents, warmth and humour breathed life back into me. It seemed so long since I'd laughed along with a group of people – so long since I'd even *been* with a group of people. I also remembered what it was to be moved by music.

Although resurrected, I was also slightly weirder. Having forgotten the fundamentals of communication thanks to my new Robinson Crusoe lifestyle, the art of effortless conversation all but eluded me. Instead I blurted fragments of the complexities I'd been facing, trying but failing to explain the implications of a lonely life in a foreign country. To my horror, I'd also developed a kind of nervous stutter. Standing offstage at Milan's Alcatraz, watching Darren Hayes croon 'To the Moon and Back' in angelic tones, I wondered if my old friends now saw me as a bit of a whinger, rather than the fancy-free producer they once knew. Were they forming theories of their own about 'the bitter one'?

Unfortunately my parole time in Italy was short. After only two days I was back in Voula, whizzing past our apartment on Labrou Katsoni in a cab, spluttering to a flummoxed driver.

'*Stammer! Tomato! Stigmata! STOP!*'

It was 7 p.m., the beginning of the gastronomic limbo period for unseasoned westernised stomachs. The evening meal in Greece can take place any time between 10 p.m. and midnight, sometimes even later, a practice enjoyed in many parts of Europe since time immemorial but which I found completely bonkers. By this time of night, back in Australia, I'd be either sound asleep or half-maggotted on cheap alcohol. The last thing on my mind would be a lukewarm plate of deflated moussaka. But on this particular evening, I was happy to hold off eating. It was a Saturday night with a difference. Dion and I actually had something to do! After more than three full months, it was to be our first night out with a couple of genuine Athenians. I was as nervous as I was excited. Predictably, nervousness got the better of me.

What if they think I'm an idiot? What if they don't like me?

I practised clever dialogue in my head to offset my fears and to ensure that our new friends would have no choice but to be enamoured.

'The Elgin Marbles? Why, it's an outrage!'

'I LOVE Athens!'

'What do I do by day? Oh, I do some work for the United Nations.'

'I once interviewed Shirley Manson from Garbage, you know. Yes, yes! I used to be an MTV producer. What was she like? Oh, charming, really . . .'

The couple we were meeting were called Yianni and Anna. Yianni was a business colleague of Dion's. He was the radio station's general manager and Dion's right-hand man. Dion adored him and he adored Dion. Anna was Yianni's wife. She was a schoolteacher and Dion liked her too. I'd never met them before in my life.

At 10 p.m., Dion and I were seated and waiting expectantly for our new friends to arrive. Somewhere around 10.45 p.m. they materialised, wandering through the restaurant as though browsing in an art gallery. I didn't yet know that in Greece, arriving anywhere in the vague *vicinity* of a nominated time is perfectly acceptable. The couple beamed at us as they approached.

Yianni, in his mid-thirties, was square-jawed and prematurely greying. He wore a smart fawn suit and 'Coke bottle' glasses that magnified his eyes at least five times. Anna was a beautiful bottle blonde with not a hair out of place. She walked with an erect posture and graceful air. She was extraordinarily well dressed in a perfectly accessorised Louis Vuitton style, a silk scarf wrapped elegantly around her delicate neck. I was wearing an outfit I'd bought off the rack from Dotti in Sydney, a shiny purple pair of trousers with a matching purple lycra top that plunged at the neckline. I thought the outfit made me look edgy, but it made me look more like a cheap slut.

'Ti kanete! Yia sas!' the couple chirped in unison, greeting us warmly. Yianni approached first, offering each of us a double-cheek kiss, then his wife followed. Of course, this greeting was an instant problem for me. You see, I didn't know it at the time, but the rule in Greece is to swiftly peck both cheeks of a friend or acquaintance with an air of sophistication. Some newcomers embrace this custom immediately, feeling all at once chic and European. I wasn't one of them. I didn't know which cheek to present or tackle first. So the result was a banging of foreheads, a nose lost in a mouth, saliva glazing an earlobe and the utmost embarrassment on everyone's part. Little did I know that once an acquaintance has been greeted with a double-cheek kiss, this constitutes a binding agreement to kiss that person upon every subsequent meeting for the duration of one's life. This initial kiss with Yianni and Anna was therefore the equivalent of signing a contract . . . in blood. I would double-cheek kiss these two individuals for the rest of my days. There was no turning back.

We all sat down to dinner, three smiles responding encouragingly to my sheepish grin. Anna turned to me. 'Milate Ellinika?' she questioned sweetly.

'Pardon? Sorry, I don't speak Greek.'

'I speak English, but mono little. I try.' Anna lowered her eyes shyly.

I soon learned that Yianni and Anna spoke nine languages fluently between them. Owing to my exclusive command of the English language, I wanted to skulk away, dragging my feet like an impetuous brat. But instead, I expressed utter amazement. Things only got worse when English words that I'd never heard before slipped effortlessly into conversation.

A waiter swooped in on us with a question for the men.

'He wunts to know if we wunt to imbibe,' translated Yianni for my benefit, smiling.

Imbibe? What's that?

I wasn't sure Dion understood either.

Yianni spoke English perfectly, but without intonation, his dialogue a verbal representation of a cardiac flat-line. He sounded a lot like Hymie from *Get Smart*.

'No. No drink for me, thantsyou,' said Anna.

'I hkaf maybe a glass,' said Yianni.

'I'll have a glass,' said Dion.

'I'll have a Jack Daniels and Coke. And maybe we should get a bottle of wine? Or maybe two, seeing there's four of us?'

Nobody responded. I was immediately ill at ease, maybe even panicked. It appeared that nobody in our party drank. Or rather they *did* drink, but unlike me, they drank *sensibly*. In fact, I would soon learn that the majority of people I'd encounter in Greece drank in order to socialise. They didn't socialise in order to drink. They didn't drink with a view to getting shit-faced, waking up in pools of their own vomit with mystery pot plants protruding from their handbags. Don't get me wrong. The country still has a high rate of alcohol consumption, but people approach drinking in a much more controlled way. It seems the Greeks know how to have a good time without obliterating themselves.

Our night at the restaurant unfolded pleasantly enough. Yianni told us that we were in one of the finest restaurants in Athens as far as Greek cuisine went. Dish after exotic dish was brought to the table, prepared beautifully, presented tastefully.

'Don't eat too much,' said Yianni, grinning. 'There is much, much more to come.'

His enormous frog-eyes danced merrily, momentarily settling on my breasts before darting across the room to focus on a shipping magnate. Yianni nudged his wife and the two began whispering to one another, lost in gossip over the magnate's dining companion, attire, conversation, menu choices and net worth. When they were done, Yianni turned his attention to Dion.

In line with his work obsession, Dion restricted his conversation to Yianni. When the two began chatting about managerial infrastructure, Anna and I went to painstaking efforts to have a conversation of our own. Because of my inability to speak Greek, I felt myself transform from mildly interesting to high-maintenance pain in the arse. I felt sorry for Anna.

'You no speak Greek?' she asked again hopefully, as though my earlier proclamation might have been a cruel joke.

'No. I'm sorry! I'm taking lessons though.'

'You like Greece?' she asked.

'Of course, it's great,' I lied as rehearsed.

'Good. *Kala*. Greece ees very difficult language.'

I gulped back another drink, by now having drunk what our entire table should have consumed. I was a little tipsy. I wanted to mix it up a little. I looked Anna in the eyes, my eyelids slightly lower than they'd been an hour earlier, and steered the conversation toward more important matters.

'You know what? You remind me of Agnetha from ABBA.'
Anna looked baffled.

'I am Unna.'

'I know. But you look like A–g–n–e–t–h–a from A–B–B–A,' I
said slowly, 'the b–l–o–n–d–e one.' I tried speaking slightly louder,
the way idiots do when communicating with the deaf.

'Who?'

'You know, the *blonde* one, from ABBA? "Money, Money,
Money"? "Knowing Me, Knowing You"? Eurovision 1974?'

Anna nervously fingered the silk scarf around her neck. Dion
glanced over at me, amused.

'Whut? No. I no know. Whut is UDDA?'

I was beginning to frighten her. Yianni interrupted, his eyes as
large as golf balls, his tone expressionless.

'Unna does not know UBBA. She knows only Greek music.'
Anna relaxed.

'Ah! Yes, I larv the old Greek singer!' Anna smiled, a faraway
look in her eyes. She had no idea that she'd intended the plural
version of the word 'singer'. Nor did I.

'The old Greek singer? You mean *Anna Vissi*?' I blurted. 'I *knew*
she was old. How old do you reckon she is? Forty? Eighty? She's
had a lot of plastic surgery, hasn't she?'

'Yes, Unna Vissi ees very good.'

I didn't know where to take the conversation from there. So I
shut up. Anna attempted mouth-to-mouth on our dying words.

'I very tired off teaching.'

'Oh, yes, you're a teacher. What age are the children you teach?'

'They little children, exi, er, six year old. I hkate them. Ees very
difficult. I work very much. I tired. I hkate them.'

'Yes, I know how tiring work can be. I worked very hard at MTV
too.'

There it was, my burning desire to validate myself through my former employment. I'd always thought it ridiculous that people identified themselves through the work they did and not through who they were as individuals. But here I was, guilty of same. To me it was imperative that our new friends were aware that I was more than a trophy girlfriend. However, Anna, like Dion's mother, didn't appear to give much of a shit about my career. Instead she began discussing the pros and cons of hiring Bulgarian nannies for her two-year-old daughter.

We left the restaurant a little after 1 a.m., heading in separate directions. Anna and Yianni were nothing like the people I usually hung out with in Australia, who by this point in the evening would be staggering around the pavement revealing intimate secrets that they'd later regret sharing. Yianni and Anna were classier, sensible and, dare I say it, a tad boring. I just wasn't the type who relished subdued evenings similar to those you might spend with a great aunt and a box of slides. I was more accustomed to life on the wild side and was very, very immature. Dion was stuck somewhere in the middle but if he thought that socialising with such people was important, then I'd do it over and over again. As Dion chirped all the way home about our two new friends, I kept the fact that meeting them wasn't the highlight of my life very much to myself.

Unlike me, Dion was a much more accepting creature, and had simple needs. All he needed was a good job, a full stomach and a warm feeling in his heart. That night, he held me tight and told me how happy he was that we were together and living in Greece. I told him I was too. I told him I loved him. We kissed one another softly.

The next day I drifted aimlessly around my favourite suburb, Glyfada. After staring longingly through a shoe shop window,

I turned to see a gypsy woman blazing a trail towards me. Her chunky, stubbled legs transported her with alarming velocity, giving the impression that her feet were somehow motorised. There was little time for an avoidance strategy. All at once she was upon me, blocking my path. She smiled crookedly as saccharine-coated words dripped from her tongue. I tried to convince myself that she was bidding me a good morning, but knew in my heart that she was actually attempting to sell me a packet of tissues. Now as tempting as this was, I declined with a polite 'no' in Greek which, even after all the lessons I'd been taking, was a substantial chunk of my vocabulary used up in one hit. I continued walking.

As I passed her by, I heard a distinct *hissing* sound cut through the air like a machete. I turned, expecting the sound to be emanating from a deflating truck tyre or a disgruntled, freshly stabbed cat. Instead, I discovered that the formerly smiling gypsy lady had transformed into a she-devil – her mouth, mostly devoid of teeth, twisting to unleash the most menacing of hisses she could muster. And her hisses were intended for me!

I'd never encountered a hissing gypsy at close range before. Or even a gypsy for that matter. Such an encounter would normally have left me somewhere between disconcerted and petrified. But now I only smiled insanely, and a laugh burst forth from my lips like molten lava. I laughed out loud like an asylum escapee, which probably confused her more than she'd confused me. I suspect I should have been terribly intimidated by what may have been a curse affecting not only me, but my future children and children's children. But I was more concerned by the fact that there was no longer any doubt that I was beginning to unravel.

I just don't know what to do with myself

Bordering on being an agoraphobic with an identity crisis, I wanted to stay inside. And yet I wanted to go out. I hit the Net to try and find people to meet and things to do, but I drew a blank. I felt cut off from the world. I had to do *something*. But what? Unable to read, write or speak the local language, it felt as though I'd been reduced to being a child all over again. I grew sadder and my self-esteem plummeted. I longed for companionship and mental stimulation yet I couldn't work or find anything to do that brought with it any sense of productivity. And after only four months, I could barely fight the urge to curl into a foetal position and whimper.

Mummy?

Occasionally Dion arrived home with a bunch of flowers in an attempt to make everything better. He was deeply sympathetic, but try as he might, he had no idea how to help me. Not that it was his role to play saviour. The guy already had his hands full. At the same time as scratching his head over my state of affairs, he was busy figuring out how best to handle a disgruntled staff member who had recently set fire to an outside dumpster.

I toyed with the idea of writing a book, but couldn't for the life of me think of anything to write about. As far as I was aware, there were no funky little courses to attend, no hot bands to check out and no potential friends to speak of. I called various embassies to see if there were any sporting teams I could join. There were none. It seemed I'd have to settle for forming a team of my own comprising a handful of my favourite Indian spirit guides.

Aside from private language lessons, I'd done little else to try to assimilate into Greek culture for three very good reasons. Well, three very good reasons to my mind at the time. Firstly, we were only going to be in Greece for twelve months. Secondly, I didn't really have a clue how to 'assimilate' in the first place, aside from buying a pair of pointy shoes. And thirdly, I was frightened of everyone and everything around me. Secure only through the love and support of my boyfriend, I came up with a brilliant personal goal to see me through the winter – the attainment of silky smooth legs. You see, I'd taken to plucking my legs daily. That's right. *Plucking* them. I'd get to work with a pair of tweezers and yank out hairs, one by one, with intense concentration for hours at a time, day in, day out. With tweezers in hand and a Holden Caulfield–type dialogue streaming through my consciousness, I caught myself, not for the first time, looping a fairly negative assessment of my life.

My life's shit. All I can do is pluck my legs. My life sucks. Why do my legs feel like sandpaper? If I just pluck a little more . . . Stupid city. Stupid legs.

This inner dialogue would be ongoing for the better part of a day. I was doing my own head in. I *had* to turn my life around. I had to do whatever it took for my sake as much as Dion's, who was on the receiving end of my growing sadness.

Eventually, I came up with the strategy of signing up for a correspondence course with the Australian Institute of Professional Counsellors and began studying counselling and psychology, which was deeply ironic considering my fragile state of mind. And maybe counter-productive considering I'd remain alone in the house with only my tweezers for companionship. However, I saw the remaining eight months as a great opportunity to learn more about myself and the puzzling people I encountered in the outside world. I buried myself beneath slabs of text. I read about rats running around boxes switching buttons on and off. I answered questions about why I so detested the cockroach. I pondered long and hard over whether Freud may have been a sexual pervert. I read and I wrote, day after day, but my stimulation levels remained at minus twenty. Despite study providing fleeting insights into human behaviour, I'd often find myself back in front of the bathroom mirror choreographing cheesy dance routines or reciting the Greek alphabet to my own reflection. I seriously contemplated offering my services to science as a human guinea pig.

This is what happens to a person who spends too much time alone.

It wasn't pretty.

The Big Brother phenomenon that was sweeping the world was kids' stuff by comparison. A bunch of people locked away from the outside world for a few weeks? *Big deal!* They had the luxury of bitchy companionship. I wanted bitchy companionship too!

Christmas was fast approaching. It was getting very cold, with temperatures averaging around five degrees Celsius and most days stony grey. To celebrate the silly season, I could think of nothing better than for Dion and me to flee the country. While I'd been to Milan, Dion hadn't yet visited any part of Europe outside Greece. He deserved a well-earned break. I began hatching a crafty escape plan.

An old tourist map I'd found in a cupboard featured an

advertisement for a travel agency. I decided to give them a try, dialling the number and bracing myself for the usual exchange: my shy enquiry as to whether the person on the other end spoke English resulting in that person throwing their telephone through the wall in response. Instead something amazing happened. Not only did the person on the other end *not* hang up on me, but they actually attempted *conversation*, first in Greek, then in English, without any hint of aggravation. I was able to make an appointment to go to their offices.

This was how I first became acquainted with Mayfair Travel, an agency run by a family of South African Greeks. They were helpful and friendly. I met with a girl, Eleni, who beamed at me more than twice, making me feel the most relaxed I'd been in Greece's service industry since my arrival. With my elbows on her desk and my hands cupping my chin, I began developing what no doubt came across as a schoolgirl crush. Together Eleni and I planned a Christmas adventure for Dion and myself from a tiny office crammed with desks, employees and cigarette smoke.

'So, Miss Lunna, maybe Kitzbuhl, Austria, could be a nice destination for you?'

'That sounds like a plan. Say, where do you get your hair done? It looks great. I've been looking for a new hairdresser myself?'

'I get my hair done here in Glyfada. Lunna, we have various accommodation options available for you. What do you think of this place?'

A fading brochure was unfurled and laid out on the desk.

'Great! So where do you go out in Athens? I've really only been to one restaurant. It was here in Glyfada. What do you do when you go out? And what's it like working with your family? It must be hard. I don't know if I could do it. Do you like Athens?' I scrunched my nose.

Over the next few weeks, Mayfair sadly became a haven, and I took up way too much of Eleni's time for the sake of human interaction. The young travel agent patiently kept business conversation on track while fielding my inane questions during one of her busiest times of year.

Unfortunately, when it came close to our Christmas trip to Austria I caught a horrendous flu. At Labrou Katsoni I faded in and out of consciousness and a doctor was called. Of course, she turned out to be an attractive young female doctor who flirted outrageously with Dion while he acted as my interpreter. *Hey! I'm right here!* I thought weakly from my deathbed. I had little strength to do anything else.

However, nothing was going to stop me from escaping Athens and experiencing my first White Christmas in Austria. On the morning of Christmas Eve, Dion mopped my brow, dragged me out of bed and raced us both over to the airport. We found ourselves caught in a gridlock caused by the entire population of Greece attempting a mass exodus. We missed our flight.

Stricken, we fought our way through the airport terminal, the scene before us utter chaos. Throngs of impatient people crammed the smoke-filled building, yelling and arguing. Strangely, Eleni the travel agent's father emerged from behind a pillar to assist us in catching another flight, a service that I doubt could be matched anywhere in the world. With our plane barely managing to overtake Rudolf along the way, we arrived in Kitzbuhl during the wee hours of Christmas morning. In celebration, I vomited.

Dion spent Christmas Day administering medication and playing nurse within the confines of a small hotel room. His gentle bedside manner soon produced results, and by the following morning I'd made a miraculous recovery. Boxing Day was therefore spent at Aurach Animal Park, set upon a snowy mountaintop. We strolled in our snow-gear, admiring reindeer, a snow leopard, yaks and a rather sick-looking wallaby. I sympathised with the creature. It was caged and in a place it clearly didn't belong.

After ten minutes' walking, Dion was panting breathlessly so we took a seat on a wooden bench. Before us was one of the most dramatic views we'd ever seen – blinding white snow-capped mountains stark against the blue winter sky. Despite the beauty, I lay across Dion's lap concentrating on discovering new methods to clear my nasal passages by way of subtle head manoeuvres. It was during this undignified moment that Dion asked an unexpected question.

'Lana . . . will you marry me?'

'Huh?'

'Will you marry me?'

'What?'

'I said, *will you MARRY me.*'

Dion sounded nervous. A few seconds passed.

'Did you just ask me to *marry* you?'

'Yes. I said, *"WILL YOU MARRY ME".*'

Again time passed. I felt the migration of a thousand butterflies surge in my stomach.

'ARE-YOU-FOR-REAL?'

'Yes, I'm for real! I love you so much. So marry me!'

I began laughing hysterically, uncontrollably. I couldn't stop. Tears streamed down my face. The laughter quickly turned to sobs. I grew incoherent.

'I never . . . and then . . . but . . . what?'

The tears and laughter continued for a few moments. Eventually I was able to form a sentence.

'Yes! I'll marry you! I love you!'

Dion embraced me hard, then looked deep into my teary eyes, cupping my face softly with his woollen-gloved hands.

'I love you too.'

Taking my hand, he bent down, ripped out a dying piece of yellow grass from beneath the snow and wrapped it around my engagement finger. We laughed and hugged and kissed, completely lost in the moment. I'd never felt so euphoric in my entire life.

We excitedly called our parents in Australia to tell them the wonderful news. After all the years we'd been together, mine assumed we were playing a practical joke and it took several minutes to convince them otherwise. My mother eventually shrieked with delight and my father offered hearty congratulations. He cracked open a can of beer into the receiver. *Pssssssssssssssssst.* They were ecstatic.

We then called Dion's parents. His father was delighted. Katerina, well, maybe not so much.

'You two be together long time now,' she lamented. And that was all she had to say. I later learned that the news of our engagement wasn't spread to Dion's immediate family for several days, and wondered if my soon-to-be mother-in-law deemed me worthy of her son.

12

Do you really want to hurt me?

Our week in Austria was unforgettable, full of romance, Christmas frivolity and Dion playing ski instructor as I slid down icy slopes on my arse. But it was all behind us now. By the time 2001 had rolled around, so too had my eyes – to the back of my head. We were back in Athens, and it was business as usual.

Effortlessly, Dion returned to work mode. You see Dion *loved* his job. *Really* loved it. He was doing wonderful things, his radio ratings jumping higher and higher with every survey. Meanwhile, back at the ranch, I was nearly collapsing with boredom. I didn't have surveys to validate my achievements. More to the point, I wasn't achieving anything. The days were long and tedious. It was cold. It got dark in the late afternoon. I wandered around the apartment aimlessly in search of a mysterious *something*.

And then, just as that feeling of pointlessness began its familiar *This is Your Life* tap on my shoulder, it began snowing in Athens for the first time since the Ice Age. It was as though Austria had followed us back to Greece. Thankful for the distraction, I skipped out into the white-powdered streets repressing an urge to throw myself onto the ground and create an impromptu snow angel. Everything was sprinkled with icing sugar and everything was going to be okay!

So what if I can't speak Greek and would rather eat a raw aardvark than a slab of feta cheese?

Like the snow, I felt my frustrations, fears and doubts begin to melt away. I skipped merrily around the streets in my loud purple anorak, smiling and childlike.

As I passed a small apartment building on Vouliagmenis Avenue, a grinning local decided it would be a sterling idea to turf a block of ice at my head from a second-floor balcony. Rock-solid and the size of a small microwave oven, it narrowly missed my skull and hit the pavement with a resounding thud. The glee I'd felt just seconds earlier was instantly shattered. Frightened, flabbergasted and fucked off, my negative thinking went into overdrive.

What could possibly motivate a person to chuck an icy missile at a passing woman's head? What? WHAT?

In slow motion, I turned. My eyes rested upon the culprit; a male in his mid-twenties clad in a navy blue parker and cute yellow snow mittens. His expression was ambiguous, although I of course interpreted it as defiant. Before I could stop myself, I unleashed a barrage of cutting remarks, my tongue having grown sharper than a surgical instrument. Obscenities that would embarrass even Eminem were delivered with a ferocity that scared me even more than the icy assault itself.

WHAT IS HAPPENING TO ME?

With hands in pockets, the ice sniper sauntered back inside his cosy apartment, closed the door and no doubt promptly forgot the entire incident after flicking on the stereo for a hit of Vanilla Ice. I, on the other hand, could not so easily forget. If the same situation had arisen back in Australia, I would have been able to quickly ascertain if it was an act of childish free-spiritedness or genuine hostility. But here in Greece, for all I knew, it could have been any-thing from a declaration of war to a 'Welcome to Athens' ceremony organised by the local council. Looking back, I'm certain no harm was ever intended. But at the time I was processing experiences on my Greek odyssey distortedly. I was driven solely by acute culture shock. Unbeknownst to me, I had been since Day One.

I needed allies . . . and I needed them fast. After yet *again* desper-ately telephoning a variety of embassies and explaining my lonely situation, I joined a social group in Athens known as Newcomers. As there were no trains in the area and I felt a bus journey would see me disappear across the border into a small neighbouring territory, I took a long-winded cab ride to the northern suburb of Kifisia.

Kifisia differs from Glyfada in that it's not coastal, it has a few different designer stores and, architecturally, homes are more palatial. In keeping with Athenian tradition, however, the town planning is equally unpredictable.

After an hour's cab ride, I found myself in a large hired room that resembled a scout hall. I was joined by a bunch of fellow new-arrivals encircled by expatriate pioneers eager to show us the ropes. There were around thirty people in total – all wearing modest tan-coloured trousers and sensible shoes. I was the youngest by about twenty years. All newcomers to Newcomers were asked to fill out a form detailing such things as name, nationality and interests. Once forms had been completed and nametags affixed to lapels – in most cases carefully avoiding cameo brooches – proceedings began in earnest. The gathering was hosted by a British veteran, with clip-board in hand, who'd slogged it out in Athens for thirty-odd years and emerged relatively unscathed. After a general introduction, I was abruptly called to attention.

'Now, today, ladies, we have an Aus-TREY-lien here with us.

Could you stand up for us please, er, Lara, sorry, Lana?' There was a pause as her eyes scoured the room. 'Where are you, Lara?'

I groaned internally and struggled to my feet at the back of the room.

'Um. Hi.'

All eyes turned to me. I gave a little wave.

'Now, it says here, Lena, that you're an animal lover. Well today has *got* to be your lucky day! Geraldine found a stray puppy on her way to the meeting this morning and we'd like you to have it. As our gift! Our gift to you. To keep!'

I forced a smile and weakly sat down again as the room erupted in a series of 'oohs' and 'aahs'. A half-dead mongrel pup was carried ceremoniously across the room and placed delicately on my lap. I attempted to appear touched by the sentiment, adopting a similar expression to that of a losing Oscar nominee.

With dog-delivery and official proceedings complete, the gathering took on a more social context. Sickly, flea-ridden puppy in one hand and obligatory cup of tea in the other, I found myself chatting awkwardly to women about domestic cleaning agents, the Roaring Forties and war veterans. My mind wandered . . .

Is this really what my life's amounted to? Wasn't I interviewing Massive Attack just six months ago? And where's that friggin' Geraldine?

I spied her across the room, excused myself from the stimulating conversation that had progressed to bath enamel, and carried the limp, semiconscious animal over to her. It bit me in the process and then drooled into my palm. Upon reaching the woman, I explained with a fixed smile that, unfortunately, I couldn't accept the kindly gesture as I lived in a third-floor, 80-square-metre apartment and this mutt happened to be a Great Dane/Woolly Mammoth cross. I handed back the poor animal and was immediately overcome by a nauseating wave of guilt.

What's to become of this poor, defenceless bitch? And what about the puppy?

At that precise moment the dog shat into the cradle of Geraldine's arm and I knew I was exercising great wisdom. As I headed towards the door, two women in tan knits stopped me dead in my tracks. One of them looked me up and down as the other put a question to me.

'How long have you been in Greece, dear?' she asked, giving her friend a sideways glance.

'Almost five months,' I replied with a shrug.

I stood respectfully as they continued speaking to each other as though I wasn't there.

'She's practically only just arrived!'

'Ha! A new arrival, eh? She hasn't a *clue* what she's in for!'

It was like Day One in a women's penitentiary. I fled the scene, as friendless as I had been before, if not more so.

Things had to fall into place at some point, right? Wrong! Not long after my sunny Newcomers' experience, I visited a pharmacy. I had a minor health problem and had opted for a quick over-the-counter remedy, thus avoiding flirtatious female doctors who required my fiancé to act as interpreter and possible love interest. It was incredibly easy to get what I wanted over the counter and I liked that. I liked that a lot.

Scanning the chosen pharmacy *Terminator*-style, I noted fifteen people around the counter: ten customers and five lab-coated staff in various states of animation. Engaging cheetah-like instincts, I went straight for a lone lab-coated girl at the far end who'd been momentarily separated from the rest of the pack.

'*Milate Anglika?*' I softly enquired of her English-speaking aptitude. The girl shook her head dismissively and pointed to a young lab-coated male at the other end near the register. As my brain issued formal orders to abort the mission, the rest of me rebelliously forged ahead. I walked behind the other ten customers – seven of them men – in order to speak to my designated consultant. 'Milate Anglika?' I once again meekly enquired. A hushed silence descended over the pharmacy. I sensed a telepathic conversation taking place amongst my fellow-consumers:

'*She can barely speak Greek!*'

'*What?*'

'She can't speak Greek! *Didn't you hear that horrendous accent?*'

'*Yeah, funny eh?*'

'*Shhh . . . listen!*'

'*Ergh! She must be sick!*'

'*What's wrong with her?*'

'*Shut up! Let's find out.*'

If they'd strained any harder to hear the next sentence that tumbled from my mouth, an ear fight would have ensued as each pair vied for top position closest to my voice box. Conspiratorial glances were shot my way. I was under surveillance from every angle. Feeling more than a little paranoid, if not violated, I nevertheless continued.

'Do you have anything for . . .'

My voice trailed. I took a deep breath. I broke eye contact.

'. . . *thrush?*'

The blood rushed to my cheeks.

After a brief silence, the predictable response followed.

'*Whut?*'

'Um . . . Do you have anything for . . . *thrush.*'

The silence was excruciating as more than a dozen pairs of eyes darted between the chemist and myself.

'Whut ees thees?'

I paused. 'Oh, ah, it's uncomfortable down . . . um . . .'

Again I faltered. Thankfully the chemist had absolutely no idea what to make of the stranger before him, and, with any luck, nor did anyone else who'd indirectly joined in on the conversation. The pharmacist called over another girl in a white coat. Her English, I was assured, was fluent.

'Do you have anything for *thrush*?' I once again whispered hoarsely.

'Whut ees thees *THRUSH*?'

There was a life-long pause.

'Um, I think it's a yeast infection.'

'A *YIST* infection?'

'Yes . . . down *there*.'

I cleared my throat and made broad, sweeping gestures with my hands around the abdominal area, occasionally pointing my index finger directly towards my nether region. I hoped that in some way the sporadic pointing would draw on feminine empathy. It didn't. I thought of a nice place I'd like to be buried.

Puzzled by my lack of direct communication, the pharmacist consulted loudly with another male in a white lab coat. This one was aged around sixty. The assistant with a penchant for screaming '*THRUSH!*' at the top of her lungs transmogrified into interpreter as our conversation was relayed from one end of the room to the other. The sixty-year-old chemist yelled something to her in Greek.

'He wunts to know . . . eef you hkad . . . eny leequid?'

All eyes settled on me, tennis match style.

'Liquid? Does he mean am I drunk? Or . . . um . . . does he mean . . . um . . . ooh, it's hot in here isn't it? Um . . . is he talking about a *discharge*?'

I had no idea why I was persisting with such self-humiliation.

I decided that a shallow grave *anywhere* would suit me just fine. But maybe a single red tulip planted on top might be a nice touch?

The female chemist/interpreter yelled something in Greek and gestured towards me. Customers and chemists alike turned and stared. After being instructed by yet another colleague, she went to the storage room and re-emerged with two huge pink boxes emblazoned with the words 'VAGINAL DOUCHE'. The boxes were so large that I was nothing short of amazed at how she manoeuvred them without the assistance of a forklift. Fleeing before the boring eyes could mutate me into a human colander, I raced home to discover that I had purchased a douche the size of a piano accordion.

That night, I poured my heart out to Dion and this time I wasn't just venting. I needed him to understand the strain that these seemingly insignificant hurdles were putting on me, and that I loved him so much that I was determined to try to conquer them. But God it was hard. I was a sensitive type. Public humiliation affected me deeply, as did being misunderstood. I didn't take kindly to being considered a moving target for ice snipers. I didn't much like being nearly run over. I didn't like people responding with sour expressions. And above all else, I hated experiencing everything alone. To put it simply, the entire Greek experience was hurting my feelings. Worse, I was beginning to feel a lot like one of those nagging, whinging housewives that I so detested.

I tried to explain what it felt like to become an unwilling introvert forced to rely on someone else to communicate on my behalf. I tried to describe what it felt like to have nobody recognising me and waving hello, nobody knowing who I was. What it felt like to have people barging into me in shops and out on the streets. Dion listened. He nodded. Then he told me things were going to be all right . . . *and that they couldn't be as bad as I was making them out to be*. He then fell asleep. It was clear that Dion was experiencing an entirely different reality from mine and that he'd probably begun engaging in a little denial. As my frustrations intensified, he seemed to withdraw. In a subtle way, I felt him retreat, perhaps in an effort to protect himself from my progressive decay. I could even say that with each passing day, Dion felt less and less 'present'.

That night I cried. And I cried alone.

Livin' on a prayer

Six months in and we were halfway there! Post-Christmas, Vagelio, my mole-chinned language teacher, had disappeared off the face of the planet as is usually the case in Greece after a holiday break, of which there are plenty. People just cease to exist. So I signed up for language lessons at a school known as Babel situated in Ano Glyfada, towards the hills behind Glyfada proper. Attending classes involved a 45-minute trudge along a dirt track lined with low-lying olive branches. Every second day I would stroll past a dead cat and note its gradual decay. As time passed, I was surprised by just how long this process took, although nowhere near as long as it was taking me to learn Greek.

Classes came with the added bonus of meeting other foreigners who, like me, were coming to terms with their new lives. My class of six were mostly older British expats who made it their business to ensure a stream of unoriginal convict-related digs, alleviated slightly by reassurances that Rolf Harris was, and is, a great entertainer. The sad thing is that I positively relished the attention, being so unaccustomed to the acknowledgement of my existence.

A typical language lesson involved my lovely, moustached and balding teacher Dimitry, working up a sweat as he attempted to explain the Greek grammatical rules pertaining to the word 'the'. I managed to grasp only a handful of excerpts:

'. . . except if . . . and except if . . . but only if . . . apart from . . . so pronounce the 'n' that is written like a 'v' . . . but only if the first letter of the next word begins with . . . And only if the word is feminine . . . and, of course, dependent upon your familiarity with the person you're speaking to . . . but only when . . . not if . . . and then don't . . . unless of course . . . so don't unless . . . and never, ever forget that although the Greek language is nothing like English, most English words are derived from it.'

The mind boggled. I spent those arduous hours tricking myself into believing that once I'd absorbed the rules of this language, the penny would drop and I'd begin talking in tongues and healing the sick. In the meantime, it was all I could do to stop myself from slipping silently into a coma.

Midway through lessons, middle-aged students undertaking phase two of 'Greek Beginners' would tiptoe into the back of our tiny classroom in order to make themselves cups of tea. They'd smile patronisingly at me and my fellow classmates, regarding us as sweet, 'kindergarten' linguists. Some would glance over at Dimitry and slip him a 'cheeky', knowing wink. As our class continued, they'd float about with an 'advanced' demeanour as I or one of my classmates stammered over a simple piece of Greek text. Little did I know that having studied Greek for less than six months, realistically they, too, knew jack shit. They just looked like they knew everything. Of course, I saw them as incredibly learned.

Despite their loveliness and unwavering hospitality, I was beginning to tire of our weekly pilgrimages to Nota and Nikos. I had taken to arriving with a book under my arm, and as the hours dragged by I'd sit at the end of the table reading. Occasionally my interest would be tweaked, say when Nota cut up Nikos' meat into convenient bite-sized pieces as though he were an incompetent three-year-old. But otherwise, I was barely an observer.

Over our usual feast irrigated by torrents of olive oil, Nota threw questions Dion's way as I chewed respectfully, quietly turning pages of my book. As always, I had no idea what anyone was saying until my ears pricked up at the sound of my own name. When 'e-Lunna' washed up amongst a thousand Greek tongue twisters, I interrupted Dion for a translation.

'She wants to know if you can speak Greek yet. I'm telling her that you can . . . a bit. Well, I'm saying you're still trying.'

Dion delivered his answer to Nota by way of a twenty-minute discourse. To this Nikos smiled kindly and threw in his usual catchphrase.

'Okay, mate?'

But Nota responded with circular motions of her hand that could have meant either good, bad or unbelievably fucked up.

'Poh-poh-poh,' she exhaled, her hand flapping about like a light aircraft propeller.

From this, I assumed she meant both bad *and* unbelievably fucked up. I felt ashamed. Nota didn't understand that I'd faithfully put hundreds of hours into learning Greek. I'd really been trying, but for whatever reason, the language was excruciatingly difficult for me and it just wouldn't stick. Of course, I didn't have the capacity to explain such things and Dion's aunt had every reason to conclude I couldn't be arsed. None of us realised that without going out into the world and practising, I could never hope to speak Greek through language lessons alone. I also didn't have the advantage of already knowing a second language, meaning the 'language' part of my brain was pretty much welded shut.

Although he wasn't the greatest language teacher in the world, Dion was very sensitive to my lingual problems. However, he'd got into the habit of telling people I could speak Greek, when clearly I couldn't. I knew he was doing it to help build my confidence, but it only served to make us both look like twits when I'd respond with a 'ne' (yes) after somebody asked if I enjoyed suffering chronic haemorrhoids.

By this stage of the game, Dion was 99 per cent fluent. Without command over the preferred parlance of my host country, I, on the other hand, was often taken for a sucker, an uneducated pillock, a novelty act that had escaped a travelling circus, an arrogant imperialist, or, even worse, a tourist – the perfect prey to be overcharged for any service on offer. The few things I attempted to arrange on my own, like, say, the repair of my beloved washing machine, invariably featured extortion. When it came to coughing up cash, locals knew I could hardly argue over an inflated price, and in any event presumed me to be a filthy rich expat. As always, it proved easier for Dion to interact with those around us.

One day I opted to take a taxi to Greek lessons rather than trudge past the pitiful, decaying cat. I walked to a cab rank of sorts outside Voula Hospital and was the first and only person awaiting a ride. I was soon joined by a woman. She put a question to me that could have just as easily been, 'Are you interested in donating any of your internal organs to medical science?' as 'Are you waiting for a cab?'

I replied with a triumphant phrase that I'd recently learned at Babel: 'Den milao Ellinika', which, contradictorily, means, 'I don't speak Greek'.

When a taxi rolled up, my dear friend made a mad dash for it, hopped in and slammed the door. I pathetically yelled, 'Hey!' as the kindly woman stared directly ahead, being whisked away to whatever engagement it was that was so obviously more important than mine. Defeated by my inability to communicate, I decided to skip language class that day, which, in English, we would describe as 'cutting off your nose to spite your face'.

Thankfully many people in Greece speak English as a second language and most are quite happy to do so. Locals like Yianni and Anna were generally patient, if not amused, as I bumbled my way through a smattering of Greek on our occasional get-togethers, completely bastardising their intricate language. Thanks to Babel, as time went on, attempting the local tongue – non-gastronomically or romantically speaking – certainly helped make life easier.

However, there were times when not having the capacity to speak fluently was as frustrating as hell. I can't recall exactly how many Greek conversations I translated in my mind as '. . . hair . . . Wednesday . . . plate . . . tomorrow' as Dion nodded emphatically, but there were definitely more than a dozen. I also engaged in more than my fair share of absurd exchanges.

Most of these played out with Athina, the world-famous Albanian cleaning lady. Each week, before my disappearing act, we'd try our darnedest to communicate with one another. One fine Thursday afternoon she began with an enquiry as to why Dion and I didn't have any children. At least that's what I *think* we were talking about. Stammering away, what I tried to say was this:

'It is actually a highly charged and confusing subject for me. It's also a little on the intrusive side. However, I will endeavour to humour you with a response. To begin with, we are not yet married. Why, it would be improper! Having said that, with our being abroad, my fiancé and I have decided to bypass this issue, it being what – at this particular juncture – we perceive to be an inappropriate time in our lives to conceive a child.'

However, with my low level of fluency what I *actually* said may have been closer to this:

'Beautiful child upon a rock please my table mister.'

The conversation then took a turn for the worse. Wiping the back of her rubber-gloved hand across her forehead, Athina responded with either:

'I work and have a baby here in Athens. It's dead easy and if I can do it, anyone can!'

or

'I work and have a baby here in Athens. It's not easy. So would you mind babysitting for me occasionally?'

To this, I responded with a generic laugh/smile/shrug and hoped like hell that it could be taken to mean either, 'Wow! Isn't it great you're managing so well' or, 'Hmmm . . . I'm not so sure about that, cheeky!' Then I briskly walked away from the conversation, but not without first noticing a bewildered look creep across her face. However, none of this was going to stop me from continuing to give the Greek language a bash . . . a bash with the linguistic equivalent of a cricket bat.

During a morning tea break at Babel, I hovered around my fellow pupils feeling extraordinarily young and Australian, intrigued by a conversation between two of the older British women.

'Did you see him?'

'See him? *Did* I? Oh my *Lord*, I almost had an *'eart* attack! He *is* darling, isn't he?'

They giggled mischievously and turned to see Keith's reaction. Keith was the only male in our class. He was also British and also, as far as I was concerned, old. He rolled his eyes.

'Blinkin' hell. 'ere I am with my life in tatters and all you two gas-baggers can do is bang on about George bleedin' Clooney!'

Keith wasn't exaggerating about his life being a shambles. You see, Keith had quit an enviable job in London, pulled his son out of school, packed up his missus and moved to Athens with a view to living the dream. His dream was to open a café that catered both to locals and the expat community; to live a slower-paced life in a sun-drenched country. Sounds simple enough, doesn't it? But Keith was foiled every step of the way by bureaucracy and a set of rules that seemed to bend and change to suit would-be oppressors. He was bullied and intimidated by local authorities and by competitors. Some would enter his café, stand in a corner and stare threateningly at Keith or his wife for extended periods. Keith was even jailed for failing to comply with a demand for bribe money by a government authority. Within six months of opening his café, Keith was forced to shut it down. He returned to Britain with his tail between his legs and a very bad taste in his mouth.

This led me to wonder if the amount of red tape encountered in Greece could in any way be linked to the phenomenon of spontaneous combustion. Sure it was purely conjecture, but when battling bureaucracy involved the illogical, the pointless, the exasperating, the fruitless and all things utterly draining, disintegrating on the spot leaving only your worry beads behind certainly seemed more desirable, if not plausible.

In Greece, something as simple as organising a telephone connection required the provision of anything from DNA samples by way of carbon dated, well-preserved ancestral toenails, to authenticated astrological charts proving that your rising sign wasn't in Sagittarius. On lucky days, a rough sketch of a waterfowl proved sufficient. Whatever the requirement, jumping through burning hoops for the benefit of unamused bureaucrats was never entirely out of the question. I began to refer to it as The Delegation Game, being hand-balled from one person to the next until my usually sprightly reflection became that of a defeated and easily startled 97-year-old. The Game included spending sixty-five consecutive dog years in queues awaiting rubber stamps, signatures and looks of contempt. The trick was not to become incensed by obscenely flippant public servants who'd shrug their shoulders and request I return another day, preferably armed with a woodcarving of a wildebeest, although sometimes specific instructions weren't forthcoming at all.

So why did everything have to be so goddamned complicated? It's a very good question and one that remains unanswered. However, I realised early on that I had to be careful lest frustration get the better of me. I learned that diving over an administration counter and feeding myself through a paper shredder wasn't a viable option. I hoped that in time, red tape would become merely as annoying as a pimple emerging the day before a hot date rather than comparable to a pole being driven through the spine and twisted several times counterclockwise. Alas, it wasn't to be.

Although Dion was quite happy to laze around doing very little at either our apartment or Aunty Nota's, I needed a change to our weekend routine. I wanted to move beyond Athens and experience somewhere further afield, say Australia, perhaps. But as that seemed out of the question for the time being, I needed another option. Upon bug-eyed Yianni's recommendations, and to celebrate my birthday, Dion whisked us away to the Peloponnese where we headed for the lovely little town of Nafplio. Seven months in, it would be our first mainland experience away from the cement metropolis and the smog.

It was March, and although the days were still cool, they were becoming brighter. After two hours, the city was a memory and by the time we crossed the Corinth Canal the scenery had changed dramatically. It was as though we'd entered paradise. The Peloponnese enveloped us with its enchanting magic and I immediately felt at ease. Dion drove crazily, overtaking everything in his path. He entertained us both with voice impersonations of people we'd known from the past. As I listened and giggled, I drank in the view. Imposing green hills sprinkled with red wildflowers arose from still, blue waters, and in the distance I could see dramatic fortresses. Any god or goddess taking up residence in Greece would surely have looked no further than the prime real estate of this region.

The former Greek capital of Nafplio is about 130 kilometres south of Athens and a renowned travel destination for tourists and Greeks alike. A castle crowns the town and there's much to discover in the surrounding areas below. There are ruins, ancient amphitheatres and a spectacular coastline. Fresh fruit, vegetable and wild honey stalls dot the roadsides. The clean air and sense of spaciousness inspire one to frolic and sing show tunes on quiet hillsides.

Dion and I had booked into the best hotel we could find, the Nafplia Palace, part of a Venetian fortress presiding over the town. We meandered in on a Saturday afternoon after multiple stops to absorb the boundless beauty. We filled in the obligatory accommodation forms and excitedly made our way to our room. The walls were of grey stone, the ceiling dark-brown wood panelling. Our separate beds had been made up with pre-loved beige covers, with matching retro lampshades. Although the room was more 1970s than a pair of flares the size of Belgium, our little balcony looked over a stunning water view. I became lost in a Lucy Jordan fantasy. Below us, Agolis Bay was a deep expanse of clear, still blue, moating the tiny island prison of Bourtzi. Lush green hilltops fringed the distant shore. As I admired the incredible outlook, a swarm of mosquitoes queued to sup delightedly on my flesh and blood, but I cared not.

Much later, as the afternoon sun began to set, I became distracted by a succession of snorts behind me. I turned to find Dion fast asleep, snoring. He didn't wake until the following morning. Once again I was left to my own devices. I began to browse through a book on the paranormal. In between page turning, I stared deeply into the corner of the room willing an apparition to appear, and convinced myself that inanimate objects on my bedside bureau were moving while I wasn't looking. I was asleep by 10 p.m., dreaming of the living dead.

The next day I doled out the appropriate punishment: 'What's *wrong* with you? Thanks to you I've become obsessed with poltergeists. Now we have to do whatever I say!'

'Okay, babe. Sorry, I was just so tired from the drive.'

We took our brunch of coffee, biscuits and cheese pastries on the balcony, and again marvelled at the spectacular view. On this occasion, my fiancé opted to remain conscious.

Later, we headed to Epidavros, home to the Sanctuary of Asklepios, an ancient outdoor theatre renowned for its amazing acoustics. Despite its antiquity, the theatre is still used today. During the warmer months, audiences shift from buttock to buttock upon the smooth marble pews. For me, the highlight was watching tourists walk centre stage to test out the acoustic perfection for themselves. Pale men in khaki shorts with camera bags slung over their shoulders would take position and self-consciously let out a quick shriek followed by a whistle. Their wives dutifully followed suit with a nippy 'hello' and a nod of the head that said, 'Yes, the acoustics *are* good here, aren't they?' It got me wondering . . . Maybe it wasn't just me. Maybe on the whole people are essentially moronic?

Alas, we were soon back in the car, returning to Athens, our time away short-lived. With every passing kilometre, my mood became more sombre. Dion chatted away happily, casually slipping into the conversation how much he loved living and working in Athens. By nightfall we re-entered the concrete jungle and my lungs and spirits once again grew heavy. Dion was glad to be back. As soon as we arrived home he switched on his computer and began working. I switched on the television, praying for some *Cagney and Lacey*.

Later that month Dion returned from work midafternoon confused and upset. A facsimile had arrived at his office that morning. He'd stubbed out a cigarette, read it, and re-read it in disbelief. It was official notice from a government body advising that his radio station was about to be shut down. Telephone calls were made, but nothing could be done. With the station looping automated music, all employees left the building.

It seemed the government had become fixated with radio station licences – a bureaucratic nightmare of its own creation. The licensing issue was complicated and in many ways irrational. The government claimed that radio broadcast signals might interfere with air traffic control signals at the new international airport that had opened that day, a claim made without any quantifiable evidence. It also argued that most stations were technically 'illegal' since their licences had been issued subject to future tender. The seventeen stations taken off the air would remain so until a High Court decision was handed down any time over the next century.

I believed in my heart that Dion's station couldn't possibly stay off the air for long. After all, thanks to his expertise, it had just that week become the number one rating station in Athens. And surely that counted for something? We tuned into Dion's beloved station, a station moulded by his own blood, sweat and tears, and at the same time turned on the television news. We saw officials with machine guns and what looked like enormous pliers climbing Mt Imittos where broadcast towers were located. The officials eventually stood beneath the towers, poised to cut transmission wires. We watched them fiddle with a piece of equipment while a split screen showed an orchestra celebrating the opening of the airport. The news commentary and orchestral music on the television competed for attention with a contemporary Greek hit blaring from Dion's radio, a cacophony of sound within our living room. We watched an official take to the wires with his cutters.

Quite suddenly, the room quietened.

Quite suddenly, the radio went dead.

Quite suddenly, Dion's station was taken off the air.

We looked at one another. The very reason we'd moved to Greece had just become null and void. I instinctively wrapped an arm around Dion's shoulder. What this meant for the station, we didn't know. What this meant for *us*, we didn't know.

My heart bled for my fiancé. He sat staring at the screen in utter disbelief, before burying his face in his hands. He then fielded calls from executives and employees well into the night. After seven months, I understood better than anyone his passion for that station. However, I confess that I secretly hoped that this might spell an early return home.

14

Losing my religion

Dion wasn't exactly doing a victory dance over what had happened to his radio station, but nor was he suicidal. Being the eternal optimist, he somehow kept his spirits high.

The Saturday following shutdown we bumped into our neighbour, Maria, outside the lift. She nodded to me politely and spoke dramatically to Dion as I hummed in my mind the musical score to *Cats*. Dion later translated that she was very distressed about losing her favourite radio station. She wasn't the only one grieving. Going by television and newspaper reports, and the flood of letters and emails from loyal listeners, the majority of Athens shared her sentiments.

We were on our way to meet with Dion's trusty sidekick Yianni, and Yianni's trusty sidekick Anna, in fashionable Kolonaki. As we entered a trendy café, the two sat solemnly stirring steaming coffees. Still uncomfortable with the greeting, I dodged a double-cheek kiss hello. Yianni moved in for the kill, kissing the air where my cheek should have been, and darted a hurt and questioning look my way. It was a definite social faux pas, and in light of the circumstances, badly timed.

Anna and I listened to the two men come to terms with the recent turn of events. I felt sick for Yianni. I obviously felt sick for Dion too, but I could see the fear in Yianni's enormous eyes. He had a wife and baby to consider, and fully understood the ruthlessness of Greek authorities. In this regard, Dion was protected by ignorance. Through stilted conversation, I gathered that Anna was none too happy about the situation either. She sipped on a coffee and shrugged her shoulders . . . a lot.

I felt it was my duty to take Dion's mind off things. Despite his intense dislike for putting one foot in front of the other – an activity commonly known as *walking* – I decided to drag him around the centre of Athens. We ended our radio post-mortem with Anna and Yianni and began an inspection of Kolonaki.

Kolonaki is one of Athens' classier areas. It bustles with traffic, cafés, trendy boutiques and alarmingly beautiful people. Dion was immediately impressed, deriving great comfort from spending wads of cash on business attire, despite being uncertain if he'd be wearing it any time soon. I liked Kolonaki too.

From there we took a quick walk to the old Royal Palace opposite Plateia Syntagma, an area that many consider the heart of the city. We watched two proud soldiers perform a variation of the goose step before the Tomb of the Unknown Soldier. These guards are known as Evzones and have been around since the early 1800s. They wear what appear to be mini-dresses, single-tasselled caps, white tights and shoes with enormous pompoms on their tips. I instantly fell in love with them. You'd imagine these elite soldiers hand-plucked from the Greek military were chosen for outstanding character and aptitude. But many a modern Greek will confide that they've merely been chosen for, well, being kind of tall and well built. And they apparently get better food than those completing compulsory military service. In any event, don't let the skirts and tights fool you. They are not, by any stretch of the imagination, cross-dressers.

Passing the Evzones, watching them effortlessly sidestep a burst of laughter as tourists did unfunny things to elicit smiles, we entered the slightly unkempt National Gardens, a refuge from the traffic and people that bustle around the park's perimeters. After gazing thoughtfully at a menagerie of ducks, pigeons and turtles, we happened upon a caged, balding parrot that to me looked embarrassed and pathetic upon its perch. It let out a screech, followed by a quick, unexpected obscenity.

'*Malaka! Malaka!*'

Also used as a term of endearment, *malaka* generally means wanker. I was very pleased to have learned this word, and even more pleased to have heard a Greek-speaking feathered friend curse. Dion and I broke into laughter, for the moment forgetting all about our uncertain future.

I have to hand it to Dion. Despite the radio ordeal, he remained composed and positive. The legalities were as confusing as hell, but he hung in there, keeping up staff morale and doing his best to clean up the shit that had stuck to his office ceiling. I did all I could to help him and felt a heightened sense of solidarity between us. No matter how bumpy this ride got, our love would always see things through. I told him that whatever happened, we would be okay, whether that meant relaunching the station or, God forbid, returning to Australia.

The legal procedure for stations applying to re-broadcast changed with alarming regularity. There was talk of behind-the-scenes bribery, corruption, backslapping and backstabbing between government officials and other radio station managers. The powers-that-be behind his network decided that every effort would be made to get Dion's station back on air. The trouble was they decided to do it *legally*. As far as I could tell, they were the only station taking this particular approach.

Dion worked harder than ever to bring things under control. Staff remained employed as a government pre-requisite to have the station reinstated, so employees rocked up to the office daily and pretended to work. Yes, *pretended*, all the way down to hosting fake radio programs that nobody heard. In the meantime, I focused on the only certainty in our lives, our upcoming nuptials.

It was decided. We would marry in Sydney in November 2001 after our year was up in Greece, and we would marry in a church in keeping with family tradition. But a question arose. In *which* family tradition? Not surprisingly, Dion's family were Greek Orthodox. Equally unsurprising, mine were not. Mine were Roman Catholic, and it just so happened that my darling Maltese grandmother was so devout, she was close to being the first living being to be canonised. My uncle, in the meantime, just so happened to be a Catholic priest.

It seemed there was a choice to be made. Greek Orthodox wedding versus Catholic wedding. Hmmm. For Dion, the decision was simple. We would marry in the Greek Orthodox Church. As I no longer necessarily subscribed to Catholic beliefs, at first I had little objection. But then the cogs of my mind creaked into action.

Hang on a minute!

Dion attended Orthodox Church about as regularly as I attended Catholic mass: let's just say 'seldom'. He could barely *understand* what was said in Orthodox Church, let alone subscribe to its beliefs. You see, Greek Orthodox ceremonies are carried out in an archaic version of the Greek language known as *katharevousa*, similar to the way Catholic mass was once performed in Latin. At least I understood what I was disagreeing with in a Catholic mass. Dion only had the opportunity to disagree with the rare snippets he grasped.

Should I marry in the Orthodox Church, thus setting a precedent that I'll submit to all things Greek? Isn't spending a year in Greece enough?

The situation rapidly moved from religious to political and I began to understand how wars began. An impossible debate arose between us. Dion was adamant that we marry in the Orthodox Church. I, however, narrowed our options down to four:

1. We could marry in the Greek Church, which my family would think was as weird as joining the ranks in a Moonies' mass wedding.
2. We could marry in the Catholic Church, which Dion's family would think was as weird as holding a wedding reception for less than a thousand people.
3. We could elope and marry under no religious jurisdiction at all, in which case both families would hunt us down and fricassee our genitals.
4. We could break off the engagement, which I guessed might bring secret relief to poor old Katerina.

It was around this time that a visit from my soon-to-be in-laws drew imminent. Naturally I was packing death. *And* naturally I had to give notice to Athina, the cleaning powerhouse. I never saw her again.

The longer I lived in Athens, the more I reminisced about Australia as though it existed on a higher plane. At the same time, it felt as though people back home were slowly slipping into the mists of nonchalance. My persistent emails were acknowledged less and less. But as it turned out, Dion and I were about to become almost as popular as a conspiracy theory at an *X-Files* convention. I said *almost*. Obviously lured by our dynamic personalities as much as by a balmy Greek summer, a trickle of relatives headed our way in the form of two of my three brothers and my soon-to-be parents-in-law. I was excited and scared – in that order.

Having been so deprived of familiar human interaction I wondered how I'd relate to even my own flesh and blood. I'd become like a displaced hermit, afraid of sharp sounds and bright objects. I worried that my brothers and I might now have nothing in common except the ability to remember only the first two lines of the Australian national anthem. I also wondered how I'd go playing tour guide in a country that quite frankly still seemed as alien to me as it did the day I'd arrived.

I met Andy and Phil at the Athens Gate Hotel across from Hadrian's Arch in the centre of town. They'd just completed a messy six-week Contiki tour of Europe and I was incredibly excited to see them. They didn't quite understand my exhilaration. Sure they were happy to see me too, but my enthusiasm was laced with a chronic desperation. Hell, I fell just short of jumping into their arms, and if they'd thrown a stick I'd gladly have galloped along the ground to fetch it. After ecstatic hellos, we hopped into a taxi and headed for Labrou Katsoni. I directed the driver, pretending I could speak Greek for the sole purpose of impressing my younger siblings. Little did they know I was merely repeating my address followed by the word 'please'.

'Wow! You're speaking Greek!' beamed Phil, his brown eyes gleaming from a tanned face

'Yeah, I know. I take lessons.' My expression was smug as I turned back to the driver.

'*Labrou Katsoni, Voula, parakalo. Labrou Katsoni.*'

Painstakingly I devised an Athens' activities schedule. It comprised one word: 'Acropolis'. Over the ensuing days I bored my brothers silly by showing them little more than the landmark that I regarded as 'okay'. We did, however, also compete in a number of walking competitions. Phil outpaced us, looking over his shoulder triumphantly.

Soon we were making plans to head to Ios, the party island I'd first visited over ten years before. Although Dion was thrilled to bits to be reunited with my 'little' brothers (they were in their midtwenties), he stayed behind to supervise his 'staff' in unwavering devotion to his nonexistent station. I wasn't sure that his enthusiasm was healthy. Unbelievably I now saw him even less than before.

Ios is a part of the Cyclades group of islands and a magnet to every young partying backpacker within a 1000-kilometre radius. It's known for its 'vivid' nightlife, though vivid is perhaps not quite the right word. People get so wankered on lethal doses of alcohol that the island has probably had as much stomach content spilt on it as it has fraudulent Stolichnaya vodka. It's chock-full of the bars and clubs for which it is famous and is known only secondarily for its crystal waters and gorgeous beaches.

When we hit town, Ios abounded with masses of pissed Australians, which was great – until they unleashed their drunken ignorance on accommodating locals. 'How much for the chips, mate? How's about I swap me T-shirt for 'em?' and other cute Aussieisms were not uncommon. Admittedly I was at least a decade older than anyone else, but I knew that the noble ambassadors representing my country weren't exactly doing me any favours. I knew that Greeks on the livelier islands often regarded tourists as uncultured, drunken freaks. I therefore resigned myself to paying their karmic debt in Athens outside of the holiday season.

I also observed how outrageously patriotic travellers can be, even if they're away from home for only a few weeks. Like I could talk, but there were kids bursting into anthemic national tributes left, right and centre.

While strolling through the labyrinth of winding alleys and whitewashed buildings in the main town of Hora, a couple of female Tasmanian cousins in their early twenties heard our accents and gravitated towards us like a couple of dorkish clowns headed for a box of abandoned bicycle horns. Within minutes they interrupted us with an impromptu rendition of 'Down Under' by Men at Work, performed with all the enthusiasm of a lunchtime shopping mall pantomime act.

Lana: 'Phil, do you remember how to count to ten in Japanese?'

(Andy's blue eyes rolled.)

Phil: 'Yes! *Itch, Nee, San, Chee* . . .'

Cousin 1, appearing as if from nowhere: 'I SAID, 'DO YA SPEAKA MY LANGUAGE?'

Cousin 2 (suppressing a giggle): 'AND HE JUST SMILED AND GAVE ME A . . .'

Cousins 1 and 2 (in unison): 'VEGEMITE SANDWICH!!!'

The Tasmanian duo giggled together rapturously – a giggle that said, 'How cute are *we?*' They looked at each other and then at each of us in turn, glowing. My face began to spasm.

The cousins joined us for a spell, as did some young friends of my brothers. As time progressed, it became more and more like an episode of *Survivor* where slowly individuals became ostracised. The Tasmanians were the first to go after it became more and more evident that they preferred to drape themselves in Aussie flags than tear from one side of the island to the other with us. I was next.

15

You drive me nervous

I returned to Athens from Ios for two reasons. Firstly, my brothers were travelling on to Turkey. And secondly, Dion's mother and father had hit the Greek capital. Katerina and Kostas were back in the old country and, in my mind, poised for a reign of terror. Dion drove alone to collect them from the airport and deliver them safely to our Voula apartment. In the meantime, I fastidiously mopped the floor and tidied the house ensuring items in our pantry were neatly aligned with the aid of a ruler. As the front door swung open, I drew a deep breath and braced myself.

With his father's help, Dion heaved seven suitcases into the apartment. His energetic mother followed. To reiterate, there were *seven* suitcases. Not two. *Seven*. We greeted one another with hugs. After some general 'how was your flight?' chitchat, I enquired about the luggage that had overtaken most of our living room. This inspired Katerina to unzip each bag and provide an inventory of its contents. There were a few items in particular that struck me as peculiar.

Packed snugly in one bag was a pre-loved bed sheet that was to be passed on to a cousin in Lesbos. It was a gift. It was *used*. Like many older Greek–Australians, Dion's parents seemed to think that Greece remained in the same state of poverty that it had in the 1950s. In another bag, a can of Fabulon ironing spray was wrapped tenderly in a face cloth. This was a gift for another relative. But most intriguing of all was the enormous pair of gardening shears that took up half a suitcase. Dion's father had brought them along should he need to attend to any emergency gardening. He proudly pulled them out of the case like a homicidal maniac, rolled socks spilling onto the floor. As I wondered whether there might also be a whipper snipper or a hedge trimmer hiding in there somewhere, Katerina approached me with a silver watch that she gently strapped to my wrist.

'Thees for you.'

Used sheets aside, Katerina was unbelievably generous. The multiple suitcases were necessary to hold what turned out to be enough gifts for the entire population of Greece. These people were incredibly giving, a wonderful trait shared by almost every Greek person I've ever known. Beware of Greeks bearing gifts? I say bring it on!

The following morning, shortly after Dion had left for work, I was awoken by an urgent thumping and groaning at my bedroom door. Straining to determine the source, I eventually discerned that it was Katerina on a cleaning frenzy, madly mopping our apartment. The mop handle bashed against my bedroom door like a call to domestic arms. To me it came with an undercurrent of accusation. It was 7 a.m. My husband was at work. I was in bed. I was *lazy*.

This was how I'd be awoken on many mornings for the remainder of Dion's parents' stay.

Dion and I had come up with a solution for our upcoming wedding. Keeping Katerina happy was a priority for my fiancé. A *big* priority. A *frighteningly* big priority. I thought it wise not to rock the boat. She was, after all, about to officially become my mother-in-law. So we agreed to marry in the Greek Orthodox Church, and afterwards participate in a short Catholic ceremony performed by my uncle. Simple!

When organising these ceremonies, both churches asked that we commit to christening our children under the banner of their religion. We agreed to both requests, but knew that one day a choice would have to be made, which seemed odd given that these religions shared almost identical beliefs. I hoped we could come up with a solution that didn't mean bypassing parenthood.

We also decided that our reception would be paid for by us, in a venue chosen by us, with a guest list approved by us. Sure it would be a Greek wedding, but it would be a Greek wedding with a twist. We'd do it *our* way. We booked our reception in the Rocks at Circular Quay in Sydney and invited 120 people. The venue was called the Italian Village, although I predicted the strong likelihood it would be transformed into a Greek one.

A few days into her visit, Katerina began acting a little strangely. Hawk-like, she sat watching me iron Dion's shirts until she could stand it no more. She stood up, gathered the shirts, snatched the iron from my hand and re-ironed each and every one of them, thus undermining the very purpose of my being.

With Dion at work and Kostas lost in the miracle of Greek television, Katerina had me all to herself. I felt uneasy, sensing something was brewing. I asked if she wanted to join me out on the balcony. She shrugged, followed me out, took a seat, remained silent and shifted about on her chair agitatedly.

Is she still annoyed with me for being a shit ironer?

Suddenly she broke her silence.

'Why you hkaf wedding reception in city?' she asked, exasperated.

Pleased that this had nothing to do with my mediocre ironing technique, I explained that we wanted a view of the Sydney Harbour Bridge and the Opera House, reminders of the city we missed so terribly.

'But you hkaf at Parramatta and you hkaf five-hkundred people, no hkundred twenty.'

Parramatta is a suburban area of Sydney's west. The last time I was there a guy with pockmarked skin, a goatee and a mullet haircut stumbled towards me at a train station and called me a profane colloquialism for a particular part of the female anatomy. Parramatta naturally wasn't my favourite place in the world. But Katerina's only concern was that our reception venue didn't have the capacity to accommodate the entire population of Lesbos.

'But we want our reception in a beautiful restaurant, with a beautiful view of Sydney, with our closest friends and family, see?' I explained simply.

'Why you no invite children? Why I no invite my cousin's friend's sister, Eleni? Why she no bring her little gerrl, Tzenni?'

I wasn't liking this. I wasn't liking this at all.

'We only want children of the immediate family there,' I offered feebly.

She huffed. She fell silent. She wiped a tear from the corner of her eye.

Oh, come on! This is getting ridiculous!

The exasperation rose in her voice.

'Why I no invite my uncle? Why I no invite my cousins? Why no children? Why Dion's godmother's friend Tzoanna no come? Why?!'

It was my turn to become agitated. It felt like my future mother-in-law was trying to *intimidate* me. It was freaking me out.

'Katerina, you have sixty relatives and friends coming. If you compare that to the number coming from my side of the family, you'll see that you're getting quite a good deal. There are only twenty of my relatives coming. *Twenty!* None of my parents' friends. None of my cousins. None of my cousins' cousins' children. We're also marrying in the Greek Orthodox Church and I'm a *Catholic*. Don't you see? Don't you see that this is *our* wedding and it's the way we want to do things?'

Katerina shot daggers in my direction. She angrily pushed back her chair, making a sharp scraping sound along the outdoor tiles, stood and waved a hand at me.

'Baahh!'

There was a moment's silence.

'But why I no invite Litza my gerrl-a-friend?'

Obviously I had little understanding of the importance of throwing a Greek wedding spectacular. Why anyone would want to invite hundreds of acquaintances to such a personal event was beyond me. Why have throngs of children sliding across a reception floor, ripping their little dresses and miniature pantsuits, the whole fiasco ending in tears? I just didn't get it. So as my relationship with Katerina slowly deteriorated over such matters of world importance, I did what any self-respecting soon-to-be daughter-in-law would do. I avoided her. And I lied a little bit.

I suddenly gained 'full-time employment'. That's right. I got a job. At Dion's radio station. The one that didn't really exist. I trekked off to work every morning with Dion and sat in his office for eight hours reading a book, playing with the printer and generally making a nuisance of myself. Dion didn't seem to mind. In fact, he appeared to rather enjoy my witnessing how much his staff loved working for him. He also quite liked yelling jibberish into a telephone receiver. I got to see for the first time how obediently staff responded to his commands. I wondered how it was possible for my soon-to-be-husband to balance daytime adulation with the night-time fears of his resident scaredy cat.

While Dion was more than happy to spare me the wrath of Katerina, he warned me not to speak too much to his subordinates. He said he wanted to maintain a professional distance, and that he could only do this if no one knew anything about his private life. He explained that if any private information got out there, it wouldn't remain private for long. His staff were gossips! For the next couple of weeks, I therefore became Dion's aloof, silent fiancée while my kitchen cupboards at home were mysteriously lined and rearranged. Oddly, one or two female staff members treated me with open contempt despite my close connection with the person signing their pay cheques, and it soon became evident that my presence there wasn't particularly welcome. My 'employment' lasted a mere fortnight.

It was a summery Saturday morning when Dion and I entered Athens' modern and pristine new airport awaiting a flight bound for Lesbos. Dion's parents had departed for the island a week earlier, opting to take a fourteen-hour ferry trip to the third largest of Greece's many islands. For Katerina and Kostas the visit had been a long time coming. They had not returned to Lesbos since they'd left over fifty years before.

At the airport, I bumped into a British girl my age selling perfume at a duty free store. Lucy lived in Glyfada and had moved to Greece after falling in love with a Greek guy. She'd been in Athens for only a month. I pounced on her like a clumsy baby gorilla.

'Has anyone got a pen? A PEN? *Anyone?*'

Lucy nervously produced a pen from her pocket, all the while staring at me. I scrawled my number onto the back of a set of Greek tampon instructions I'd found in my handbag.

'Now you call me. You're new here, I've got no friends and we've *got* to hang out.'

Lucy never called.

Our first day on Lesbos, Dion and I headed for a beach at the coastal village of Eressos. Nimbly avoiding sea urchins, we entered the deep, cool blue water.

'Is that Turkey over there?'

'No, it's a boat.'

'Is that Turkey?'

'No, it's a small child wearing a flotation device.'

'Is that Turkey?'

'No.'

'Is that?'

'No.'

We never sighted Turkey. For a start, we were on the wrong side of the island. But our spirits soared regardless. Hand in hand, we walked into the yard of the ancestral family home only to be confronted by a lamb, tied up and dangling upside down from a tree. Kostas knelt beside it with a butcher's knife in hand. He smiled at us before lackadaisically slitting the throat of the formerly frolicking beast. Blood gushed from it and splashed around his boots, forming a ruby-red lake in the centre of the garden.

I screamed.

He asked if we'd enjoyed our day at the beach.

The small stone house smelt stale, and was being shared with Katerina, Kostas, Nota and Nikos for the duration of our stay. The men sat and did jack shit on the narrow balcony while Katerina, Nota and I competed to see who could work the hardest in the kitchen. I lost.

I emptied the bucket that acted as our kitchen sink in the dry dirt yard outside and pulled Dion aside.

'Should we give your mum and dad their wedding invitation now?'

'Yeah, let's do it!'

One of my 'duties' at the radio station had been working on our wedding invitations. We were both quite excited. My gorgeous fiancé put his arm around his mother and handed her a cream, polished envelope with a double-heart silver seal on the back. She opened it with hardworking, leathery hands and began reading. She then began speaking sharply to Dion in her native tongue.

'What's she saying?' I interjected, panicking, forgetting Katerina could speak English.

'Um . . . she's saying their names should be on the invitation first, before your mum and dad's.' Dion looked embarrassed and a little sad.

'Oh. So it should say "Katerina and Kostas are pleased to invite Katerina and Kostas to the wedding of Dion and Lana"? Yeah, that makes a lot of sense!'

Not one to shy away from a drama, Katerina slumped down on a chair and cradled her head in her arms. Dion patted her on the back. I wrestled myself to the floor to stifle a groan.

That night we were to attend a fiesta at the local village. While this was the type of cultural experience that backpackers and hardy travellers crave, I can safely say I wasn't looking forward to it at all. For a start, I'd spent the majority of the day, post-wedding invitation calamity, receiving funny looks from an endless parade of friends and relatives that streamed in and out of the house. To make myself feel better, I mused that technically they were all 'Lesbians', being native to the island of Lesbos.

Olives, feta cheese and bread were brought to the table at five-minute intervals by a frantic Katerina, desperate to placate the smiling and toothless. She spoke exclusively in Greek. Since the

Great Wedding Invitation Disaster of 2001, Katerina was no longer on speaking terms with me, although as people barged through the door, she would tilt her head in my direction and mutter something by way of a hasty introduction. That's when I'd usually be on the receiving end of a strange stare. After a while, Dion began to snigger.

'What's so funny?'

'Ahhhh . . . how do I break this to you. She's introducing you as "Lana, my son's fiancée, who's thirty-three" and then introducing me as "Dion, my son, who's thirty-one".' Dion continued chuckling. I wasn't laughing quite so hard. But worse was yet to come after I broke our vow of silence to admit to Katerina that Dion hadn't brought a pair of trousers with him.

'*WHUT? NO TROUSER?* Whut he wear tonight?'

She stared at me, eyes scanning my face, crow-like.

'*WHUY YOU NO PACK TROUSER FOR HKIM?*'

'What? *Me?* Dion forgot them, not me! We didn't even know he'd be needing them.'

'BUT YOU ARE HKIS *WIFE. YOU* PACK BAG FOR HKIM!'

'Pack his bag? . . . I'm not his wife! And I'm not his mother either.'

An expert in the various methods of calming his mother, Dion interjected, cool as a cucumber.

'Mum, who cares about the trousers. I can wear the shorts I brought.'

Katerina began hyperventilating, her chest rising and falling.

'SHORTS? *SHORTS?*' she wailed.

Dion presented the shorts he had in mind. She snatched them from him, disgusted, and with great, agonised sighs folded out a screeching ironing board.

'Do you want me to iron them?' I offered meekly.

Katerina was so distraught that she actually let me apply my substandard ironing technique to the shorts, and stormed out of the room. I pictured her throwing herself down onto the creaking bed in the adjacent bedroom and sobbing violently into a pillow.

That night, we visited a packed town square filled with the delicious smoky scent of scorched lamb. There was singing, dancing, eating, drinking and wild celebration – wild celebration for everyone except Katerina and me. Katerina could never celebrate when her son was wearing a stupid pair of badly ironed shorts. I could never celebrate when I was about to inherit a mother-in-law who so obviously saw me as unworthy.

The following morning we awoke to the sound of Katerina singing Dion's name.

'Dionysi! Dion! We go soon, Dion! Hkurry! You be late!'

It seemed that 'we' were expected to join an expedition to visit an ill, elderly uncle of . . . someone's. I never did quite work out who he was, but it didn't seem to matter so much. Our vivacious group trudged through narrow streets waving *'Kali mera!'* (good morning) to everyone we passed. Some of our party periodically stopped to pick ripened figs from trees and insert them into each other's mouths.

We soon entered the darkened hovel housing the prostrate figure of the aged uncle. My prognosis was that the old man was not long for this world. As he began muttering Greek nouns at random, Dion and I took a step back out into daylight to recompose ourselves.

What the hell are we doing in the room of a dying stranger?

The cries of a goat-herding family friend summoned us back into the room, presumably to say our final goodbyes.

'Ela! Dionysi! Ela!'

The moment chosen for us to impart our blessings came just after the oblivious old man had been half stripped – of clothes and dignity – and propped up onto a potty in the centre of his bedroom. As I offered a quivering, token *'yia sas'* (goodbye), I got the distinct impression that his retort came only in the form of him laying cable.

Three months after their arrival, it was almost time for Katerina and Kostas to leave the old country for the second time in their lives. To my great relief, two-thirds of their visit had been spent in Lesbos while we were safely back in Athens, although over the weeks I was never sure if they'd suddenly appear on our doorstep. When they did finally return, it was only a matter of days before their departure.

As Dion set off for work and Kostas handcuffed himself to our sofa in front of the television, I offered to take my soon-to-be mother-in-law to the Acropolis. I didn't have the heart to tell her that I thought the icon was 'okay'. I just wanted her to see that I wasn't the inadequate, incompetent human being she presumed me to be.

Knowing that she was only forty-eight hours away from returning to Australia and her grandchildren, Katerina had mellowed considerably. In fact, with nobody else around, we openly enjoyed one another's company. Katerina was softer, more sympathetic and understanding. She spoke not unwisely of the importance of a successful marriage and I wondered if her little performance in Lesbos was nothing more than a dramatic improvisation exhibited for the benefit of surrounding friends and relatives.

Katerina and Kostas left the next morning, following desperate requests to bequeath half-used bottles of talcum powder. All of us seemed to be a little sad. In spite of myself, as they walked out the door bound for the airport, I began to cry. And to my astonishment, I wasn't crying tears of joy. I cried because I realised I'd soon be alone again. And I cried because at the end of the day, despite the hiccups, Dion's mother and father were two harmless creatures who were responsible for bringing the love of my life into being. I'd grown accustomed to the threat of them blowing in and out of our home like gale-force winds. After they'd closed the door behind them, Labrou Katsoni fell deathly silent once again.

16

Mad world

'Hi-it's-me.'

It was Dion putting in his daily phone call from the station, speaking at an incredible pace.

'Have-you-switched-on-the-television-today?'

'No. Why would I? I never switch it on during the day. I painted my toenails different colours though.'

'A-plane's-flown-into-one-of-the-Twin-Towers-in-New-York-City! Turn it on! It's unbelievable!'

'Nah. I don't think so.'

'WHAT?'

'What for? I'll see it at some point. They re-run stories like these over and over . . .'

Such was my disconnection from the rest of the world that I couldn't understand the implications of what had occurred. Granted, a plane colliding with a city building was nothing to sneeze at, but I didn't know that September 11, 2001, would be seen as one of the worst acts of terrorism against the 'free world'. Not once did I turn on the television that day. In fact I knew nothing of the magnitude of events until Dion returned home, sat me down in front of the TV and patiently explained what was going on in the world. I was shocked.

What does this mean?

Is World War III about to erupt?

Is the world about to end?

Should we return to Australia?

I watched the news footage re-run over and over that evening and cried for all of humanity.

Dion told me that one or two of his staff members had commented that the USA deserved everything it got. It was the first time I learned that many Greeks held reservations towards America, possibly as a result of US support of the right-wing military junta that ruled Greece from 1967 to 1974. And as for the territorial dispute relating to Cyprus, an island divided by Greek and Turkish rule, many Greeks believe that the Americans favour Turkey, Turkey being an important ally bridging the US and the Middle East.

For us, September 11 marked a year in Athens. Dion's contract was expiring, his radio station was still off the air and the world was going mad. While I'd definitely had enough of Greece, Dion hadn't. He explained how important it was for him to get that goddamned station back on air, and for the first time mentioned that he wanted to renew his contract for another twelve months. Before I fell apart, he held my hands and explained that he was confident that it wouldn't be long before the airwaves were once again revived. He had unfinished business to attend to.

While I had every reason to want to flee to the safety of our home country, I heard in Dion's voice a sincere plea, a plea that rang with the importance of achieving all that was yet to be achieved. I wanted to see Dion do well, to make the most of an opportunity while it was there for the taking. *The first year's always the toughest, right?* I told myself.

I can do this!

Who am I trying to kid? NO, I FUCKING CAN'T!

Yes, I can.

Cannot.

Okay, MAYBE I can.

I concluded that despite the challenges so far, perhaps our story in Greece wasn't quite over, and that life was all about the satisfaction that results from overcoming difficulties and making the most of opportunities that often come cleverly disguised. Although I was yet to reap any rewards and hadn't yet proven my proclaimed adaptability, I strongly believed that fate had surely brought us to this part of the world for a reason. I didn't want to give up. I was deeply in love and had a wedding to look forward to. So, unbelievably, I agreed to Dion renewing his contract for a further year. And just like that, my one-year sentence was doubled!

He smiled gratefully, scooped me up in his arms and swung me through the air.

'You're the greatest, babe!'

I was going to get the hang of this country, even if it killed me.

Act II

For when two join the same adventure, one perceives before the other how they ought to act; while one alone, however prompt, resolves more tardily and with a weaker will.

Homer, *The Iliad*

A sort of homecoming

Post contract renewal, my gaze had settled upon it often. It was a dusty bottle of cooking sherry that sat winking at me from our kitchen shelf. Thank Christ I had something slightly more productive to keep me from succumbing to the seductive lure of alcoholism. It was my wedding! From an Athens living room, I frantically made long-distance arrangements, adding to a never-ending list of things to do. My daily chores now looked a little something like this:

> Choose menu
> Arrange fittings
> Order place cards
> Decide on flowers
> Figure out what bombonieres are
> Add Litza to guest list

A certain movie had also captured my attention. It was called *My Big Fat Greek Wedding* and was a box-office smash that was receiving rave reviews all over the world. It had begun screening in

Greece only weeks before our magical day. The timing was unbeliev-able. So Dion and I traipsed into a cinema complex behind youths modelling the latest in telephone technology, unable to resist. As we watched the eccentricities of the Portokalos family unfold, I squirmed uncomfortably in my seat, my popcorn left untouched. I noted, shocked, that the non-Greek in the film, the xenos, was not being readily accepted by a dominant Greek family member. *Hello?* I also watched the non-Greek calmly get his head around Greek culture and concede to marry under the Orthodox religion. Okay, so the xenos in the film was much more composed than I was, but still, this fucking comedy was practically the story of my life! Had film creators been spying on me? Is that what this experiment of *Truman Show* proportions was all about? How could a portrayal be so frighteningly close to my own reality?

As the xenos headbutted resistance and Mr Portokalos rattled off English words that had Greek at their root, the word 'xenopho-bia' unexpectedly popped into my head in a private act of defiance. I slunk lower in my seat. I felt a little evil as I listened to Dion chuckle obliviously beside me. And so it was that – as far as I was concerned – Mr Portokalos and Katerina melded into the one being. I anticipated the big fat day, not too far into the future, hoping that Katerina would wrap me in her loving arms rather than rap me across the knuckles.

When my departure day for Australia eventually dawned, I awoke serenely. I was jetting out of Athens two weeks ahead of Dion to finalise preparations. The only audible sounds that morning came courtesy of an old woman knitting on the next floor up and a priest poaching an egg three blocks away. Otherwise the world was still. As my slippers shuffled along the floor, I deliberated quietly over whether I should put in a quick call to Cadbury Australia, manufacturer of the Cherry Ripe. I thought it through. It surely wouldn't hurt to encourage them to double their production rate and predict an unprecedented rise in sales to the Board. Seconds later, the disco-ball-dazzling enormity of what lay ahead smacked me in the face.

I was going HOME!

I was going home to get *MARRIED*!

And I was going home to eat CHERRY RIPE!

Before I knew it, I was disembarking at Kingsford Smith Airport and staring at a life-sized 'Welcome to Sydney' poster depicting people at Bondi Beach unashamedly parading bikini line shaving rash. I'd been in and out of Sydney airport countless times, sometimes returning after much longer stints away, but never before had I done what I was about to do.

On hearing their familiar and friendly accents, I found myself practically insisting on a group hug with Australian immigration officers. The fact that they all sounded uncannily like Steve 'Crocodile Hunter' Irwin was unimaginably reassuring. But while the distinctive twang brought great comfort, something also snapped. I began to chuckle mischievously, like a psychotic person holding onto a twisted secret. I was very lucky not to have found my arrivals card marked with a special symbol alerting customs to search my baggage and person for illicit drugs.

Next I became engrossed by a Sydney infomercial being screened on monitors above the baggage carousel. As I absorbed the familiar landmarks of my home city, I felt my heart begin to swell with unadulterated pride, if not adoration. My face contorted into grotesque expressions from which, I'm sure, onlookers expected to see an alien burst forth. By the time I'd collected my bags, satisfactorily cleared customs and determined through blurred vision the outline of my parents, I began to howl with the intensity of a newborn.

I bawled and sniffled my way down the arrivals ramp, making a beeline for Mum and Dad, and a spectacle of myself at the same time. My parents tried their best to mask their concern over my public display of emotion. While being as sympathetic as people can be as mucus trails from the nose of a hysterical grown woman, their eyes betrayed their fear that I'd returned home an utter basket case. Sobs permitting, I assured them that my tears expressed only joy at being home, *not* despair over being returned into their temporary custody. We nevertheless all felt a little bit awkward.

In the days that followed, I discovered that going home was for me what coming up for air is to the drowning. Suddenly everything seemed perfect. I loved things like drains, basil, newsreaders, chops and bank tellers. I felt positively euphoric over being able to speak to my ever-friendly country-folk again after a year of relative silence and perceived hostility. I found myself speaking at great length with traffic wardens, tax agents, scientologists and anyone else I'd usually avoid.

While I attempted to blend back into the scenery gracefully without looking like a rerouted piece of Eurotrash – my Athenian garb seeming out of context and, well, quite ridiculous – I simultaneously got to hang out at all my favourite places with all my favourite people. In comparison to my 'other' life, everything around me made complete sense. The fresh air knocked me out, and everything else about Australia that I'd once taken for granted stuck out like a pair of oversized elephant's testicles. As I kissed the ground upon which I walked, hugged trees and professed undying love for things such as reliable electrical wiring, very few of my friends truly understood my joy. They were too busy manning tug-o-war teams, trying to pull me in a thousand different directions. It seemed everyone wanted a piece of me. It was exhausting and delicious.

As I paraded myself around various parties, I fielded the same questions over and over again.

'When did you arrive?'

'Why did it take you so long to call?'

'When are you coming back for good?'

'How's Greece treating you?'

'What language do they speak over there?'

In between organising our wedding I found myself zipping here and there, never really spending much time with anyone. Looking back, the only quality time I truly spent was the five minutes I had alone with my mother's cat. And after only a relatively short time away, I was distressed to find shifts occurring in friendships. I was moving in a different direction from everybody else. It was scary to realise that I no longer had the opportunity to change with the people that I loved. Not that I had much time to reflect on such matters, for I had a wedding approaching faster than a speeding locomotive.

I arose from slumber, slowly shrugging off the freedom of dreams.

WHO AM I AGAIN?

Oh, that's right. Lana.

WHERE AM I?

Australia. Good.

WHAT DAY IS IT?

OhmyGod!

IT'S MY FREAKIN' WEDDING DAY!

I tumbled out of bed, near-vomiting with nervous excitement. I raced over to a mirror and took stock of myself. I looked like shit. I glanced out the window. It was grey and cloudy. I didn't care much about either.

IT'S MY FREAKIN' WEDDING DAY!

The morning flew by as a giddying blur of hairdressers, bridesmaids, make-up artists, jittery relatives, nosey neighbours, champagne, photographers and shiny vintage cars. I was transformed from wicked witch to fairy princess in a mere matter of hours. My brother Geoff materialised wearing an Armani suit and a Gene Simmons KISS mask, documenting proceedings with a video camera.

The next thing I knew, I was in a white Bentley with my mother and father heading for St George's Greek Orthodox Church in Sydney's eastern suburbs. My father was quiet as my mother made pointless banter with our driver. We may as well have been taking a taxi ride to an RSL club for a cheap lunch and a whirl on the pokies.

Arriving at the church, a sea of familiar faces surrounded the car and cameras clicked in time to obligatory exclamations.

'You look beautiful!'

'Aw, you're just like something right off the top of a wedding cake!'

My three bridesmaids and gorgeous little flower girl assembled by the car door as I made my grand exit, my wrist firmly affixed to my slinky dress. A bracelet belonging to my grandmother had become caught on the satin bodice, my arm stuck in a 'V' position as though in an invisible sling. My dress began to fray. We were off to a rip-roaring start.

My bridesmaids, father and I congregated at the back of the blonde brick building, looking down the aisle we'd soon be walking. Dion faced the altar, rigid, like a large mound of petrified rock. So too did his mother. I suddenly felt sick. This was it.

'I can't do this,' I whispered hoarsely to my father. 'Really . . . I don't think I can!'

'Yes ya can. Ya have ta!' My father shot me a look he normally reserved for those he presumed to be 'galahs'.

With my father firmly linking my arm to prevent escape, we were soon tailing my bridesmaids along a narrow strip of red carpet. When I arrived at the altar, Dion was too terrified to even look at me. His sweaty palm grappled for mine and we held on for dear life. What followed was unfamiliar ritual. A gold-covered Orthodox Bible was thrust into my face by the priest. I wasn't sure what to do, so I hesitantly air-kissed it.

Was that right?

I didn't know. There had been no time for a rehearsal. I broke into a nervous giggle, and looked across at one of my brothers, who joined me. The priest nodded and smiled.

Two small white hoops were then produced and crisscrossed over our heads, like a magic act where a ball is placed beneath one of two cups and the cups are then shuffled. This, I'd been told, symbolised the union of two becoming one, of 'I don't know where you end and I begin', or something along those lines. I didn't quite get it, but I liked it. Dion and I were then invited to circle the altar three times, taking our first steps together as husband and wife. I faced those in the church thrice with a self-conscious smirk on my face. Dion's family looked reverent, my brother solemn (thankfully minus the KISS mask), the remaining non-Orthodox half of the church amused. One guest actually laughed out loud, cupping his mouth with his hands. We were officially married!

To celebrate, as we left the church, Dion's father Kostas chucked a handful of rice directly into his newly married son's face. We went for photos with our families on the cliffs by the Vaucluse apartment we'd left behind just a year earlier. Katerina was nowhere to be seen. Had her sons and husband forgotten her in all the commotion? We next saw her in the front row of the Catholic church at Watson's

Bay, her mouth a grim horizontal line. A parade of our nearest and dearest friends and relatives took to the pulpit to offer prayers and readings, many resenting us for having made them a public spectacle. Twenty minutes later, our token Catholic ceremony was complete as well.

It was official. We were married. *Twice*, just in case. We'd declared our love loud enough for all of heaven to hear! We happily accepted a never-ending stream of congratulations from those we loved, and during private moments, gazed into each other's eyes. Overwhelmed, my new husband wrapped me in his arms and I breathed him in. This was the man that I loved, the man of my dreams, the one I would grow old with. He lifted me high into the air and we laughed as I glided slowly back down to earth like a feather. We whispered secrets and held hands, unable to let go of one another, for we were united, bound by love and drunk on a happiness that fizzed inside us like champagne bubbles. This was undoubtedly the greatest day of my life.

After the ceremonies there was nothing left to do but celebrate . . . and go into damage control with Katerina.

We entered the Italian Village as husband and wife, a moment I'll never forget. Before us was a sea of linen-covered tables, each with candles and white lilies emanating soft light and sweet scents. Every table had a familiar face beaming up at us. It was the closest I'd come to a near-death experience, minus the dark tunnel.

Behind us stood the magnificent Sydney Harbour Bridge and the stylish eggshells of the Opera House, both lit up against a night sky. I smiled and looked over at Katerina. She didn't smile back. And something else was amiss. She was seated at the far end of her table, away from us. *There must have been a mix-up with the place cards. This is all I need!*

I went to her.

'What happened to you earlier with the photos? And why are you sitting at the wrong end of the table?'

'No worry, doesn't matter,' she replied wearily, her expression a study in martyrdom.

Is this a wedding or a wake?

I returned to my seat unfazed in my tight white silk. Nothing was going to ruin this day for me. Nothing.

Dion made a heartfelt speech honouring me before all present. He talked about my inner and outer beauty, my love and patience. He talked about his first meeting with my family and how dedicated they were to me. He said he'd soon understood why, then turned to face me, microphone in hand.

'My wife, Lana . . . I can say that now! That and things like "My wife and I would like a table near the window." Thank you for giving me the unconditional support and love I'd only dreamt of having. You have made all my dreams come true. Love at first sight? You betcha! You are, and always will be, my sweet princess.' Then he vowed that from this day into eternity, he would walk over hot coals for me. The sincerity in his voice and in his eyes brought tears to my own. My hand fluttered to my heart. I looked over at Dion's father, Kostas. He wasn't paying any attention. Instead he waved a cassette tape at me.

I was brought back to the moment by a tug on the hand. It was my Dion. It was time for our first dance together as husband and wife. The stirring sounds of 'Gorecki' by Lamb filled the room:

If I should die this very moment, I wouldn't fear
For I've never known completeness, Like being here
Wrapped in the warmth of you, Loving every breath of you
Still my heart this moment, Or it might burst

Could we stay right here? Til the end of time, til the earth stops turning?
Wanna love you til the seas run dry
I've found the one I've waited for

Post bridal waltz, Dion's relatives began closing in on the dance floor. I knew what was coming. First the staccato sound of the bouzouki. And then The Circle. It slowly began moving clockwise in time to the music. More and more people joined in. The Circle got bigger and bigger, the music louder and faster. Australians, Maltese and Greeks alike threw their heads back in laughter. To the Australians and Maltese it was a novelty. To the Greeks, a celebration. Katerina looked proud. People grabbed plates handed out by waiters and waitresses. As the music got faster and faster, plates exploded in the centre. Plate smashing was a redundant Greek tradition that Dion and I very much wanted kept alive.

The Greek track finished and was replaced by carefully chosen '70s and '80s cheese. As Dion and I left the room for photos, people began cutting disco moves. Kostas again waved a cassette in the air from a far-off corner of the room. We returned to find the dance floor cleared except for a small rotation of Greek elders. Ultra-traditional Greek folk music crackled through the speakers while a small leg-scissoring group carouselled, leaving the rest of our guests to look on with what Katerina probably presumed to be deep admiration.

At the end of the night, we went around the room bidding farewell and accepting warm wishes from our friends and family. My father asked Dion to take good care of me. Dion laughed. *Of course he would!* A drunken guest spilled a glass of red wine all over my white dress, ranting something incoherent about Duran Duran. I kept moving among the guests, doling out hugs and kisses, looking like a bride with multiple stab wounds. Eventually I reached my mother-in-law. She wasn't smiling. In fact, Katerina looked suicidal. This, I gathered, was her official way of welcoming me into the family.

The following day she told me that she'd cried every day for a fortnight leading up to the wedding. I asked her why.

'Becowse I no think you make my son hkappy.'

These were her exact words.

18

Start of the breakdown

After a three-day express honeymoon in Byron Bay, our visit to Australia regrettably drew to a close. I tried to ignore the incessant nagging of the Dark Mistress of the Aegean, but could hear her from across the globe, screaming like a double-crossed, tantrum-throwing banshee. My new husband, on the other hand, was quite happy to pander to her whims. Our respective families were in bits. Nobody, myself included, could believe we'd be gone for another full year.

Our wedding became a fast-fading dream. Back in Athens, Dion went back to reining in his staff – who still did nothing – while I reverted to seesawing between agoraphobic and lunatic.

A few days after returning, I forced myself out of the apartment. As always, there was no real reason for a Glyfada gallivant other than to check in on the CD pirates, world-weary retailers, beggars and stray dogs. There was no real reason to wear a new pair of glittery blue thongs that spangled with every step either. I'd purchased them in Sydney. As Greece began its grey descent into an icy winter, temperatures plummeting, sporting thongs was clearly delusional. The sad thing was that my decision was conscious. To survive the yawning year ahead I'd made a secret pact with myself to live as though I'd never left Australia. It didn't exactly work. I was soon scurrying about the quiet streets like a frazzled rodent with purple frostbitten toes while those around me strutted past in fur coats and preposterously pointy thick leather boots.

After eating a lunch in silence from my preferred easy-to-order fast-food restaurant (hkkamburger), I made my way home. A car navigated by a solitary male slowed to a snail's pace and began tailing me, the driver offering a provocative smile that bordered on a sneer. This wasn't the first time this had happened, but on this occasion the driver pulled up alongside me, opened the passenger door and lunged in an attempt to physically drag me into his car. I ran – flip-flops a-flappin' – with a view to outpace his horse-powered vehicle. I disappeared momentarily after toppling into a conveniently located roadside ditch. I was petrified. The evil menace thankfully drove away, more than likely back to his mum's for a spot of lunch.

Later, the ever-protective Dion agreed that despite Athens being statistically and comparatively safe, it was probably best that I wrap myself in cotton wool and stay tucked away in our apartment for a spell. So for the next month or so, I barely left the house. I hasten to add that reading the words 'for the next month or so I barely left the house' is slightly less arduous than actually living it. Dion, like me, was quite oblivious to its implications.

I resumed my counselling studies, practised Greek and, of course, ironed. I spent days at a time in my pyjamas. I reasoned there was no point in changing out of them when night would soon return. Once I'd forced myself out of bed each morning, I com-menced each day with a lengthy 'to do' list:

Counselling course
Greek

Wash
Iron
Email

After writing a daily summary to my mother detailing the amazing events that had transpired over the previous twenty-four hours (*'Yesterday I washed, studied and ironed'*), I'd spice things up a little by emailing the marketing departments of various worldwide conglomerates. My emails ranged from suggesting changes to packaging (*'after pressing in your plastic lid, I find your milk splashes onto my wrists'*) to moralistic tirades (*'have you really thought about who you're targeting and what message you're putting across to young women with poor body image?'*). To my surprise, no one ever responded.

After many weeks of this, the pull of the outside world proved overwhelming and I pleaded for day release. So, one Saturday, Dion suggested we hit the road to nowhere. Mystery drives were a rare specialty that would often lead us to main-road pasta establishments as though breaking at a truck stop. I couldn't wait.

Jumping up and down all the way to our Labrou Katsoni lift, we bumped into Maria the neighbour, who pounced on Dion to find out when the radio station would be back on air. As always, her coloured blonde hair and make-up were flawless, nay, invincible, and, as always, she conducted a long-winded conversation with Dion while I pondered how women would cope if not for hair dye. But this time, as Dion shook his head, I knew what he was saying – he had no idea when the station would next broadcast. Nobody did. Not even the army of legal representatives who now had enough cash to put down a tidy deposit on a small island.

Later, as the car bumped along spidery roads, I observed Dion carefully to ensure the grim radio situation wasn't affecting him more deeply than he was letting on. He flicked through the handful of stations still broadcasting. His mood, as always, was light. In fact, it was joyous. Mortified, I watched him begin morphing into a stereotypical character who might be portrayed by comedy actor Nick Giannopoulos.

There he sat, in the driver's seat, passionately singing along to a traditional Greek folk ballad, beaming as he rocked his head and body from side to side. He drew dramatic breaths in between song lines to make his delivery as loud and heartfelt as possible, surreptitiously increasing the stereo's volume at fifteen-second intervals. While the song in question made my ears bleed and had me considering the repercussions of squeezing my body through the air-conditioning grille, Dion appeared to be thoroughly enjoying himself. He definitely wasn't drowning in the dire consequences of ongoing radio dilemmas.

Shocked, I plummeted back into my own reality, staring out of the passenger window to see the remains of yet another run-over stray cat, the rubble of another unfinished road, and the aerodynamic phlegm of another one-limbed refugee. Unbelievably, this was the defining moment when it dawned on me that while my husband had been adapting to life in Greece alarmingly well, I hadn't. At all. A nauseating fusion of homesickness and culture shock smothered me in one fell swoop and held me captive. And in that instant I became the antithesis of *Shirley Valentine*. I felt as though I were losing my only link to sanity – my husband.

Adding insult to injury, this day also coincided with Australia Day. I knew that the closest we'd come to acknowledging our country of origin would be by way of a subtitled documentary on marsupials we'd stumble across later that evening. In keeping with my ingenious new 'Why, I'm Not Even Here! I'm Still in Australia!' strategy, I therefore silently recited a medley of Australia-inspired lyrics by Rolf Harris, GANGgajang and Men at Work – tying my kangaroo down to a patio during a lightning storm to watch men chunder.

As Dion's cat-strangled vocals clashed with the music in my mind, I entertained the idea of heading to the seedier outskirts of Omonia Square for a dodgy yellow and green 'Made in Australia' tattoo. I was *this* close to buying a pair of shiny red shoes, a powder-blue pinafore and proclaiming with a click of the heels 'There's no place like home!' *And we'd only just returned!* There was almost a whole year of this ahead! My mind began to wobble.

I sat in the passenger seat brooding over the fact that despite working at a non-functioning radio station, Dion was loving life. He had a new bride. He had recognition, meaning and something that could be loosely described as an extended, albeit slightly dys-functional family in the form of his employees, and his Aunty Nota and Uncle Nikos. There was little discontinuity between his former life and his new one.

Not so for me. I'd trotted along behind him – stopping only for the occasional unsuccessful territorial marking – and become a non-working personification of confusion. In twelve months, I'd changed from an independent, working wild-child into a needy, sweat-pant-wearing house sitter – introverted, shy, paranoid and ultra-sensitive. I'd lost most traces of the self-confidence I'd once possessed. This was the 'new me' . . . and I *hated* her! The only good thing I had in my life was Dion. And now Dion suddenly sang trad folk ballads with all the passion and gusto of a Hellenic-raised Pavarotti doped up on horse tranquilliser.

While envious friends and family in Australia made it clear that they now regarded me as a 'kept woman' or even a 'princess', a more appropriate description might have been an 'unemployed liability'. Sure my new life afforded me the time to read, study, meditate, investigate archaeological digs, uncover the secrets of the Masons, reflect on the complexities of love and, of course, make an impact on the packaging of consumer goods, but sadly it wasn't enough to distract me from facing myself. I had no idea I could be so annoying!

So after our short little road trip, homesickness, culture shock and loneliness finally amalgamated into one big, fat blob and descended upon me like a giant turd. I remained housebound, knowing that if I stepped outside I'd encounter something that I didn't particularly want to face. I was becoming as frightened of the outside world as I was of myself. And as always, I struggled to find constructive ways to ignore the fact that I didn't have anybody to play with, including trawling the Internet for information on the dietary benefits of the crouton. As interesting as that was, I couldn't help but conclude that my Australian life was a lot more interesting and purposeful. And more than ever before, I began to feel really, really sad.

Although Dion was a brilliant companion, I saw him for about an hour each day – just enough time for him to be fed and watered before he drifted into a blissful slumber in front of the television. This was the only 'real' human contact I had. Obviously I needed to go out and make me some friends. But how? I'd tried Newcomers, an organisation that apparently doubled as an animal adoption agency, and left empty-handed. I'd surfed the Internet for friends and found none. I'd even asked Dion if I could work at the radio station, but this time for real. I was sure there'd be *something* for me to do that would involve meeting new people. However, in light of the fact that his station was off the air, Dion wasn't exactly 'hiring'.

Making friends didn't usually require a clever fifteen-point strategy outlined in a PowerPoint presentation but that's virtually what it had become. Unfortunately, I didn't have the luxury of an instant group of people to select from in order to carry out a compatibility study, commence the process of bonding and thus forge everlasting relationships. So I resumed a lonely life that seemed even lonelier now that we'd committed to another year.

One night after dinner, I squeezed the now-familiar question into Human Interaction Hour.

'I need to make some friends desperately. What should I do?'

Dion fiddled nervously with his ear.

'I don't know, babe, but you've always got me! *I'm* your friend!'

He made his hand into a duck's bill and 'bit' me on the arm before marching to the kitchen for a strong cup of coffee. I sensed my situation made him feel powerless, maybe even somehow responsible. Worse than feeling lonely, I'd now reached a place that was nothing short of soul destroying. I'd become even more out of touch with reality, separated from the world and everyone in it. And as I continued to slip, I took to playing Unkle's 'Lonely Soul' over and over again, a brooding reflection on isolation that hinted at cutting life's cord. I figured if nobody else was gonna feel sorry for me – aside from a helpless Dion – I might as well feel sorry for myself.

I tried turning to Anna, the beautiful wife of Dion's colleague Yianni. Over a Sunday taverna lunch ordered by the men, I opened up to her for the first time, steering the conversation away from the usual perils of nanny hire to something slightly deeper. I explained in slow English that I was experiencing loneliness to a frightful degree and starting to lose the plot. I announced that I had no friends and didn't know what to do. She paused to digest the information and offered an insightful pearl of wisdom:

'I theenk you must make friends.'

With that, she sat back, popped an olive into her mouth, and brushed the blonde frond of hair from her eyes to allow her to concentrate on more interesting things, like the seagull crapping on the footpath just past my right shoulder. You see, Anna didn't get it. Nor did Dion. Unless people had experienced this type of isolation for themselves – this quicksand sensation of suffocating in emptiness – they would *never* get it.

I clung to Dion at night as we willed the problem away.

'It'll be okay, babe,' he soothed.

I lay in bed, my body rigid with anxiety, and braced myself for the coming day.

It's funny what can happen to a person when they feel disempowered and alone. Well, not funny, but interesting. As long as it's not happening to you.

To be certain, on the surface my life seemed idyllic. I lived in an exotic country. I got to travel. I didn't have to work. I had a fabulous husband and we didn't have any financial struggles. What was so hard about that? *Nothing!* And I certainly didn't take any of it for granted. But unfortunately the positives were severely outweighed.

Unlike the life I'd known before, there was no synchronicity, no weird and wonderful coincidences that opened new pathways, no friendships, no sense of belonging, no human connection, no learning, no 'a-ha' moments, no nothing. Only confusion. Athens appeared unyielding. I never could have predicted the implications of surrendering myself to the unfamiliarity of a foreign land. I hated my domestic role. I didn't particularly enjoy studying. I didn't care much for museums or the incredible history that abounded. I was totally crap at the language. I was friendless, if that hasn't been stated enough. And I couldn't cope.

My life became less about discovering this new 'world' with a sense of wonder, irony and wit, and more about surviving each day.

While I'd heard that most people giggled and begged for another turn after riding the 'Relocation Roller-coaster', others begged to get off . . . or simply barfed. There are no prizes for guessing which category I belonged to. All over the world relocators boasted about blending into utopian existences in their new countries, merrily renovating Tuscan homes and whatnot, while my adaptation felt like being dragged kicking and screaming across a rocky terrain with a scorpion affixed to my arse. Why did it feel as though half of my brain had been removed and I'd been forced to watch a ten-hour-long documentary on the life and times of Michael Jackson? Most of what I understood as acceptable and unacceptable had become irrelevant. I didn't get why people acted the way they did, or how *I* was supposed to act. Nobody could explain any idiosyncrasies sufficiently and, as a result, I felt as though the remaining portion of my brain had been flicked hard by an industrial-sized rubber band. There *had* to be something wrong with me.

An omnipresent sadness hovered like a black cloud. I awoke most mornings with a sense of dread. I stopped smiling altogether. Little did I know that depression was sadistically creeping up on me as I innocently pitted olives in preparation for yet another Greek salad.

I woke one cool, sunny day drowning in a darkness I hadn't known before. I began crying. I cried the entire day. As Dion slept, I cried throughout the night. I awoke crying, barely able to drag myself out of bed. I cried for days on end. I cried for nights on end. The days and nights turned into weeks. And it seemed that I'd continue bawling until all fluid had drained from my body and I was nothing but a pile of desiccated flesh on the floor, identifiable as human only by a pair of lips and eyes sadly staring up at anybody who cared to notice.

As my mind began to contort I had no one to turn to except my husband. Dion did his best.

'Please don't cry, babe. Everything's gonna be okay.'

'You don't understand. I wish I was dead, but for all intents and purposes I *already am*. I feel dead, Dion. DEAD! God, please help me!' I collapsed into shuddering sobs.

Dion's face was ablaze with fright.

'I'm gonna go buy you one of those little chocolate cakes you like, okay?'

He left the house, shooting me a frightened glance before slamming the door shut. As much as he tried to understand the abyss of infinite sadness, he simply couldn't. I'd never considered Dion to be particularly attuned to wayward emotion before, so I knew I had to be scaring him half to death. All he could think to do was buy me a fucking cake, for God's sake! I felt misunderstood, but also terribly sorry for him. On top of everything else, I was overcome by guilt.

Once again, Dion thought my sorrow would pass of its own accord and by day he drifted off to work, no doubt grateful for the respite from his sobbing wife. By night he promised to take me home to Australia if it all got too much. I only had to say the word. In the meantime, I tried to hold on. I tried to hold on as hard as I could.

Not only was my life unravelling, but also Lana as I knew her. From my counselling studies, I wondered if I was experiencing the various stages of grief. I knew that I'd already gone through a warped version of denial. That was pretty clear when I began slapping about in a pair of glittery blue flip-flops in the dead of winter. Denial eventually gave way to anger . . . and boy was I suddenly mad! I was mad at Dion. How *dare* he not experience the same hardships as me. How dare he not get what it was that I was going through.

How dare he shoot through an escape hatch and find solace in a radio station. God help him when he returned home each night. Without fail, I'd be red-eyed and still in my pyjamas.

'Yeah, I spent the day doing jack shit again. Oh, hang on. I *tidied* and *cried a lot*, that's right. Can't you put your plate in the dishwasher for once!'

'Okay, okay! I'll put it in the dishwasher. But why are you talking to me like that?'

'Because I'm sick to fuck of feeling like this and I'm sick of playing housewife.'

'I know you're not happy, but don't take it out on me. I can't stand it!'

Sadly, an even-tempered yet exasperated Dion bore the brunt of my frustrations in the absence of any other available punching bags. But not only was I angry at him, I was angry at *the world*. I was angry because I could no longer have a decent conversation with anybody familiar *about* anything familiar. I resented friends and family back home for not returning emails and never calling. I was angry at the lack of green grass, the pollution, the coriander deprivation and the near feral dog around the corner that got off on attacking my shopping trolley on the odd occasion that I dared step outside my prison. I was even angry at Athenians for wearing impossibly extravagant shoes! Yeah, I was angry at the whole world, and worst of all, angry at myself for being so angry.

I knew that I should have felt enormously grateful for what the gods had bestowed upon me. *But I didn't!* I'd lost control of my self and my life. I came to feel that if I didn't communicate in tumultuous tirades with Dion, my existence would be all but forgotten. Our formerly civil, light-hearted conversations had now been replaced by me wailing about the inconsistencies of Greece and the pain I was enduring. He'd nod back blankly in return.

Thankfully the anger eventually subsided and gave way to bargaining. I bargained with Dion until he agreed that we'd definitely return home at the end of this twelve-month period. Although this gave me at least *some* sense of control, I noted a slight hesitance in his promises.

'Okay, babe. But you never know what's around the corner.'

What the hell was THAT supposed to mean?

So I turned to God. I promised that if He stopped the pain, I'd at some point build an orphanage. That didn't work either. The Almighty knew I was full of shit. I found myself defeated and slipping into an even more formidable stage: the dark and debilitating stage of depression.

I mourned for what had been and looked upon my new circumstances with disgust. I saw no way of changing them and felt paralysed, useless and melancholic. It has to be understood that this was much, much more than feeling 'sad'. It was all-engulfing, as though I were lost in a black hole from which I'd never emerge. As the weeks passed, the tears continued. I *couldn't* leave the apartment; it was no longer a choice. I tried telephoning our international health insurer in the UK who offered a 'free counselling hotline'. I lay on the floor, my chest heaving with agonised sobs, my face hot and streaked with tears and I remained on hold for over an hour. *Over an hour.*

'Thank you for holding. A trained counsellor will be with you shortly . . . Thank you for holding. A trained counsellor will be with you shortly . . .

'Thank you for holding . . .'

A trained counsellor never came on the line. I learned later that the number had been changed.

I called a friend in London at random who similarly didn't answer. I tried a friend in Australia who didn't know what to say.

I didn't want to panic my family, so I decided then and there to keep the pain to myself. It was my cross to bear, and mine alone. I continued to sink lower and lower, rocking back and forth through the days, going gradually insane. I remained lost in this void for two hellish months that felt more like a thousand years. By fuck, this was the exact opposite of integration. This was *dis*integration.

Dion continued to wait for the phase to pass as my mind cracked and shattered. I tried to explain my emotions as best as I could and he listened intently, yet helplessly. He simply didn't know what to say or do. He could only hold me and remind me that he was there. And I could only collapse into his arms as my body either convulsed or went limp. I wanted to crawl inside him and draw on his sanity like an emotionally disoriented parasite. I clutched at him as desperately as I did the vapours of my fast-fading identity.

19

Emotional rescue

Before moving to Greece, I dreamt of escaping the rat race and leading a Carmelite nun-style existence that involved a vow of silence and minimal interaction with the human race. This, I thought, would allow me to evolve spiritually until I tranquilly ascended towards the heavens upon a cotton-ball-soft cloud. I got the 'escape' and 'vow of silence' parts right, but instead of spiritual tranquillity, I scored myself a breakdown. Be careful what you wish for.

As I spiralled out of control, I finally confided in my parents, leaving out the bit about me usually being found in a crumpled heap on the floor. Too ashamed to admit defeat, I revealed only that I was feeling dangerously sad and lonely. They read between the lines and planned a holiday to Greece at the same time as practising techniques similar to those used to coerce kittens from trees.

As I awaited their rescue, I discovered an English-language newspaper, the *Athens News*, full of news and classifieds that I actually understood. Awestruck, I flicked through its pages and a tiny ad suddenly sprang from the 'Therapy' section like a heralding from the angels. It advertised a counsellor in an area known as Zografou in central Athens. I made a phone call, forced myself to climb out of my burrow, which was no small feat, and began attending weekly sessions with a counsellor named Kristie.

A Greek-Brit in her mid-forties, Kristie was impartial, empathic and actually gave a damn. I'd hate to think what might have happened if I hadn't found this amazing woman. She first gave me a book on depression that helped me understand what I was facing. We then began the slow process of untangling the knots. Each week, we explored how living in Greece had affected my self-perception and, to our horror, it became evident that I saw myself as a completely worthless, partly incapacitated, fully intimidated and hideously ugly piece of shit. There was work to be done! We agreed that since I'd formerly had a healthy self-esteem, we could get back to that place without the use of medication. And we agreed that despite Athens having the potential to be as frustrating as hell, it wasn't unconquerable.

Kristie set weekly tasks to help me overcome my culture shock. Sometimes I'd write pages on how bleak everything seemed and then we'd discuss it realistically and bring things into perspective. At other times, we'd discuss shopping techniques. Her suggestions had nothing to do with pretending to be preoccupied by Pythagoras' theorem. No, she suggested that if shop assistants made me feel uncomfortable, I should ignore them. *Ingenious!*

As I trialled my counsellor's strategies, I ever so slowly resurrected. Sure I'd re-experience the odd day of feeling discouraged, confused and cushioned by about as much support as a cupless bra, but now there was a difference. I didn't take it all on board and blame myself. Nor did I blame the people around me. The alienation I felt didn't mean there was something wrong with me, *or* them. Kristie explained that living in a new country put my self-concept to the harshest of tests, and if anything I deserved wild applause, even if it sometimes felt that people around me were poised to throw rotten tomatoes instead.

After two months of Kristie's kindness and expertise, I was ready to take Athens by the balls. Although rattled by my breakdown, Dion was thoroughly relieved to have his girl back. Throughout the ordeal, he'd been concentrating his efforts on solving a problem he saw as slightly more tangible. The way he saw it, getting the radio station on air would also mean getting our lives back on track.

As my strength returned, so did my confidence. I soon resumed grocery shopping and took a giant leap into the world of clothing retail to update my wardrobe. Before I knew it, I was even exploring Athens' public transport system. Yes, I was actually able to catch a Greek bus! Sure figuring out a Greek bus route and timetable was about as easy as translating the *Mr Ed* theme song into Sanskrit, but I did it. I sat smugly on a modern Athens omnibus, staring at pedestrians through a dusty window and feeling more than a little empowered.

Well accustomed to the personal space invasion that sometimes featured in the Greek capital, I wasn't even all that fazed when joined by a short and sweet elderly gentleman as we headed for the city centre. By 'joined' I'm of course talking about an instant Siamese-twin type merger where the old fellah all but sat on my lap instead of taking advantage of the available seat space beside me. A minute or two into the journey, he struck up a conversation.

Establishing that I could speak very little Greek, he used a few simple words and a lot of gesticulation to indicate that the woman sitting across from us – with crazy hair, a vacant stare and an enormous bale of hay on her lap – was *insane*. As I pondered this rather obvious 'revelation', I noticed that the elbow of the old man had gently worked its way into my right breast. Not wishing to cause any undue embarrassment, I said nothing and instead tried shifting in my seat upwards, then downwards, and then contorting my face and body so that I was pressed flat against the bus window, nose and lips upturned in a ghastly display of nostrils, gums and teeth. I was forced back into my original position when a small child in a passing car took one look at me and promptly burst into tears.

'Greece eees veery, *veery* goodt cown-try,' the old man interrupted, his rogue elbow making its way back to its new favourite position.

'Yes, I *love* Greece,' I replied with a forced smile as though a simultaneous molestation wasn't taking place.

An internal argument raged within. I felt compelled to give this old man the benefit of the doubt. Maybe his arm was bionic and in some way malfunctioning? Maybe he hadn't realised his elbow was in an uncompromising position? I just couldn't bring myself to accuse this sweet old thing of something that was probably perfectly innocent. I couldn't even bring myself to change seats. Strangely, I didn't want to offend.

The unacknowledged arm and breast wrestle continued for a full forty-five minutes until the fact that this dear, sweet man was in reality an A-grade sleazebag was angrily confirmed by a young man who'd played witness to proceedings from a vantage point behind us. Upon disembarkation, this unsung superhero flew from out of nowhere and into the old man like a human bullet, taking it upon himself to defend my honour. What a guy! And what a city!

Fresh out of my black cloud, the situation left me obviously shaken. I'd formerly been able to sniff out sleaziness a mile off, but during my long days of solitary confinement, I'd almost forgotten how. I'm ashamed to say that this was a pivotal moment where I made the conscious decision to be a bit mean. It probably didn't suit me and it probably wasn't exactly what my counsellor had in mind when it came to re-adjusting, but from that day forward, should some hapless soul have shot me a sour look from behind a shop counter, I resolved to whack a double-dose right back. Even if they offered no expression at all, I'd sneer. And once I'd started, I couldn't seem to stop. Appallingly, I was doing unto others what I'd despised them doing unto me.

Dion was extremely protective of both me *and* the Greeks. He loved us all! However, after the old man had copped a feel, he more fully understood how formidable the territory seemed through my eyes.

'God, I can't believe he *did* that to you. Are you sure he was touching your boob?' he asked.

'What do you mean "am I sure"? Of course I am! It's a wonder his elbow didn't leave a permanent indentation.'

'Sorry, babe. How's about I make you a milkshake or something?'

'I've had enough milk shaken for one day, thanks.'

Things between us were getting back to normal. Dion recognised in me the same woman he had married: someone mildly courageous and questionably humorous. Our love and solidarity thankfully intensified after hurdling recent events and Dion was once again able to devote himself to his wife and to Athens' airwave resuscitation.

Back in Australia, yoga had been an important part of my life and I wondered if it might be the missing ingredient in creating a more peaceful existence. I knew it would certainly be the perfect accompaniment to my healing and, by a stroke of luck, the same day that I'd been molested on the bus I'd also stumbled across a yoga advertisement on a bookstore noticeboard. Lessons were conducted by a young local girl, Irini, who taught door-to-door, meaning I could practise from home. Calling her, I found she spoke English quite well and so invited her to Labrou Katsoni to discuss her services further.

Dion was working from home that day, which was a great rarity. Poised over his laptop at the lounge-room table, he found it difficult to concentrate as Irini and I enthused about the benefits of yoga. After ten minutes, she sprang to her feet.

'I get change?' she asked.

I said, 'Okay!' winked at Dion and waited on the sofa. I had no idea what she meant, but knew that whatever it was, it was bound to be interesting.

Disappearing into our bathroom for a while, she re-emerged with a yoga mat tucked snugly beneath an arm and wearing a Nike bra top and a pair of pale blue leggings. She unfurled the mat, stood stoically for a few seconds, and suddenly began heavy breathing. Concerned she was hyperventilating, I half stood, but before I could offer any assistance she was down on all fours arching her back. Apparently she had launched into a yoga demonstration. Dion and I exchanged amused glances.

Ten minutes passed, and still the routine continued. I bit my lip to suppress a giggle. Apart from the sounds of the stranger's writhing and Darth Vaderesque breathing, our humble lounge room was otherwise silent. Dion had stopped tapping away at his computer, awestruck by the human pretzel twisting around our living room.

Fifteen minutes passed and I noticed sweat seeping through her leggings, particularly around her bum crack. I glanced at my watch.

After twenty minutes, I began to feel slightly agitated.

Twenty-five minutes passed.

Thirty minutes.

Thirty-five freakin' minutes.

I remained conscious only through sheer determination. Dion looked across the room at me with questioning eyes. I returned the same expression, shrugging.

At the forty-minute mark I began to feel pissed off. Not so much at the stranger sweating and groaning on our lounge-room floor, but at how things tended to unfold in Greece. Why was nothing ever *normal*?

Forty-five minutes . . .

Fifty minutes . . .

Fifty-five fucking minutes!

Finally, after ONE FULL HOUR, Irini assumed a catatonic pose, panting á la Michael Flatley post-performance, and picked up her mat, looking satisfied.

'Any question?' she asked sweetly.

I told her I'd be in touch.

Dion and I debriefed after her departure.

'*Why did she do that?*' I asked him, eyes wide.

'Dunno, babe. I guess she just wanted to give you a demo.'

Dion was one for stating the obvious. He still didn't get that someone like me needed to understand the why behind every single Greek occurrence. Nor did he understand my frustration when the answers weren't forthcoming. The motivation behind her routine and whether she'd trained under the careful eye of an Indian guru will forever remain a mystery, for I never contacted Irini again.

Thankfully, right after my counselling sessions had drawn to their natural conclusion, along with Irini's 'salutes to the numb', I soon had the comfort of my parents to bring a real sense of normality back into my life. Suddenly, there was Dad perched on our flower-filled Labrou Katsoni balcony with a can of Amstel super-glued to his hand and a wicked twinkle in his crystal-blue eyes, Mum positioned close by to comment on his excessive alcohol consumption.

'Want another beer, *Dad*?'

Dion liked the fact that he could now officially call my father

'Dad'. The word 'Dad' ended most sentences. In fact, sentences were spoken for the sheer hell of saying it.

'You beaut. Yes, please!'

'Don't encourage him, Dion!' Mum would chastise. 'But can I have one too?'

'Sure, Mum. Here you go, *Dad.*'

After a compulsory visit to the Acropolis, I took my parents bowling at a run-down alley in Glyfada with Coca-Cola – lacquered carpets that reeked of stale cigarettes. We were the only three patrons there. As I dropped ball after ball with a clumsy thud into the gutter, I listened to the familiar intonations of my parents shouting behind me.

'Go you little bea-U-ty!' (My father.)

'You can do it, Lana! Go! That's *great!* Wow! Ooh-ah!' (My mother.)

It literally brought tears to my eyes. I wasn't accustomed to hearing such words of encouragement. Here were my parents in Greece, at my aid, trying to convince me I was good at something I was obviously shit at. I hadn't appreciated or needed them this much since I was a helpless, screeching infant.

Later, Mum pulled me aside and asked me to go for a walk as Dad perched himself on a wrought-iron balcony seat with a beer to his pursed lips. 'This is the bloody life!'

I walked with my mother towards the ocean.

'Are you okay, love?'

'Yeah, Mum. I'm over the worst I think. It was horrible, though. And I'm still so lonely. Thank God you and Dad are here.'

'Poor thing. You used to have *so* many friends. I feel so sorry for you. But you've got Dion and he's such a great bloke.' Mum paused. 'Sometimes it's good *not* to have friends too, you know? Then you don't have to worry too much about other people while you're busy concentrating on giving us grandchildren.'

'*Grandchildren?* Mum, are you *mad?* I can't even look after myself here, let alone a baby. And I can assure you that spitting out kids is the last thing on my mind. I think we'll start worrying about stuff like that when we're safely back home.'

'Okay, I suppose you're right,' she replied, gently nudging my ribs. We both fell silent, lost in our own thoughts concerning miniature Lanas and Dions, cuddles and soiled nappies. Parenthood would come, but all in good time.

Wanting to make the most of their time in Greece, my parents and I decided to go on a quick jaunt to Santorini. Dion, unfortunately, had to continue supervising his employees' magazine-reading and smoking habits. So we headed to the port of Piraeus and wound up dodging truncheons wielded by the army. They were there to break up an angry mob that was beating the hell out of a bunch of dockworkers. My father removed my mother and me from harm's way as the riotous group fell towards us like a toppling dominoes display. Although our ferry failed to depart owing to the unscheduled violence of the waterside dispute, the following day we were sailing the deep blue waters around breathtaking Santorini on an organised tour aboard a schooner.

Joined by a battalion of Brits, tour organisers offered us cat's urine in plastic cups that they tried to pass off as 'wine'. All on board necked as much of the stuff as they could – my beloved parents included. A few hours later, the formerly reserved British tourists were draped over one another chanting ditties that often included the word 'bucket'. Even this couldn't detract from the majesty of the volcanic island flecked with white. As she took in the view, my mum's deep brown eyes were full of the mischief that only cheap alcohol can induce.

'See the white buildings?' she asked, suppressing a chuckle.

'Yeah?'

'Don't you reckon from here they look like bird poo all over a big brown rock?'

My sweet mum thought she was being really naughty. At least she had the excuse of being drunk. It was how my mind worked sober.

At the end of the cruise, we clambered aboard a coach to be dropped at various accommodations in the town of Fira. Sitting beside my mother, her toes just brushing the floor, I peered across the aisle to throw a smirk my father's way. To my surprise, he was looking more than a little bewildered, his grey hair styled at a right angle fixed by ocean spray and a stiff sea breeze. He'd been joined by a woman in her mid-fifties, a fact not perplexing in itself. But upon closer inspection, I understood why his eyes had formed stunned question marks. The hands of the woman next to him were coated with the former contents of her stomach. So too was her handbag and the smuggled bottle of wine cheekily poking out of it. And so too was my father's now-speckled trouser leg.

My parents' Greek visit came to an end after only ten days. They also had Malta on their agenda, my beautiful mother making her first trip back since leaving as a child. I was lucky enough to join them on this historic occasion, documenting every movement, burp and fart with a video camera. Having caught a separate flight to my folks, I stood poised at Malta's humble international airport to record Mum's initial reaction to her homecoming. She finally emerged from behind a herd of travellers looking remarkably unfazed.

'Welcome to Multa!' I shrieked in my best Maltese accent.

'Thanks,' she replied shyly.

'So . . . tell me. How are you feeling right now?'

'Um. Good thanks.'

'How does it feel to be back?'

'Good.' Her head wobbled nervously before she put a hand to the lens and giggled coyly. 'Stop it, Lana. It's embarrassing.'

'Come on, can't you at least drop to your knees and cry or something?' I had an idea. 'Dad, pinch her!' I shrieked.

He refused. I stopped rolling.

After checking into our hotel, we strolled along the Sliema promenade. This was the town where Mum had lived until she was four and, despite her nonchalance, I knew she was re-experiencing something special. In a faraway voice, she expressed how happy she'd been here, back when the town was a fishing village. It had lost little of its charm. We paused at a café by the water to nibble on cheese pastizzis washed down, in my father's case, by Cisk, the local beer. Peering over the bay, Mum reminisced about the day her brothers had dived into the water to retrieve peaches that had floated to the surface after a ship had sunk nearby.

Her voice trailed as she became lost in nostalgia. We meandered into the residential part of the town, passing Victorian and Art Nouveau villas before reaching Mum's church and primary school. The house she had grown up in was now a garage. Mum seemed confused, until she caught sight of a large sign.

'Oh, God! Would you look at that?'

Right next door was a shop proudly bearing her maiden name. We entered, me armed with the video camera like an invasive current affairs reporter, my father behind me and my mother lost somewhere in our shadows. We all stood silently. The shopkeeper stared at us. The camera whirred quietly.

'Do you remember the family who used to live next door with the same name as this shop?' Mum finally asked.

'I rememberrrr de family,' said the wiry old man, his r's curling from behind the counter. 'But I am no relation to dem.'

'That was *my* family!' Mum exclaimed proudly.

'Yes! I remember dere were many of you.' The old man strained hard to retrieve files from his memory banks. I zoomed in closer. 'You were noisy! You went to Australia!'

Mum's eyes sparkled happily.

We awoke early the following day with a sense of adventure. Riding in a horse-drawn carriage around the capital of Valletta, with its baroque buildings lining hilly streets, I commentated loudly, again with a fake accent. I realised regretfully that I could speak more Greek than I could Maltese.

'Made up of de several islands, Multa is de speck beneat Sicily. It is in Valletta that my grand-moderrrr had de clothing shop. And you still see signs today of de Knights of St John. Look! St Elmo's Fort! And de many buildings!' I gestured madly. My father joined in.

'Valletta has de population of 6000.'

He sounded like the Swedish chef off the Muppets. We laughed so hard that my mother shed tears. Later, however, her tears were of sadness as we took in a documentary on Malta's history. It was through this that we saw the devastation caused to the tiny country during World War II. As we watched footage of forlorn faces, and towns reduced to rubble, we remembered stories shared by my grandmother. During the war, she'd survived for days on only an egg and had given birth in a bomb shelter during a German attack. For the first time, what she'd told us seemed real. Pieces of my family's history fell into place.

After three magnificent days, my parents travelled on to London and I was back to being an Australian in Athens plucking my legs.

Dion continued to throw himself headfirst into his work and it eventually struck me that he must have considered me to be much more self-sufficient than I really was. I worried about the implications of his workaholism and my lack of autonomy. If he continued to work this hard and leave me to my own devices, how was that ever gonna work? It hit me harder than ever that it was ludicrous to rely on him to try and play husband and friend in between his enormous responsibilities. After my parents' visit, I decided I was no longer prepared to exist without companionship. I was determined to turn my life around. So I started *imagining* I had friends! That's right. *Imagining*. Not as in hallucinating, mind you. Now *that* would be crazy. No, what I did was I closed my eyes and imagined a world where I was surrounded by cool people that I got along famously with. And I chanted a lot during the process.

Aaaaauuuuhhhhmmmm . . .

I had every intention of carrying out this action every morning and night until my humble desires became a reality. It was a foolproof plan. Cool, compatible friends would soon be wished into existence, guaranteed.

You're my best friend

For several weeks I chanted like a moronic novice monk. Then, one day, out of the blue, a former work colleague from Australia sent me an email saying she was planning a trip to Greece. I assumed she was seeking complimentary accommodation and made for the linen closet to make up the spare bed. But she didn't care if we put her up or not. No, she'd already made arrangements to stay with *'other friends'* in Athens.

Other friends?

OTHER FUCKING FRIENDS?

OTHER FUCKING FRIENDS IN ATHENS?

I was outraged!

Why hadn't I been informed sooner?

I called Dion, and we immediately engaged in exaggerated westie dialogue.

'Wait 'til ya hear this one! Maaarleene has other fuckin' friends in FUCKIN' ATHENS!'

'Get fucked! Ya fuckin' shittin' me!' Dion reciprocated. 'Who?'

I went on to tell him that these 'other friends' to whom she referred hailed from New Zealand. I needed to hunt them down and make them my own. I emailed her back and begged for their telephone number. A week later, the number flashed at me from my computer screen. I dialled immediately and tapped my fingers against the tiny mahogany desk where our telephone sat, ignoring the happy chatter of birds outside, and listened intently to the sound of a ring tone.

'Hello?' a neutral voice answered.

'Hi. Is that Tim?'

'Yis,' the voice responded, betraying a New Zealand accent.

'Oh, hello, Tim! This is Lana, a friend of Marlene's. I heard you're living in Athens and just *had* to give you a call! So how are you? How are you finding this crazy city?'

'Oh, et's great.'

Tim's voice remained monotone, but it was more than his flat expression that bothered me. He'd used the word 'great' to describe living in Athens. He was one of *those* people who'd effortlessly assimilated. I just knew it. So I proceeded with caution.

'Say, what are the chances of you and me hooking up? Would you like to meet for a coffee or something?' I asked casually, failing to mention that I didn't drink coffee.

'Okay.'

'Okay?! Ohmygod, you have no idea how bloody great it is to hear that! I don't know how long you've been here, but I've been here for eighteen months and guess what? *I've got no friends!* How's that? What about you? Do you have any?'

'I had one, but she's gone. I've been here a year.'

Tim seemed to be a man of few words.

'Well, maybe you and I could be friends then? It kinda makes sense, doesn't it?'

I was sounding desperate and I knew it. But I didn't care.

'Maybe . . .' came the understandably hesitant reply.

We made plans to meet the following day in Kolonaki, where Tim lived with his partner, Shane. I asked whether he might be so kind as to wear a pink carnation for ease of identification. He didn't laugh. I made a last ditch attempt to be instantly lovable.

'This is strange, isn't it? I mean it's like we're going out on a blind date or something!'

'See you tomorrow. I've kinda gotta go.' Tim hung up.

It was a brilliant sapphire-blue day, as hot as it gets. As I bussed along the artery of Vouliagmenis Avenue towards the centre, I peeked beneath a shutter that had been pulled down to block out the blazing light and heat. I spied the now-familiar Mister Baby store, then the Acropolis and knew I was getting close. I alighted outside the 'Neoclassical Trilogy', comprising the Academy of Athens, Athens University and National Library, just past Syntagma Square. Despite being built during the 1800s, these magnificent samples of ancient Hellenic architecture for me evoked images of Socrates spouting philosophical epiphanies to anyone who cared to listen. I walked by, staring admiringly at the regal columns. It's strange to say that sometimes buildings can lift one's spirits, but these ones really did. I'm sure the fact that I was about to meet a fellow human being had something to do with it as well.

As I strutted along the paved forecourt that brought me to the street parallel, I dialled Tim's mobile number nervously. He answered, his voice cracking slightly. With my mobile phone pressed firmly to my ear and eyes darting, Tim guided me towards a fruit stand located amidst bustling commuter buses and their outpouring of fumes. We continued speaking until we practically shoulder charged one another to the ground. We laughed, hung up our phones in unison and then embraced clumsily like the complete strangers that we were.

Upon closer inspection, I couldn't help but notice that Tim was one of the hottest guys I'd ever laid eyes upon. He was tall, tanned and trendy. His short light brown hair had been cut and groomed in a style that was so beyond 'now', it was tomorrow. He wore Diesel clothing from head to toe. Lean, strong and possibly fifteen years my junior, his smile won me over instantly.

We began walking to nowhere in particular, talking over one another, babbling and giggling excitedly. Our conversation was the antithesis of the one we'd had the previous afternoon. Tim was animated, his green eyes sparkling with naughtiness. Although I'd promised myself that morning to remain civilised and demure amidst the beautiful people of Kolonaki, we stopped at a café at Kolonaki Square and proceeded to get shit-faced, diving headfirst into as much vodka as our antipodean kidneys could tolerate.

As the afternoon flew by, the scene grew increasingly incongruous. We were the only two throwing back alcohol in a sea of sophisticated coffee drinkers. On adjoining alfresco tables sat coffee cups, biscuits and cigarettes. Our table was two parts vodka to one part cigarette ash. Shredded cigarette packets floated in tiny swamps that had formed around our elbows, a pile of empty glasses adding to the overall disaster. As the afternoon traffic whizzed past, conversations between surrounding sophisticates were no doubt politically and philosophically driven. Our amplified and slurred shit-talk related only to the comedy of errors that had become our lives in Greece and was punctuated by raucous, drunken laughter.

Tim instantly became the girlfriend I'd been so desperate for over the preceding year and a half. At last I could discuss emotions, consumerism, beauty products, Dannii Minogue, menstruation and Athenian hardships while taking the piss out of anything and everything that moved. I had a partner in crime. In one short afternoon, a whole new world of consumerism and alcoholism opened up before me. In one short afternoon, my life changed.

Blind drunk by the time the moon replaced the sun, I telephoned Dion and did my best to pretend that I always spoke as though my tongue had been velcroed to the roof of my mouth. I invited my husband to join us – me and my New Best Friend. By the time he arrived, Tim and I were slumped in our seats like a couple of rag dolls, our arms draped across one another's shoulders.

'Hi, baby! Look! Tim! Ish Dion . . . Hey, Dion? *Dion?* Ish Tim!'

Finger extended, I pointed at Tim beside me with great emphasis. Tim responded with a high-pitched squeal of laughter.

At first Dion attempted to make sane conversation but quickly surmised that we were a couple of drunken fools. While he was pleased I'd made a new friend, he did find it disconcerting that I was now seen inserting cigarettes up my nose in public and asking Tim if I looked like a walrus. Tim was convinced that I did.

Timothy was twenty. Although born in New Zealand, he'd spent the better part of a decade growing up in Cairns in northern Queensland, Australia. Tim had even less of a grasp on the Greek language than I did, but unlike me, he didn't particularly care. In fact, it barely affected him. Sure he was unaccustomed to the culture and disliked being misunderstood from time to time, but for Tim it was water off a duck's back. This only served to highlight my own extreme sensitivity. But in his words, why would he let it get to him when everyone around him was so goddamned good-looking?

Like me, Tim was unable to work in Greece, having entered the country on the arm of a sole provider. In my days of bouncing off the walls like a flea in a jar, I'd taken to referring to myself as a 'manbag': an occasional accessory found dangling from my husband's arm. I shared this idea with Tim, who didn't appreciate being lumped into the same category. Although financially reliant upon his partner Shane, Tim remained fiercely independent and, unlike me, able to retain a strong sense of identity.

Shane worked for a prominent insurance company and was high up in the food chain. He spent as much time in Athens as he did outside of it, taking care of business all over the Middle East. Shane and I would grow to have a mutual respect for one another, although he most likely saw me as a drunken Aussie sometimes found lurking creepily in the shadows of his Skoufa Street apartment. Bonded by an innate understanding of loneliness and alcoholism, Tim and I decided we would become inseparable, although Tim warned that he tended to spend a considerable amount of time travelling outside the country. The intrepid Kiwi was making the most of his time abroad, sunning himself all over Europe's hot spots whenever Shane relented, which was, well, always.

In the days that followed, Tim and I spoke daily on the telephone, discussing grooming, fashion and the pros and cons of plastic surgery. He was very much pro. By night, Dion would suffer summaries of the day's conclusions.

'Tim reckons if you get an eye-job, it takes ten years off your age *and* you can't even tell.'

'That's great. But you're not getting plastic surgery.'

'But can I, if I want, later, when I get older? Tim says it's *so* worth it.'

Tim and I made plans for our second rendezvous, deciding on a nightclub called Venue close to Voula. I hadn't been out to a nightclub for a year and a half and didn't know what to expect. Worse, I didn't have a thing to wear.

Dancing queen

I first met Tim's boyfriend, Shane, before making my debut on the Athens nightclub scene. It was one of the few occasions that Dion was out of town on business. In his absence, I felt like an unsupervised teen whose father had been awarded custody despite constantly thrashing about in a work deluge; or a wayward pubescent renowned for teaching others how to do the draw-back behind the school library. Shane, also like a parental guardian, dropped Tim at our apartment before racing off to attend a meeting. When he rang our doorbell, he came face to face with an Australian woman who'd obviously had a fistfight with a cosmetics factory and come off second best. In addition to pantomime make-up, I wore spray-on jeans, a slutty top and a pair of stilts that could only be loosely described as 'shoes'. To me it seemed logical to don the Athenian uniform.

I, on the other hand, was greeted by a well-groomed, thirty-something man who radiated high intelligence. Despite his angelic features, within moments Shane struck me as a highly strung sort. Thanks to my poor directions – including an instruction to 'turn left at the grey building that has a roof that looks like an orange squeezer' – the couple had become hopelessly lost and it seemed that Shane didn't suffer fools gladly. As he attempted to point out my lack of navigational skills, his head shaking and hands flapping, I realised I couldn't understand a word he said. A heavily accented Kiwi, his speech was delivered rapid-fire and I found myself smiling and nodding vacuously. I was exasperated, not only because I was probably being told off, but because I couldn't even understand English any more.

After we waved Shane goodbye, I turned to Tim.

'I'm really sorry, but I couldn't understand a word your boyfriend said!'

'Thet's okay,' Tim said comfortingly. 'He doesn't hev an Australian eccent like me from leveng in Cairns. Forgit et!'

Jumping out of a smoke-filled cab, Tim and I argued.

'Rachel Hunter es so much sixier then Elle Macpherson.'

'Is not.'

'Es so. Do you thenk either of thim have hed any work done?'

Tim brushed a hand thoughtlessly through his well-moulded hair, his remarkable thick brows framing his gleaming eyes. He looked and smelled stunning. I looked and smelled funny.

We entered Venue. The club was relatively empty, catering to a crowd of around sixty, although with a capacity for hundreds. It was, after all, a Wednesday night. Disco lights flashed on vacant tables and a bereft dance floor. Regardless, it was a great-looking club, partially open-air and backing onto the ocean. Most patrons were wearing all-white ensembles and opting to chat and look fabulous rather than move to the music. Tim looked the part, but moved through the world with an air of devilry.

The well-stocked bar was duly noted and we helped ourselves to a few warm-up drinks before getting the party started. As is always the case in Athens, the drinks were lethal. And as a result, we were the first twits on the floor, trying our darnedest to cut moves and look cool, one of us succeeding more than the other. Not surprisingly, the super-high shoes strapped to the ends of my legs meant performing a balancing act to a generic dance beat. I wasn't so much dancing as *swaying* like a willow tree caught in a storm. Tim moved to the beat in a new millennium kind of way, as only twenty-year-olds can.

'Thes song es great.'

I'd never heard it before. As he stared off into the distance, looking sexy and mysterious, I yearned to return to the safety of my bucket of Jack Daniels and thimble of Coke. Using Tim as a crutch and any other solid object I could lay my hands on, I lurched back to my bar stool like Frankenstein and fell into seated position. When Tim eventually rejoined me, I begged him to walk or if necessary *carry* me to the water's edge. Right after Tim had asked if I'd ever consider getting a boob job, we overheard two British girls chatting. We glanced at one another and reached a simultaneous conclusion. *New friends!* We honed in on them like seagulls to chips.

'Hey, you girls are Bretish!' Tim blurted.

'Yes, we live here,' one of the girls responded politely, shocked by the interruption.

'SO DO WE!' I sang, as though divine intervention were at play.

The girls forced a smile.

'Oh.'

There was an awkward silence during which we all smiled hard.

'Okay. Bye!' one of the girls finally said.

They walked away. Briskly.

Tim and I looked at one another for a split second before bursting into laughter.

We didn't need them. We had each other. That night I slept alone, drunk and positively jubilant.

A couple of weeks after my night out with Tim, I experienced my first *bouzoukia*. For the uneducated, the bouzouki is either a three-, four- or eight-stringed instrument, something like a lute. A *bouzoukia* is nothing less than an eight-hour extravaganza, and something like a Greek wedding reception on steroids. People of all ages participate with unabashed extroversion, hundreds cramming into smoke-filled venues and losing themselves in hedonism. There is nothing else quite like it.

At most Athenian *bouzoukia*, long rectangular tables placed within inches of each other are filled with excitable Greeks. A bottle of scotch or vodka is provided for each table and at around midnight the celebrations begin. Most people begin chain smoking. Many throw back drinks and pelt tray after tray of red carnations at on-stage entertainers who perform traditional bouzouki ballads or more up-tempo contemporary numbers. Towards the end of the night, many punters can be seen up on tables dancing. Performers continue to sing and play into the early hours of the morning. A frighteningly high proportion of audience members take to the stage around them, slipping and sliding on flower petals, women dancing seductively like belly dancers who've ingested high doses of full-strength Spanish fly while under the spell of Aphrodite.

Now that that's in your head, try slotting me into the picture. It isn't easy, is it? Let's recap a few things about me. Firstly, I can't understand Greek, so could never hope to interpret a single lyric. And let's not forget my natural aversion to Greek music. And let's also bear in mind that I don't, under any circumstances, belly dance. But if ever there was a bouzouki night where I came close to storming the stage, it was the night I went with Dion, Yianni,

Anna and a host of their friends to see Sakis Rouvas perform. I could communicate effectively with only Dion, Yianni and Anna. One of Yianni's friends attempted stilted conversation in English, then gave up. The music was too loud, the conversation too boring. The remainder of our table stared through me and smoked.

Sakis Rouvas is arguably Greece's biggest heartthrob. With slick jet-black hair, hazel eyes, glowing white teeth, high cheekbones and a lithe body, he is the embodiment of a modern-day Greek god. He sings. He dances. He *gyrates*. The night I saw Sakis take the stage, I witnessed not one but *two* of the greatest moments in entertainment history. Flanked by Dion and a cigarette-wolfing stranger, I waited anxiously for the show to begin.

'Sakis!' shrieked young women in the audience.

'Sakis!' shrieked Yianni, whooping and clapping like an excitable schoolgirl, his eyes like spiralling saucers.

'Saarkeys!' shrieked Dion with a forced Australian accent.

The stage curtains parted. Women screamed. I held my breath. Yianni cupped his mouth with both hands. And there, moving across the stage in rigid, motorised bursts emerged a mammoth fibreglass purple and green dragon. That's right. A *dragon*. The size of a garbage truck. It was the type of stage prop *Spinal Tap* would have killed for. And roosting casually upon the dragon's head lay Sakis Rouvas, leaning back on his elbows, one leg extended over the other, as though sunbathing. The crowd went berserk. My eyes filled with tears. It was the single greatest thing I'd witnessed since KISS performed at the Sydney Entertainment Centre on my date with Dion all those years before. Dion looked at me, threw his head back laughing and clapped his hands. He was relishing the spectacle as much as I was. And there was more to come.

Midway through the show, we saw Sakis suspended from the ceiling by invisible wire. He wore a mermaid suit, or, rather, a mer*man* suit. In keeping with the marine theme, he mimed the act of swimming across the stage, his giant rubber fishtail flapping from left to right. It was perfect. I could only pray that the Olympic Games' opening ceremony would match the immensity of this theatrical ingenuity.

So we had *bouzoukia*. We had nightclubs. We had Tim and Shane. We had Yianni and Anna. Things were looking up! And now that I'd elevated myself to a social standing similar to Rachel Greene's in *Friends*, I wanted to make up for lost time. I became ludicrously enthusiastic about experiencing all that Athens had to offer to the point of punching the sky after learning that *Riverdance* was coming to town. Yes. *Riverdance. That's* how enthusiastic. Understandably, nobody shared my fervour. We didn't end up going.

But what we did end up doing was eating a lot. Almost weekly Dion and I began double dating with Tim and Shane as though we belonged to some kind of gastronomic-obsessed cult. I was delighted to learn that dinner in Athens wasn't all about *tavernas*. Hundreds of fabulously trendy restaurants thrived, each brimming with the middle to upper class. Some restaurants even successfully managed to deviate from the Greek culinary precedent. We began our gastronomic journey with a place on the water known as Privilege.

Privilege was like no place I'd ever been before. For a start it had billowing white outdoor curtains floating in a balmy evening sea breeze. We had the choice of either being seated upon comfortable, funky lounges or at one of many outside tables that oversaw a floodlit ocean. As we were led to a table by a model-type waitress scantily clad in all-white as though fresh from the set of *Barbarella*, we passed a backlit bar that displayed an immense array of bottles of different shapes, colours and sizes. I distinctly saw them reflected in Tim's widening eyes. Eyes to bottles. Bottles to eyes.

As Shane and Dion discussed work and the intricate mechanics behind well-crafted time pieces, Tim and I discussed emotions, stroked one another's forearms and fell off our chairs. Tim always re-surfaced without a hair out of place.

Looking around it seemed we'd infiltrated the natural habitat of the Beautiful People. The place was positively crawling with Athenian princes and princesses. It was where the flawless congregated. Sweeping invisible hair from his face and glancing at his reflection in a strategically placed mirror, Tim intrinsically knew he was amongst his own kind.

Being in Greece as the US invasion of Iraq drew near was a strange experience, to say the least, and impacted us in ways quite unexpected. On the whole, the Greek people were against the invasion. Vehemently. When it was announced that Australia would join the so-called War Against Terror, I felt as though my country had lost her innocence. A CNN report described Australia as 'one of America's closest allies'. My paranoia ran riot. I worried that the latest turn of events would not put me in good stead with the local population. I was right.

While purchasing faux Byzantine earrings for Katerina in Plaka, in the hope of at last winning over my mother-in-law's approval, I noticed a local falter after I told him where I was from. Nine times out of ten, the merry response that had followed a revelation of my origins usually concerned cousins living in Melbourne. But not any more. Instead there was silence. I was so accustomed to people reacting favourably after mentioning Australia that I was taken aback. And to Tim's delight, I took to telling people I was from New Zealand. It was a very strange time indeed.

We heard that an American expat's car tyres had been slashed in the dead of night. If Tim and I were together in public we rarely spoke so as not to attract any undue attention to our foreignness. The world we lived in was becoming increasingly mad, the volatility in the air tangible.

As I ironed an afternoon away, my telephone rang. It was Tim, right on cue. He called at the same time every day to update me on the progress of his lasered chest hair. Not surprisingly, he had succumbed to the bombardment of billboards advertising hair removal. I gladly flicked off the iron and sat cross-legged on the couch, poised to discuss hair and the nutritious ingredients of our respective meals planned for the evening. I answered the phone.

'Good afternoon. All Kiwis Suck Incorporated. How may I help?'

I heard a hiss on the other end of the line.

'Lana! Sometheng tirrible's just heppened. You've gotta hilp me!'

Over Tim's drowning words, I heard sirens and angry shouts.

'What's going on?' I sat rigid on the edge of my seat.

'I was walking through a protist outside the US Imbassy . . .'

For a moment the line dropped out.

'Tim? *TIM?*'

'Yeah, I'm here. Shet! I was walking through a protist, and iveryone was going crazy. I tried to get through and . . . I thenk I've been *maimed*. Fuck!'

A horrible scenario played out in my mind. I saw my gentle and handsome Tim trying to make his way through an angry crowd only to be pummelled violently.

'They sprayed fuckeng *tear gas* en my eyes!' he wailed.

'What? *Who did?*'

'The police! They just started sprayeng iveryone. It went right en my eyes! *I can't fuckeng see!*'

I didn't know what to do. While I may have grown up on the

wrong side of Sydney, it wasn't quite the same as growing up on the streets of Beirut. I felt helpless. And scared.

'Oh God! Are you okay? What can I do?'

'I dunno. I dedn't know what ilse to do except call you. Shane's away . . . and . . . oh my God . . . *my eyes*! I can't tell you how much they steng.'

'Okay. Are you away from the crowd now?'

'Yis.'

'Can you sit down somewhere for a minute?'

'Yis.' There was a pause. 'I'm okay.'

There was relief in his voice. He was calming down.

'You poor, poor thing. What the hell were you doing walking through a protest outside the Embassy? You know it's not the best place to be taking a stroll right now.'

'Yeah, I know. But I hed to . . .'

There was another pause.

'I hed to keep a facial appointment weth my beautician.'

A few months later, when the Iraqi 'liberation' unbelievably went ahead, I spotted fresh graffiti near our home painted in angry red capitals. It read: 'MURDERERS GO HOME!'

The words were written in English. I pointed them out to Dion. And even he was unnerved.

22

Golden years

Dion and I began to outgrow our little love nest, or, rather, I was just plain over it. I didn't really need to be constantly reminded of the walls that had confined me. There was nothing wrong with Labrou Katsoni of course, but I needed a change to mark my ascension into an agreeable Greek existence and Dion was happy for a change of scenery. Weekends therefore became devoted to house hunting in and around the greater Glyfada area.

We scoured the classified pages of the *Athens News* and quickly learned to translate advertising terminology. Furniture described as 'classic' became 'classic' much in the same way as a joke can be. 'Fully furnished' sometimes meant a three-legged table and upturned washing basket dining set. We were also introduced to unfamiliar real estate rituals, beginning with disclosure of personal details on real estate forms. For whatever reason, Dion was always required to include the full name, date and place of birth of his parents. A variety of real estate companies would be commissioned to flog off the same property, so there was always a certain amount of frenzy surrounding viewings.

After encountering many agents, there was one in particular

who stood out beyond the rest. A peroxided dolly-bird, she attended a viewing wearing a pair of seven-inch heels, camel-toe jeans, a child's pink V-neck T-shirt squeezed over a Wonder Bra and a face-full of clown make-up. She flirted outrageously with my husband, her cheap perfume all the while punching me in the face. She flicked her hair often, giggled a lot and touched Dion's shoulder, her hand lingering much longer than necessary, should it have lingered at all.

Excuse me! I'm standing RIGHT HERE!

She reminded me of the vixens Tim had warned me about who'd do anything to get their hands on a 'rich' foreign man or, more to the point, his bank account. So it was for this reason that I didn't rush over to help her when – courtesy of her mental 'shoes' – she fell over outside a dodgy apartment, her denim-clad legs pointing skyward. In fact I was actually delighted. Dion politely clasped her by the elbow and pulled her to her feet.

At most viewings, landlords were also present. Sometimes impromptu lunches would be organised with a view to forging immediate kinship. As glasses of weak cordial were raised in a *stin yeia mas* salute – the Greek equivalent of 'cheers' – I'd sit and stare at far-off lemon trees as Dion did all the talking. I wondered if through landlords' eyes Dion was seen as 'the man', the one to decide on our new home, and if I was seen as 'the mail order bride', the one who would cook in his kitchen. During these long, drawn-out meetings, I'd fantasise about plucking a lemon from a tree and throwing it at a landlord's forehead just to see what would happen next.

All in all, the properties we saw were disappointing. Most were a lot older than our Labrou Katsoni home, and internally were cluttered with dark-wood, 'classic' furniture. We realised how lucky we were to have scored our little modern apartment in the first place. Still, we persevered. We reasoned that not all real estate agents were porn extras or sharks, that not every dwelling was better suited to accommodate livestock. And we knew that the perfect place would eventually fall into our laps and – with any luck – not on top of us.

One Saturday afternoon we were scouring the paper as usual when an ad jumped out at us. Enticing words such as 'sea view', 'pool' and 'barbecue' led to dancing and swirling visions of a perpetual Greek holiday. We promptly organised a meeting with the owner, who spoke English fluently.

A born salesman, the short and stocky landlord – whom we shall call 'Yiorgos' – wore petite-legged dark trousers and an open collared shirt. He greeted Dion warmly, acknowledged me vaguely, carefully avoiding eye contact, and proudly showed us around an apartment that rivalled Labrou Katsoni. It was brand new, freshly painted, and had two generous light-filled bedrooms, an enormous living room with wooden floorboards, a state-of-the-art kitchen and two well-appointed bathrooms. The entire complex, comprising six apartments in total, was perched atop a hill. Wide verandas offered expansive views of stark-white buildings below, the enticing emerald Aegean Sea and commanding rocky hills. It seemed we'd struck gold.

With a cigarette smouldering away in the corner of his mouth, Yiorgos put his plump hands on his hips and looked rather pleased with himself. These apartments were his pride and joy. He explained at great length the hi-tech security systems he had in place to protect his turf: towering electric gates, cameras, alarms, police on 24-hour standby. It was not the first time we'd noticed over-the-top security measures. Around Voula and Glyfada, security seemed to be an obsession. Precisely what everyone was so diligently protecting themselves from, we'd never really established. Thankfully Yiorgos offered an explanation. The smile briskly disappeared from his chubby, tanned face as he shared with us a story.

A few weeks prior, his wife had been at his mother's place when two men – in broad daylight – entered the house and stole his wife's handbag. Not good. Yiorgos' emotions went from sunny to stormy in the blink of an eye, his face turning beetroot red, his eyes welling with hot tears. Yiorgos knew, without a shadow of a doubt, who had carried out this heinous crime – *Albanians.* He reasoned that if Greeks carried out such an act (which they wouldn't) they'd have had the courtesy to put all the papers and credit cards into an envelope and mail them back to their rightful owners so as not to cause any undue inconvenience. This is what he told us. My mental scoff was so loud, I feared it was audible. Dion didn't flinch.

So as mentioned, Yiorgos was angry. *Very* angry. As he reached the crescendo of his story, his voice grew shrill. He began to visibly shake. A cascade of tears trickled down the smooth terrain of his ruby splashed cheeks. I became entranced by a blue vein pulsing at the centre of his forehead as he worked himself into a state before us.

With a conspiratorial whisper, he then revealed he'd been harbouring a secret intention to hunt down the culprits . . . and *KILL* THEM! You know, kill, as in murder. As in an unauthorised termination of existence. And I wasn't at all convinced that this blood-curdling proclamation was figurative. Yiorgos continued to divulge that he'd even figured out the best place to bury his victims and described the precise location he had in mind for shallow graves, falling just short of dropping on all fours and carving a map into the floorboards with a penknife. My neck muscles tensed and my head twisted involuntarily to the left. I wondered if we were about to become accessories to murder.

We weren't entirely sure at this point how to respond to the bloodlust of a man we'd only just met, especially since this man was using quite an unusual sales pitch to lure us into becoming tenants. I later learned that Dion, who'd remained placid and smiled serenely throughout, had managed to take this potential landlord's rantings with a grain of salt. He was equipped with an inbuilt Greek bullshit detector that I didn't yet possess. In the meantime, my face continued to twitch.

Abruptly the murder talk ceased and Yiorgos trotted around the apartment, resuming the tour. He switched to a more pleasant line of conversation, to that of his passion for pit bull terriers. He owned three of them, and one was a champion fighter that had left several dogs in its wake. 'Ripped their faces off' were his carefully chosen words. Outside, by the swimming pool, he released the hounds. Thankfully the first canine that threw itself at us was only seven months old. The two adult dogs arrived a few seconds later and began mating somewhere around our legs. We pretended not to notice, unlike our potential landlord who laughed hysterically, elbowing and interrupting Dion mid-sentence.

'Look! Look! Hke's *hkumping* hker! HKA HA HA HA HA HA!'

The breeding pit bulls and their jocular, potentially murderous owner lived one floor below the apartment we were considering. Our landlord, as is often customary, would therefore also be our neighbour. It became apparent that his pit bulls would join us every time we dared use the communal swimming pool. Call me crazy, but I didn't much fancy the idea of treading water, encircled by three pit bull terriers, while my landlord watched hysterically from his kitchen window.

'Look! Look! Hke's *keeling* hker! HKA HA HA HA HA HA!'

Our search for a new apartment continued. In the meantime,

out of the blue, and after a full year's silence, Dion's station bolted from the stables. For reasons that weren't ever made clear, it was suddenly allowed to broadcast again, although still at risk of being shut down at any given moment for any given reason. With all the momentum that was now behind it, there was no stopping it. And there was no stopping Dion either.

Okay, so Yiorgos was slightly off the wall and not the best representation of an entire nation. But now that I'd straightened my own head out, I felt in a stronger position to try and get inside the heads of the people of Greece. What made them tick? With Greek forefathers playing a major role in shaping the worlds of art, politics, philosophy, medicine, mathematics and architecture, there was an immense amount of wisdom and intelligence prevailing that fuelled a strong national pride. Desperate to comprehend, I embarked on a little research.

I learned that Greece had faced Turkish oppression, Balkan wars, two world wars, a civil war and junta governments, leaving many starving and dead along the way. Modern Greeks had emerged from a turbulent past and a long history, a history that was very much in contrast to that of white Australia. I figured that the things I perceived as 'strange' were always going to look that way when approached with my own cultural expectations.

I began to understand that the people of Greece weren't 'strange', but different from those I'd encountered before. So gradually, day by day, I found myself accepting more and judging less. I began to see that misinterpreting what was often neutral behaviour had caused me a lot of undue grief. Slowly I began to break through barriers and be rewarded with reciprocated friendliness rather than the stoniness I had come to expect. Sometimes I'd smile so hard that my whole body would spasm, but the results were amazing.

After two long years, I finally began eliciting smiles from the locals. It was all in the timing. It was all in the sincerity. It was all in the expectation. As I began to accept the people around me, it seemed they began to accept me too. By now, even genuine offhandedness and underhandedness barely registered on my radar, a combination of a new-found understanding and simply being accustomed to general Athenian behaviour. In places, even the city itself seemed beautiful.

The Greeks I'd encountered, on the whole, seemed to be creatures of contradiction. They thrived within a sprawling metropolis fuelled almost by a village mentality, and were disorganised, passionate, hospitable, illogical and giving. If they didn't know you they could be 'rude' by my interpretation, and while they possessed perhaps a more animated or mercurial temperament, once they did know you they'd look out for you, even bend over backwards, as the ever-reliable Yianni had proven time and time again.

I do believe that I was finally coming to understand the place. Weirdly, at the same time, a sense of displacement set in and I started to feel as though I didn't necessarily belong in Australia any more. And yet, despite recent breakthroughs, I continued to feel that I didn't belong in Greece either.

I'd successfully reached a state of limbo.

Yiorgos of Murderous Intent, the Porn Princess of the Realtor World, weak cordial and amorous pit bull terriers were all but forgotten when an unbelievable opportunity presented itself. On the grapevine, Dion heard of a newly built rental home available in a place called Lagonisi, thirty minutes from Voula. Lagonisi is a sparsely populated area away from Athens, set on a magnificent piece of Aegean coastline. It has a perpetual holiday atmosphere, except, of course, during winter, which was when we went to check it out. Despite temperatures around the zero mark and gale-force winds that whipped my hair violently against my cheeks, I knew that this was *exactly* what we'd been looking for, in Dion's case genital shrinkage aside.

We were looking at a brand spanking new, ridiculously spacious home the likes of which we never could have dreamed. It was set within a security compound that included a communal tennis court, a helipad, bountiful gardens that lined a long, winding driveway and five enormous luxury homes, painted in Mexican reds and Tuscan yellows. And it didn't end there. The house came complete with a full-time Albanian handyman and security guard named Sultarn, and a cleaner, Clariana, his wife. They both lived in a tiny dwelling somewhere on the compound tucked out of sight.

The available apartment was a whopping forty squares on the ground floor with the sea right on its doorstep. It comprised two enormous bedrooms, three bathrooms, a humungous living and dining area, an office and a new-millennium kitchen. Being tiled throughout with large slabs of shiny off-white marble, the potential to host weekly roller-discos didn't pass by unnoticed. The master bedroom and lounge room looked directly onto a red tiled veranda that preceded a small, wild piece of yard. Viewed through large glass sliding doors, it yawned with sparse winter foliage, feral cats and in the summer – we were told – the occasional wild turtle. Beyond that, spread out forever, was cobalt blue.

The piece of land on which we stood neighboured property formerly belonging to the Onassis family. I had visions of slipping on a pair of black Jackie O's. This was it! This *had* to be our new home. We signed the papers, waved bye bye to Labrou Katsoni and Maria the neighbour and moved in on a blustery, cold grey day just prior to Christmas 2002.

When the subject of contract renewal arose once again, this

time the prospect of staying for another year seemed nowhere near as daunting. Having friends and more of an understanding of the country certainly helped. And so too did the idea of living in luxury by the sea. Plus another carrot had been dangled. Not only would Dion be running Athens' number one station, but he had the chance to run a second one, too. His network had already begun purchase negotiations. It would be a career breakthrough. So, effortlessly and less moronically than you might think, we came to a unanimous decision. It was time to enjoy our days in the sun.

As I unpacked and arranged our belongings at Lagonisi by day, Dion moved his busy staff, including new employees, into a new building that included his own palatial office complete with kitchen, shower and fireplace. As far as I was concerned, my husband was the crown prince of Greek radio. Perhaps sharing similar thoughts, his work dedication intensified.

We spent Christmas with Tim and Shane at Lagonisi – or 'Laggers' as Dion and I liked to call it – Tim spending most of the day making vain attempts to convince us that the pavlova meringue cake was a dessert that originated in New Zealand. I couldn't resist baiting him.

'Tim, for the last time, pavlovas are fucking *Australian*. Go back to New Zealand where you belong!'

Our Lagonisi home was breathtaking. Each morning the ocean would take on a different shade of blue, each dusk a different shade of pink broken only by the silhouettes of distant islands. But paradise was to be shared. The second level of our home was occupied by an eccentric old Greek man who'd been responsible for building each home on our property with his own bare hands. He was patriarch to a clan of five, each having a stake in one of the five buildings on his land. His name was Stavros and he was almost completely out of his mind, almost completely deaf, and spent most of his days and nights noisily rearranging his furniture. From the sounds that came through our ceiling, he could have just as easily been rolling across the floor in a barrel as he could have been herding cattle.

A level up from Stavros was the 'weekend' home of our landlord, Tasos. Tasos was in his mid-thirties and the eldest son of Stavros. He was an intelligent, rich and handsome active type who flew helicopters in his spare time. Being married didn't stop him from falling hopelessly in love with my husband. Right from the start, Tasos couldn't get enough of Dion, lavishing upon him a bizarre form of hero worship. While I wasn't exactly seen as an annoyance, I was certainly incidental. From the moment we met, Tasos was unable to look me in the eye. And I really, really hated it.

Tasos' gorgeous wife, Despina, was a knockout with unruly blonde curly hair, a killer body and brains to match. She was studying medicine, spoke a multitude of languages and was exceedingly kind and patient with me. Once we'd settled into Lagonisi, we all made pained attempts to become fast friends, some trying a little harder than others.

23

Life in the fast lane

Things were great. We'd moved to a beautiful place and I was getting into the swing of things. We had friends, and to top everything off, Dion had negotiated a rental car for me into his contract. His company *really* wanted him to stay. When it came to driving, I knew I'd have to become either more courageous, or more suicidal. For want of a better expression, I decided to face my Athenian driving fears *head on*. The day Yianni delivered my automatic grey Hyundai Accent, I couldn't have been happier. Sure I was secretly shitting myself. After all, I did actually have to drive the thing, but the car spelt freedom. Living in a more remote area, it had become a necessity.

Dion accompanied me on my debut drive. Within minutes, I skidded off the road in an attempt to avoid crater-sized potholes at a speed of 100 kilometres per hour. With a trail of dust behind us, we both laughed nervously. I then narrowly missed a motorbike whizzing along in my blind spot as I attempted to get back into my lane. A helmetless female passenger on the back turned to lovingly offer me a thrust-open palm. This gesture is known as *moudza*, and pretty much means 'get fucked'. I'd heard it symbolised shoving excrement into the face of another.

'You'll get the hang of it,' Dion assured me. I wasn't sure if he meant driving or people suggesting I eat shit.

My hesitancy to drive in Athens had little to do with driving on the opposite side of the road to which I was accustomed. Rather, my concern was that I hadn't developed my psychic ability enough to pre-empt the bizarre road tricks that other motorists might pull from out of their behinds. It seemed that driver behaviour was not so much dictated by road rules as by rules based entirely upon chaos theory.

On my first solo mission, I daringly headed for the centre of town along the gorgeous coastal road. I took a blind corner ten minutes from our home to discover a parked taxi, its hazard lights flashing, blocking my lane. With cat-like reflexes, I swerved and narrowly missed its rear end as mine did things of its own. Somehow I avoided sideswiping a vehicle to my left, just as my heart threatened to burst forth from my chest cavity, splatter against the windscreen and slither into a clotted puddle on the dashboard.

Clearly the taxi's hazard lights and precarious parking indicated an emergency was in progress. As I passed, I looked back to see if any assistance could be offered. As inconceivable as it was, however, I saw that the emergency was linked only to the driver's bladder control. Having completed his leisurely leak on the side of the road, I took a mental snapshot of the middle-aged man zipping up his fly. He casually sauntered back to his vehicle, oblivious to the fact that his urinal urges had almost confined me to a wheelchair.

As my journey continued, I noted that driving within lanes was entirely optional. Although white lines were once presumably intended as a means of dividing roads, it was now acceptable to drive either between them, or *over* them, as though following bread crumbs through a beguiling forest. This meant that if a driver decided to take the follow-the-white-line option, he'd claim ownership of the better part of two lanes, meaning other motorists couldn't pass unless their vehicles had the capacity to halve their size and squeeze past. This was just the way things were and gladly accepted by everybody. Bar me.

Inexplicably, though, this obligatory ducking and weaving worked. Traffic generally ebbed and flowed, cars eventually moved out of the way as required, and despite first appearances, the on-road chaos, for the most part, was kind of effective given that the vast majority got from A to B alive.

When I eventually arrived in Kolonaki, things became trickier. See, my car was slightly thicker than the width of a toothpick and it proved near impossible to navigate down narrow streets crammed with double-parked vehicles. However, as nuts as it all was, I will say this: the bizarre parking rituals, kamikaze driving styles and flagrant contempt for the law felt strangely liberating.

I'd had an epiphany! I would henceforth be known as . . . 'a writer'. And I would write . . . 'a guidebook'. Yes, I would write a guidebook and I would ingeniously entitle it 'A Guidebook to the City of Athens'. Who better to expound on the bounties of this promised land than someone who'd just spent a couple of years indoors going gradually insane? This guidebook of mine had been commissioned by nobody and had not been researched to gauge its validity within the guidebook market. Yet I made it my goal to steer people around the city of Athens in black and white like I was some kind of authority on the subject. I committed myself to it with sincere dedication. And sometimes I'd give Dion a page or two to read. More often than not, he'd slip into a coma mid-sentence.

Despite assigning myself this rather immense undertaking, I still felt like I was idling. I wanted to do more with my life and squeeze as much out of our Greek experience as possible. So when I found an ad in the *Athens News* searching for volunteers to help save the endangered loggerhead turtle, I felt sure it was my destiny.

I immediately made an appointment with MEDASSET, the Mediterranean Association to Save the Sea Turtles. It made perfect sense. After all, the things I'd seen in Greece had made me a closet animal-welfare lobbyist: a Great Dane confined to a cage the size of a shoe box; six half-dead beagles tied up and hanging out of a passing car boot; street cats fighting over a piece of souvlaki; malnourished stray dogs lying around the streets as though stoned; an Alsatian confined to a small apartment balcony without any shelter or exercise. The very least I could do was something for the poor, defenceless turtle.

Greece is home to many important loggerhead-turtle nesting sites, the most densely nested being the island of Zakynthos. Here, the main problem is tourism. You see, Zakynthos is a major draw card, frequented mostly by sausage-and-egg eating Brits. And it's no wonder – the island, with its clear green Ionian waters, is stunning. But the inevitable results of tourism, including garbage, traffic, pollution, lights, noise and the blades of passing speedboats, don't quite work for the loggerhead turtle. In turn, the government, local landowners and developers don't quite give a shit. It's a case of tourism versus environmentalism that's involved the European Court of Justice on more than one occasion. And it was a matter that was about to involve me. After my great success in retrieving the Elgin Marbles, nothing would stand in the way of my latest crusade.

The cluttered and claustrophobic offices of MEDASSET were located around the corner from Tim and Shane's apartment. I met with a young, full-time worker named Vicki who looked remarkably like a turtle herself, with her large brown eyes and little round face. She seemed innocent and fragile. She told me I could help MEDASSET by writing press releases for them in English. I was rapturous. At last I could do something beyond my 'guidebook' that actually contributed to the world. So chuffed was I, in fact, that I promised Vicki I'd speak to Dion about an on-air production to alert people to the plight of the turtle and the importance of keeping waterways clean. Vicki's soft, turtle eyes brightened at the prospect.

As soon as I arrived back at Laggers, I excitedly called Dion. He was eager to help, too. He agreed to produce an ad as a gesture of goodwill. Delighted, I composed a script and forwarded it to both Dion and Vicki for approval. Dion loved it. But Vicki didn't respond. And after a series of unanswered emails, telephone calls and a holiday break, Vicki seemed to have vanished. I was kind of expecting that an effort of this magnitude would be met halfway. But I seemed to be doing all the chasing. Was my writing *that* bad? Or was I getting more of a taste for the way things happened in Greece? I guess I couldn't always boast about crossing the finishing line. And in the end, I gave up trying, perhaps now a product of my environment. A short message hailing Mother Earth went to air on Dion's station regardless.

24

The lovecats

As we settled into our home a new life began to emerge. During the week, I'd stay inside, sheltered from the cold, watching beautiful little red-bellied birds bob up and down on leafless rosebush branches outside. The glass doors would almost buckle from buffeting sea winds. It was as though I captained a ship that had run aground.

Despite being only thirty minutes further out from Athens, I felt more disconnected from the capital than I expected. Dion would leave the house earlier and arrive home later as he juggled two stations. I saw him less and less. Tim and Shane left the country for three months, and loneliness and boredom returned with a sinister wave and cheesy grin. I felt pretty much back where I'd started, only this time in one of the most beautiful settings imaginable.

I'd withdrawn from the counselling course to make way for my guidebook, and spent my days writing and trying to ignore the sounds of Old Man Stavros upstairs tap dancing across the floor in what sounded like a pair of wooden clogs. Each *crack* that reverberated through the ceiling, each flick of a page and each keystroke echoed through the apartment, reminding me that I was again alone. I tried to ignore it, but I'd been here before and knew that this was dangerous territory.

I became grateful for the almost daily power shortages that at least brought with them an interruption. Blackouts would last a couple of hours and force me to use my 'me time' in creative ways that had become my specialty over the years. Obviously, I resumed plucking my legs. I also began reciting hypnotherapy scripts verbatim should I one day choose to attempt to put someone 'under'.

'Your eyes are growing heavy. You're sinking deeper and DEEPER into relaxation.'

I spoke this into a hand-held tape recorder. I'd run around the lounge chairs and every so often drop into a push-up or assume the 'plank' position, sometimes followed by an impromptu 'downward dog'. I drank litres of water and kept a written record of the number of times I urinated in a day. I weighed myself every few hours for no good reason and became convinced that one of my pupils was larger than the other. I also began practising a little magic.

After reading about self-proclaimed Indian avatar Sai Baba and his alleged powers of materialisation, I was again motivated to explore creative visualisation. I figured that if a fat guy with an enormous afro wearing an orange caftan could do it, then so could I. Hell, I'd brought my existing friends into being, hadn't I? This time, I thought it might be nice to conjure up a pet.

So one day, after a week of blackout-inspired visualisations, I began to type up random thoughts on my personal understanding of the Greek capital. Bored, I looked up and spied outside our glass doors the kind of creature normally found seated at the right hand of Satan. It was a mottled grey and white beast, with a coat that more resembled a collection of used Steelo pads than it did fur. It had only one and a half ears. Its dull yellow eyes were malevolent, its expression fixed in a savage sneer. As it ambled across our balcony, it passed me a dirty look. And as it did so, I guessed that this filthy animal was probably a member of the feline family, although twice as large as any cat I'd ever seen.

With morbid curiosity, I ventured outside to take a closer look. As I approached, the cat stopped dead in its tracks, crouched and stared. It seemed to challenge me to step closer. I slowly extended my hand, and made gentle, reassuring sounds.

'Here, *Cleany*. It's okay. Come on!'

The cat arched its back and hissed, displaying a tiny row of angry, razor-sharp teeth. My magic technique needed some work.

Cleany, the disgusting feral creature hailing from the underworld, took to hanging around our yard and while I was in awe of his ugliness, he wasn't quite what I'd had in mind. So, over the next few blackouts I persevered in trying to visualise his return from whence he came, which was obviously hell. I hoped to do a deal with the devil in which I traded him in for a new furry companion.

Two weeks later, a fresh looking ginger tomcat bounded up to our back veranda and sat with a look of expectation in his clear green eyes. Like Cleany, he was of gargantuan proportions, reminding me of a cross between a mining truck and a weightlifter, but he had a strangely knowing and friendly look about him. He was young and energetic and had a head the size of a slightly deflated football. He also had an enviable pair of enormous ginger balls.

I went to him. This cat showed no wariness towards me as I began patting his course, rough coat. Then he raised a paw and allowed it to dangle in mid-air. I assumed he was gay. He purred a deep purr and began head-butting my thigh. I was in love.

He was imaginatively named Ginger on the spot. From the bushes to the right of us, Cleany looked on jealously. Cleany and Ginger became my close companions . . . and one another's arch enemy.

Although it remained chilly, I started taking early-morning strolls across the usually deserted stretch of pebbly coastline that neighboured our home. They were beautiful, thought-provoking walks where I pondered leg-hair stubble, life and, naturally, things that bothered me. This list included the stray dogs that charged at me barking and the odd, lone male that occasionally crossed my path. But what bothered me most was the rubbish that spoilt this otherwise perfect beach. As I watched a rat the size of a Rottweiler run over a plastic drink bottle crowning a pile of garbage just beyond gently lapping waves, I began to formulate yet another wily plan to change the world.

I dwelt upon the contrast between the Greeks' fastidiousness within their own homes and their tendency to toss their refuse into the outside world with as much gusto as carnations around a *bouzoukia* nightclub. I gathered that very few locals ever pondered whether a plastic lid might choke an unsuspecting dolphin to death. It was another paradox difficult for my Australian brain to comprehend. Why was it so? Remembering that the Greeks were only a generation past the threat of starvation, I guessed the plight of the environment seemed less vital than personal survival, or so I concluded on those morning strolls. I'd also been told by a Greek native that littering hinted at anti-establishment feeling towards the state, foam coffee cups seen as anarchic missiles.

Back in my luxurious seaside palace, I placed a call to Clean Up Greece. I explained to a woman breathing heavily on the other end of the line that I was the wife of a man who ran two prominent radio stations and suggested that something be formulated to spread the word to the masses. In basic English, the woman at the other end agreed that, yes, this was a good idea. Or maybe she simply agreed it was an idea.

Dion soon held meetings with Clean Up Greece and the

organisation proposed that his station sponsor a small concert, which was certainly a start, but not what I'd had in mind. No, I wanted to shout an environmental message from the rooftops, to broadcast an ongoing campaign to a wide audience, to educate, to make an impact. But it wasn't my radio station, it wasn't my environmental group and it wasn't my language. I could only light the cracker, run for cover and watch the glowing wick fizzle out. Despite grand plans to leave a positive imprint on this glorious corner of the globe, I felt sure I'd leave behind only a barely detectible smear.

Thankfully, as the Olympics drew nearer, Athens became more environmentally conscious and began sprucing itself up. All I could do was hope that the city's new look would make an impression on people and that the environment would be maintained after the Games had been and gone. It remained to be seen.

In the meantime, the months at Lagonisi rolled by, my weeks filled with cat-watching, writing and wondering whether Stavros upstairs had taken to building an ark in his living room. I'd resumed language lessons at Babel, graduating to the 'Beginners B' class, although, embarrassingly, I could still only speak a minimal amount of Greek. This didn't stop me, however, from shooting a knowing wink at the teacher whenever entering the 'Beginners A' classroom.

Despite the amazing stimulation of not being able to learn a language, I felt a tug on my sleeve from my old friend loneliness. This time I used a variation in technique to ignore her. Like an adrenalin junkie I began suggesting new endeavours to my frazzled husband.

'Why can't we do more together? I don't see you any more. Why can't we be more adventurous? Let's take up scuba diving. Let's go on a safari. Let's go to Malta. Let's *do something!*'

'Babe, I'm so tired and I've got so much programming to check through.'

'*Programming?* What about parachute jumping?'

'Do you want to go to Nota and Nikos' at the weekend?'

'No, I don't want to GO TO NOTA AND NIKOS' AT THE WEEKEND.'

'Why are you talking to me like that?'

'Like what?'

'You're yelling.'

'No I'm not.'

'Don't yell.'

'I'M NOT!'

As the weather grew steadily warmer, the small winter birds vanished as the shrubs in our yard bloomed in iridescent pinks and ruby reds. The sun became more intense until it was finally warm enough to enjoy the outdoor life. The water I'd been gazing at for months beckoned. Hardy, wild flora stood to attention in a guard of honour as I descended the paved walkway from our house until I reached the charming stone archway made by Old Man Stavros. Beyond it the ocean winked and flashed endlessly, disturbed only by far-off islands rising like precious sculptures from the ocean bed below. Stepping through the arch and into the picture, I followed a narrow metal walkway over rocks and unceremoniously plopped into the water like an indolent walrus, catching my breath. It was cold but invigorating.

Soon my morning routine included a daily dip where I avoided the walkway and ambled along boulders that had crumbled into the sea like tremendous mounds of honeycomb. Like a faithful dog, Ginger would accompany me most of the way, routinely embedding his teeth into my ankles. Despite the thin trickle of blood that would drip to my heels, I found this irresistibly cute. Ginger, it seemed, was a wild and courageous sea cat who would have delighted in swan diving into the water with me if it weren't for his pesky cat

DNA. Cleany would remain at a safe distance, watching us hatefully like a jilted lover.

While my weekday rock scrambling was a solitary affair shared only with my ginger companion, my weekends with Dion soon became cooking fests as we entertained Yianni and Anna or Tasos and Despina. Tim and Shane were soon to return, promising a wonderful summer ahead.

Dion finally rose to the challenge.

'Okay, you want to do something, let's go to Hydra.'

'Really!'

Excited, I jumped to my feet and bounced towards him like a rabbit with my two hands dangling at my chest like paws.

'Please don't tell me you decided on Hydra because you see me as a multi-headed serpent.' I butted my head softly into his shoulder and he wrapped an arm around me.

'No, babe . . . despite the recent yelling.'

'*I WASN'T YELLING!*'

'Okay, don't yell! You're probably right anyway. I've been working so much, I need to get away.'

So we found ourselves in Hydra, a quaint little island with a complete ban on motorised transport, much to Dion's disappointment considering he wasn't a fan of walking or, for that matter, any form of exercise. Luckily, though, Hydra town is concentrated around a tiny port and our accommodation was close by. We arrived at the port, walked to our room, checked in, walked back to the port, and sat at a taverna and gorged on food for two solid hours. The menu included charred octopus, zingy tzatziki, fried potato chips, spinach and one of my all-time favourites, fava beans mashed with lemon juice, oil and raw onion. I relished spending quality time with my man as much as I did the food. We ate and we talked – really talked – and laughed like lovers and friends. It had been a while.

Dion looked at me with a serious expression. 'You know what? You're the greatest.'

'Dion! Thank you! Where did that come from?'

'Nowhere. You just are. Everything's okay now, isn't it? You like living in Laggers?'

'*Like* it? I *LOVE* it. I'd never imagined living anywhere so incredible.'

'I told you everything would be okay. It took a bit, but we got there,' he continued.

'Well, we're not quite "*there*" yet. I still feel out of place sometimes. And this still isn't home.'

'Yeah, I know. But you have to admit, it's pretty damned brilliant.'

'Granted. And so is Australia. And so are you.' I leant over and kissed him on the forehead from across the table. 'I just wish things had clicked into place a little faster for me.'

'Me too.' Dion raised his glass. 'To Greece!'

I raised my own. 'To Australia!'

'To you!' Dion countered.

'To us!'

After gaining an extra kilo and an outright refusal from Dion to mount a donkey, I forced my husband to his feet and we walked along the water's edge towards the western side of the island. We passed a variety of rusty cannons and small bobbing fishing boats then finally reached a panoramic vantage point.

The miniature port town below didn't conform to the Greek island standard blue and white. Hydra's architectural colour code included yellows, brick reds, stone greys and sandstone, and there were more than a few mansions set amidst the spectrum. Hydra was renowned as the fat cat playground of yesteryear and it was easy to imagine aristocrats and tycoons hosting decadent parties here.

As expected, the ninety-year-old within Dion began to protest about the walking and he insisted on heading back to the port. We spent the remainder of our time sitting and drinking, lying down and sleeping, sitting on a small boat that took us to a beach, lying on deckchairs and sitting on a ferry bound for Piraeus, Athens. All in all, it was the perfect weekend.

In addition to our *Fantasy Island*–style Lagonisi compound, there was yet more at our disposal. The public beach next door that I'd strolled along in the colder months had transformed into a crowded watering hole, offering three makeshift outdoor cafés. Buses would drop off hordes of beach-goers from all over Athens daily. Cars and motorbikes were stacked anywhere they could fit off the Athinon–Sounion road, sometimes parking us into our home. People ambled along our 'private' road in their favourite dickstickers and floral underwired bathers like herds of cattle, blissfully unaware of the sound of our car engine revving impatiently behind them.

Back from the beach, however, Lagonisi remained a sleepy, forgotten town. There was little more than a tiny supermarket and hairdressing salon in one direction, and a pharmacy and even tinier supermarket in the other. Houses had sprung up here and there, but unlike Athens central, the town had a Greek island sense of space. Like Athens, however, there were many houses under construction – grey concrete shells that never seemed to progress. I eventually came to learn that these buildings simply represented the way things unfold in Greece, that is *slowly*. And in many cases, people simply run out of cash.

I attempted to gain a sense of community by patronising the local supermarkets and hairdressing salon. This had quite a lot to do with hair becoming my latest fixation. Behind closed doors I'd begun staring at my lank, dark locks in the mirror, saying aloud the

Greek word for hair like a barking chihuahua.

'*Malia! Malia! Malia!*'

Although I'd recommenced language lessons out in the world, I remained as foreign as ever, and people responded to me with little more than confusion whenever I spoke. Eleni the hairdresser was no exception. Not to put too fine a point on it, Eleni was a bit of a bitch. Or perhaps she was just perpetually sad. How would I know? I could only go by her facial expressions and how viciously she tugged at my hair. I tried to overlook the fact that a pair of gardening shears may as well have completed the set of cutting implements laid out on her hairdressing trolley.

In any event, sour-faced, she would tease my hair 1980s-style while dousing my head with the entire contents of an industrial-sized can of hairspray, effortlessly ripping yet another hole in the ozone layer and transforming me into a sideshow freak. During one of our kindergarten conversations, I lied to Eleni. I told her I'd been living in Greece for six months, such was my embarrassment at *still* not being able to speak the language. However, this did little to lessen her hostility. In fact, short of using judo manoeuvres to pin her to the ground, my linguistic disability left me powerless to stop her from hair teasing and going sick with a hairspray can.

After one appointment, Eleni managed to make my head look enormous and somehow *square*. You know you've had a particularly bad haircut when your head defies the laws of physics and reflects the combined cranial volume of The Jackson Five. After visits to Eleni, I'd often be seen zipping around Laggers with my monster hair bending angrily beneath the confines of a Hyundai roof.

Still, I was determined to discover what set Lagonisi apart from the rest of Athens. One Saturday, as Dion attended an outdoor beach broadcast to which I wasn't invited, I noticed a market in progress and thought I'd scout around for something interesting.

I slammed my car door shut. A stumpy, crumpled man staggered past holding seven squawking chickens upside down by the feet. If I had been on holiday, I guess I might have seen this as a little bit *National Geographic*. But I wasn't on holiday. And I didn't find it particularly compelling. This was where I lived, among chicken danglers! It momentarily knocked me off balance. I saw that while I lived in a picture-perfect setting, it didn't alter the fact that I was still a long way from home and a true understanding of a Greek way of life. I still missed Australia.

Things deteriorated further that day when I bumped into Maria, our former Labrou Katsoni neighbour, on the streets of Glyfada. As our eyes locked in recognition, Maria, it seemed, was delighted by our unexpected reunion.

'How *are* you? How is Lagonisi?'

This was Maria speaking – the woman who for two years lived next door without uttering a single word to me in English while I contended with an indescribable loneliness that nearly cost me my sanity. She could speak English perfectly *all along*. I was surprised to say the least. When Dion returned later that afternoon and I shared the breaking news, he was as shocked as I was.

Truly, madly, deeply

Tasos and Despina, our landlords, were getting to know us on a much more personal level than is customary in Australian landlord–tenant relations. We were invited to hang out with them whenever they were around. Let me just repeat a part of that last sentence: *whenever they were around.* As in every waking moment of every single weekend.

Saturday mornings would usually kick off with an early-morning phone call from Tasos to Dion's mobile phone.

'You wunt to go for a swim, Dionysi?'

'You wunt to go for helicopter ride, Dionysi?'

'You wunt to go for coffee, Dionysi?'

Soon it would be lunchtime.

'You wunt to go for a swim, Dionysi?'

'You wunt to go for helicopter ride, Dionysi?'

'You wunt to go for lunch, Dionysi?'

And then it would be night time.

'You wunt to see a movie, Dionysi?'

'You wunt to come upstairs for coffee, Dionysi?'

'You wunt to go for souvlaki, Dionysi?'

Which would lead us into Sunday and the cycle repeating over.

Greeks are exceedingly hospitable and social if they call you a friend. While we were grateful for the extended friendship, it was clear that Tasos was besotted with Dion. I thought it was hilarious – at first. It became less and less funny.

You see, through no fault of his own, Tasos assumed I had some sort of a life of my own. The first time Dion was invited for a ride in Tasos' helicopter, both Dion and I were beside ourselves with excitement. We went to the helipad, Dion climbed aboard and the next thing I knew I was being asked to step away from the aircraft. I removed my leg from the passenger door. Who knew it was only a two-seater? The helicopter was soon hovering over the ocean like a drunken dragonfly. I remained at ground level, waving idiotically, trying to look as though I never expected to go up with them in the first place.

On many occasions, Tasos, Despina, Dion and myself would get together and play happy couples, sitting for hours drinking coffee and eating, a favourite pastime of any self-respecting Greek. This would take place either at our landlords' funky third-level apartment or ours while Old Man Stavros played living room croquet on the floor in between. The only problem was that Tasos still couldn't look me in the eye, include me in conversation, hear or acknowledge me in any way, shape or form. It made me want to take to myself with a blunt pencil to establish whether or not I was still alive. Tasos found me either astounding or insignificant, I couldn't tell which. Dion didn't notice him not noticing.

Despina, on the other hand, was gentle and patient. She was always ready with a Greek language tip as she helped me with my homework or with an invitation to meet her to go shopping. The trouble was, as hard as I tried, I could never truly connect with her. I had a secret passion for music, drinking and discussing the manifestation of cats while she had a less secret passion for tea-totalling, medicinal studies, sophistication and maturity. While she could speak English perfectly, it didn't necessarily mean we spoke the same language.

As our relationships blossomed to varying degrees, we lunched one afternoon with Despina and Tasos at a taverna renowned as a carnivore's paradise in a nearby village called Kalithia. Dion admired a piece of steak on Tasos' plate.

'Mmm. That looks nice, Tasos.'

Dion bit into his lamb chop.

Tasos looked at his plate, then over at his wife's.

'Despina, give Dionysios you meat.'

Despina dutifully stabbed her steak with a fork and slapped it onto Dion's plate, no questions asked.

Dion was embarrassed.

I thought it was hysterical.

Tasos thought it was normal.

Despina ate her spinach.

During our dinners and marathon coffee-drinking sessions, I'd either grow bored with the conversation, which usually involved aircraft instrumentation, or I'd become consumed by methods that forced Tasos to acknowledge me. But as with Dion's mother, anything I attempted to reveal about myself would pass by unacknowledged. I began to wonder if it was considered uncool for women to talk about themselves. Or irrelevant. Or boring. I couldn't figure out which. As I pondered such nuances, Dion negotiated the cost of Tasos giving him helicopter lessons.

When the telephone rang late on a Sunday night for another coffee session to mark the passing of yet another triumphant weekend chock-full of solidarity and its record-breaking intake of caffeine, I finally did an imperceptible Michael Jackson 'Moonwalk' away from the posse, or *parea* as it is known in Greek. I opted to stay downstairs and slob about in my pyjamas instead, figuring my presence wouldn't be missed anyway. Dion was happy to head on up alone and discuss rotary wing aircraft. He quickly became lost in the world of aviation and the free time he'd once spent working at his laptop was replaced by studying a variety of helicopter manuals.

Hang on a minute! Since when was working at the laptop *optional?*

I grew resentful that I had to share the little 'Dion time' I had with helicopters, a guy who may or may not have disliked me, and a lovely woman with whom I had little in common. It was a case of me choosing between solitude and feeling a certain awkward boredom. I chose solitude. Me. The girl who'd almost died of loneliness not too long before.

One Saturday night Dion and I were invited to a party at our wealthy landlord's other dwelling in a groovy section of Kolonaki at the foot of Lykavittos Hill. Floor boarded throughout, the old-style apartment felt dark and confining despite its immensity. Despina, looking stunning with her lion's-mane of wild blonde hair, welcomed us and then floated off to work the room. Tasos fell just short of holding Dion's hand. I made for a makeshift bar in the corner of the living room, attended by a bored, bow-tied bartender. Out of the forty guests, I was one of only three who requested an alcoholic beverage. I was poured a green cocktail and made my way to Dion's side to listen to Tasos introduce him to anybody who inadvertently made eye contact from across the room.

'Thees . . . ees Dionysios Giamoreyos.' A hand would dramatically gesture towards Dion.

'Aaaaaahhhhhhh!' Would come the response. 'Ti kanete! The radio station!'

Eyebrows would raise. Smiles would broaden. Hands would be shaken. Dion would then introduce me.

'And this is my wife, Lana.'

'Yias sas!' they would say before their eyes magnetised back to him.

'The radio station!'

I sucked back as many alcoholic concoctions as it took to numb my senses. A polite couple attempted to strike up a conversation. I fumbled my way through a witty quip that got lost in translation. They stared back at me, presumably brooding over the unfair slow execution of Socrates, and floated away.

I surveyed the room. Guests stood around holding plates of lukewarm pasta and speaking softly. Nobody was laughing. Nobody was dancing. Everybody was stone, cold sober.

Isn't this supposed to be a party?

I greatly admired the intelligent, sane drinking going on around me. I truly did. But this didn't mean that the sheer sensibility of it all didn't drive me to drink. I found myself fighting an uncontrollable urge to get completely wankered and make a public spectacle of myself. The more I drank, the more I considered jumping onto the table and belting out a rendition of 'Fame'.

The night culminated in Tasos putting on a two-hour home video of shaky helicopter footage, mostly focused on the control panel. Everybody huddled around a television screen. Dion became engrossed. I felt slightly sick. And it wasn't entirely attributable to the consumption of mysterious green cocktails.

I sent an SMS to my brother Phil in Sydney, in an attempt to convey my concerns in a brief message.

At shit boring party watching helicopter footage. What should I do?

Thankfully my brother had all the answers.

I say whip it!

I took a moment to reflect upon the profundity of his words. If no one was prepared to party, then I'd party on my own. At a safe distance behind those staring at a close-up of an altitude gauge, I silently began eighties dancing, arms swaying from side to side.

My smile froze as I remembered the barman. I glanced over my shoulder. He stared back, as bored as he'd been upon our arrival. I scurried into the crowd and gazed at the television screen breathless, like every good party-goer should.

While Santorini had afforded me the opportunity to see my father's trouser leg spray-painted with British stomach lining, Dion had never visited the island before. On learning this, many looked at him as though his brain had haemorrhaged through his anal passage. He began to develop something of a Santorini hang-up, so some weeks after the party to end all parties we arranged a romantic dash to Santorini that meant leaving behind choppers, landlords and the sounds of Old Man Stavros nailing himself to the floor. I was stoked!

Rather than stay at the main town of Fira, where eager shopkeepers might have attempted to convince us that enormous gold leopard brooches bejewelled with semiprecious stones were the perfect accompaniment to my torn Mooks T-shirt, we opted to stay in the quieter town of Oia (pronounced 'eee-ah').

Oia is embedded in a cliff top at the northern tip of Santorini. Like Fira, it boasts magnificent views over steep volcanic cliffs and an azure sea. Unlike Fira, Oia is low-key and more atmospheric.

We positioned ourselves in a modest little room amongst whitewashed houses and sky blue domes. Our view over the water was dizzying. We strolled from our room passing a large Orthodox church on a town *plateia* before reaching a variety of classy shops selling paintings, sculptures, jewellery and handicrafts.

Our first afternoon was spent gazing into the sunset for which Oia is famous. We weren't the only ones. Santorini's entire tourist population zoned in on precisely the same spot – the teeny-tiny area mentioned in every Greek travel guide known to humanity – jostling for the perfect photo opportunity. As the sun slowly set, the sky changed from blue to pink, and the sun from orange to red. The wildly appreciative crowd whooped and clapped madly as a small red blob slowly vanished over the horizon like a Jaffa plonking into the sea. I too gave a standing ovation, but with raised eyebrows and a sly smile sailing Dion's way.

'Woooo-hoooooooooooooooo. Yeah!'

Which, for Dion's benefit, actually meant:

Listen to all the morons clapping a sunset!

I could afford to be a spoilt, cynical bitch. I saw a sunset not dissimilar almost every afternoon from our Lagonisi balcony. Dion let out a sarcastic 'whoo' and we both had a chuckle at everyone else's expense. Our patronising cockiness was sickening.

We returned to our room to play with a grey and white kitten that enjoyed puncturing our flesh with its tiny kitten teeth. With Ginger blissfully unaware, we lavished love on the furry creature that we called Bitey. As the night sky deepened, Bitey was banished and we played with one another instead.

Later we dined at a pleasant little taverna, an orange moon as big as a pizza pie filling the sky. I stared into the familiarity of my beloved's dark, happy eyes. We laughed, admired one another and shared secrets.

'God, Dion. We're going to look back on all this and remember how lucky we were.'

'I know, babe.' Dion took my hand. 'I love you, you know.'

'I love you too. Thanks for persevering with me over the years. I know it's been tough sometimes, but who knew what this adventure had in store? And I've started thinking about something. Something extremely "adult" . . . Is it time?'

'Time for what?'

A warm smile buttered my face.

'Do you think it's time to start thinking about making babies?'

'*Babies!* Really! Do you think you can handle it?'

'I don't know. Maybe. No one really knows until they have them, right? If I fall pregnant now, by the time I'm ready to pop, we'll be back in Australia.'

'God! Babies! Do you think? This is HUGE!' Dion squeezed my hand and I squeezed his back harder.

After more than six years together, we were in love and in Oia, Santorini. *And talking about starting a family!*

26

Agadoo

Hooray! Tim and Shane were *finally* back in the country and we proceeded to celebrate. On a thick and balmy summer night, we attended a dinner organised by Shane at an outdoor club-bar-restaurant called Akrotiri. Athens is positively littered with establishments that defy one-word descriptions, although it is essential that the word 'club' be found somewhere amongst the infinite succession of words used to describe them. Always in English, descriptions tend to borrow from the following combinations:

Club
Club-Bar
Club-Restaurant
Club-Bar-Restaurant
Café-Club
Café-Club-Bar
Café-Club-Restaurant
Café-Club-Restaurant-Bar
Bikini-Club
Bikini-Bar-Club

Bikini-Bar-Club-Restaurant
Club
Club-Club
Club-Club-Club
Club-Club-Club-Club

The main contenders of the Club-Bar-Restaurant scene, such as Balux, Destijl, Island, Privilege and Venue, would swap locations from season to season, meaning the city was always in a permanent state of flux.

At 11 p.m. we arrived at Akrotiri in an area called Kalamaki. Like most places of its ilk, its setting on the water's edge was marvellous. A restaurant area backed onto the ocean with tables and chairs set around a large, tastefully lit swimming pool.

Our dinner was attended by eight: Tim, Shane, Dion, myself and four colleagues of Shane's. Dressed to the eyeballs, we ate and drank pleasantly, commented demurely on the pleasing surroundings and blended effortlessly into a typical Athenian dining experience. It was all very sophisticated, that is until Tim and I began a secret drinking competition. By our fifth glass of wine, guzzled between fiery spirit chasers, we began debating loudly whether Christina Aguilera or Britney Spears would be the next Madonna. The others discussed work.

By 1 a.m. our party members began drifting off into the night with sensible notions of slumber. But for Tim and I, leaving was not an option. After bidding farewell to our respective partners, and with determined grins on our silly faces, we promptly made our way to a bar at the far side of the venue overlooking a dance floor. We threw back a couple of shots. They were free. They tasted like methylated spirits. We didn't care. We ordered more. On some level we understood we were the only two pissed mutants in the entire establishment. To onlookers, we were just another couple of freak tourists with substance-abuse problems. Again it occurred to me that I'd never seen a staggering, drunken idiot in Athens, day or night, unless I happened to catch a glimpse of my own reflection.

I guess the trouble really began when I spied a pineapple perched innocently on the edge of the bar. It was part of a summer fruit cocktail display. In the wily ways of the pineapple, it seemed to beckon seductively, begging me to caress it, to hold it, to take it as my own. As Tim danced wildly amidst a subdued crowd, the pineapple vanished swiftly from the bar's edge, clutched to my breast like a prized trophy. I strode over to the dance floor and presented it to Tim, holding it high as though it were the Son of Man. Tim shrieked with delight, reinforcing my understanding that the pineapple was in all ways good. He then snatched it from me, shoved it down his Diesel trousers, and continued dancing, the pineapple's green spiny leaves protruding like thick, gangrenous pubic hairs from his waistband. Our state of intoxication was such that this seemed to be the single most hilarious thing ever to have transpired. Doubled over laughing, I looked at those around us and pointed at Tim's groin encouragingly.

It's a pineapple!

I wanted everyone to join in on the joke. Unlike Australian establishments where such a display would entice every drunken maniac to gravitate towards us, nobody inched closer or even cracked a smile. Essentially, the sober and sane saw us only as fuckwits. To me this wasn't good enough. Surely they misunderstood. I removed the pineapple from its underpant nest, held it out for all to see, and pointed to it.

It's a pineapple! A PINEAPPLE!!

The youth of Akrotiri didn't want to play. They thought we were stupid. They were right. But that's beside the point. In all my time in Athens, I still hadn't seen anyone being silly. Not one person. I found it disconcerting.

While we may have been ostracised from the rest of the Club-Bar-Restaurant fraternity, we were inseparable that evening: Tim, myself and the pineapple. The following morning I was discovered unconscious, my body strewn across Lagonisi bathroom tiles, a half-rotten pineapple beneath my head as a pillow. An army of ants trailed along the floor to the pineapple, crawling around my face and down my arms and legs. I hated myself. And I no longer cared much for the pineapple either. Dion was none too keen on either of us. A weak smile barely masked his underlying chagrin.

Dion was working so hard on the two stations that I became convinced I'd married the Invisible Man. There was compensation, however, in the weekly pilgrimages Tim made to Laggers armed with a teeny-tiny pair of shiny spandex diving shorts covertly tucked into his day bag.

'I love *you*, not your backyard ocean, Pinrose!' he assured.

'Yeah, right. Whatever, user.'

'Know any potential frinds with a wenter chalet in the ski regions?'

We'd make a salad together, our waistlines taken into high consideration, before Tim barged past racing me to the water. Cleany would regard Tim's taut buttocks hatefully. Ginger would gallop after us with a sense of adventure. Tim and I would soon be wading, continuing an ongoing debate about teeth bleaching versus porcelain veneers.

Outside of this, I was pretty much left to my own devices and in between bouts of guidebook writing I entertained myself aquatically. Once a snorkelling mask was affixed to my face and fins to my feet, my entire world changed. While I may have looked like an even more amphibious version of Yianni, my eyes suctioned out of their sockets and magnified, I felt at peace. Aside from the occasional Greek man who would emerge triumphant from the depths with an octopus in hand just prior to bludgeoning it to death against a rock, the piece of ocean at our doorstep was almost entirely mine and I couldn't have been happier with the arrangement.

The sea became a daytime playground where I'd pass hours at a time playing a guest-starring role in an imaginary episode of *Flipper*. My diver's mask became a window into a world of tranquillity and wonder. I would see green and orange fish zipping in and out of rocks and schools of fish of different shapes, colours and sizes darting this way and that. Occasionally I'd spy a sea snake or a curious long and thin Dr Seuss–type creature, the length of a pencil, with a dopey looking snout. The underwater world became a secret, parallel universe. It was every Piscean's dream.

One day I spotted an immense school of fish that flashed an electric blue when the sun hit it a certain way. There were literally hundreds if not thousands of fish swirling together as one co-ordinated entity. I swam through the centre, as though swimming through a galaxy of shimmering sapphires. It was one of the most wondrous experiences of my life. In that moment I completely appreciated the great privilege of living in such a beautiful and exotic location. I felt an all-encompassing serenity that I've rarely known. It was a serenity that would prove to be fleeting.

A week later, on a hot summer night, I sat transfixed by a documentary on Charles Manson courtesy of satellite television. Wearing a little pink silk nightie best suited to a five-year-old, I spread lazily along the sofa. Dion was sound asleep in an all-too-familiar perpendicular position on the couch opposite, snoring noisily.

Despite my finger being so far up my nose I was close to practising brain surgery, the extent of Charles Manson's evilness soon
overcame me. I looked at the sliding glass doors that led to our yard
and the ocean, but tonight saw nothing, only an inky blackness.
As a still shot of Sharon Tate looking vivacious and alive filled the
screen, I switched off the television, revolted. I shuddered. It was
way past midnight and time for bed.

I shook Dion awake and went to the bathroom. He stumbled in
behind me in a pair of boxer shorts, his hair in a state of confusion.
As I plonked myself on the toilet, I watched the back of my husband
as he brushed his teeth, his head shaking from side to side with
each short brushstroke, his little behind moving in the opposite
direction to each stroke. I had a brief chuckle to myself.

When I turned to flush the toilet, pure terror ripped through
my body like a bolt of lightning. Peering at me through the frosted
glass of our bathroom window was a large oval face. And the face
was *smiling*. *SMILING!* As reality sank in, a sound exploded off
the bathroom tiles that I'd never heard before, and, to my horror,
the sound was coming from *me*. I was screaming uncontrollably,
as though starring in a B-grade horror movie.

The face disappeared from the window, a phantom. Dion, still
half asleep, dropped his toothbrush and began screaming too,
although why he didn't know.

'Aaaah! WHAT? What's wrong?'

'A face! THERE WAS A FACE AT THE WINDOW. Someone
was watching me . . . on the TOILET! Dion, the face was S-M-I-L-
I-N-G! THERE'S SOMEBODY OUT THERE!'

My wavering voice was not my own. We ran through the house
terrified, bolting every door and window.

'THERE'S SOMEBODY OUT THERE!'

'What do we do now?'

'Call Sultarn,' I croaked. Sultarn was the Albanian handyman-security-guard who lived in our complex. Despite the late hour, Dion called him at once and within five minutes he was at our door. Dion explained what had happened in Greek. Sultarn responded, looking at me as though I were, well, pretty much committable.

'What did he say?' I asked.

'He said there's nobody out there.'

HOW THE FUCK WOULD HE KNOW?

Shaking, I walked the two men into the bathroom and pointed at the window.

'Tell him the man was looking through there.'

Dion garbled something in Greek. Sultarn responded, shaking his head.

'What's he saying now?'

'He's saying you wouldn't be able to see someone's face through frosted glass. He thinks it must have been your own reflection . . . or your imagination.'

My imagination?

I felt insane. Had the Charles Manson documentary played tricks with my mind? Had psychosis finally set in?

This is it, folks. She's finally stepped over the edge.

'Dion, I swear to you I saw a face. It was fucking *smiling*. I'm not going crazy. Get Sultarn outside. Let's see if we can see him through the glass.' I couldn't stop shivering.

Dion relayed the request. Sultarn shrugged, a gesture that said, 'Okay, whatever floats your boat, sister.' And we waited for him to go outside, me still shaking, Dion holding me and offering strokes of comfort.

Was it my own reflection?

'I really did see someone,' I whispered feebly, my voice trembling unconvincingly.

Sultarn made a mobile call to Dion from outside. He was right. We couldn't see him through the window. My head grew heavy, I felt hot and dizzy. I'd finally lost the plot. I walked closer to the window. Nothing. Just the outline of my own face reflected back at me, looking shocked and old. But then I thought I saw something, some movement outside to the right. I took a closer look.

'Why is Sultarn standing next to the window with his back against the wall? Ask him to put his face up to the *glass*.'

Dion again relayed instructions into the telephone. Sultarn complied. A chill ran down my spine. There at the window was clearly a man's face. Somebody *had* been watching us. And do you know what? The face at the window in that second looked remarkably like the one I'd seen only fifteen minutes earlier.

The following morning, Tasos, Despina and Old Man Stavros went into damage control. They provided blinds and curtains for every window in the house. They organised external security lights. A giant 20-metre-high fence was erected at the side of our house to deter intruders from the large vacant lot of land to our left. The irony was that it was Sultarn doing all the erecting.

From behind a curtain, I peered at him hammering away.

I know it was you.

I was desperate to ask his wife, Clariana, about his movements the night before. Of course all I could manage were the words 'window' and 'hello'. I got the impression that Clariana wanted to offer comfort, delivered via a succession of frowns, shrugs and smiles. As always, though, her body language could just as easily have been conveying amusement over my brilliant articulation.

Dion took an interesting stance. He reasoned that if Sultarn was in fact a pervert, at least it was someone we sort of knew and not a complete stranger. I never quite understood the logic. Yet again, I remained housebound for a spell, too spooked to go anywhere near our handyman, curtains and blinds drawn to shut out a blazing summer sun and Peeping Toms. There would be no more snorkelling for quite some time.

27

Wind of change

We were now three years into our Athenian adventure. It was September 2003 and Dion's work contract was once again up for renewal. Despite Freddie Kruger patrolling the grounds, overall my life was great. By comparison, Dion's was nothing short of incredible! His radio stations were both topping the ratings, he'd been given a brand-new top-of-the-line SAAB convertible, he lived in a luxury home worthy of an Onassis, his work colleagues kissed his arse, he'd moved into an enormous office complete with an ensuite and fireplace, he was sometimes seen zipping through sunny blue skies taking helicopter lessons with Tasos and he not only spoke Greek fluently but now even dreamt in Greek. Oh, and he also had me.

Dion felt invincible and was eager to renew his contract. Who could blame him? I wasn't too far behind in the enthusiasm stakes either. While I still faced the usual communication dilemmas, overall I felt much more at ease. I fully appreciated our island flits. Driving had given me a sense of independence. Tim and I were having a fat old time. I had a goal in the form of writing the guidebook to end all guidebooks. And in Lagonisi, we had an unbelievable setting in which to snorkel and breed.

'Just one more year!' I told Dion with a wry smile and wave of the finger.

But as we came to the end of our third summer, the winds of change began to blow: so subtly at first that they were barely detectable. Something was slightly amiss with my man. Little warning signals began firing in my mind.

The first tiny flare went off when it dawned on me that Dion no longer telephoned me through the day any more. Nor did he ever mention Australia. As in he never mentioned it at all, ever. It was as though the continent where we grew up no longer existed. He stopped talking about our families, our past, or any cute Australianisms that we formerly laughed at together. He no longer shouted, 'Aus-tray-ya!' if Nicole Kidman's head popped onto a television screen. He no longer referred to Australian music, or put on an exaggerated Australian accent when we were mucking around.

He also began defending to the death anything associated with Greece. If I mentioned an illogical encounter I had with a Greek person or an amusing idiosyncrasy, I noticed that he no longer laughed it off and told me not to worry about it. Instead, he stuck up for the country and the ways of its people, no matter what effect the encounter had had on me. He had become more solemn, more serious.

As our second wedding anniversary approached, we decided to visit the island of Rhodes, which I hoped would bring back Dion's sparkle. In between Lagonisi power blackouts and our telephone lines going dead, I logged onto the Internet, did some not-so-solid research as was my 'thing' and decided it would be preferable to stay within the medieval section of the island. I made an online reservation at a hotel.

We arrived late on a Friday night and grabbed a taxi that drove us through fortress arches built by the Knights of St John of Jerusalem.

Bumping along cobblestones in the darkness, I felt instantly transported back in time. We entered the stony, medieval façade of our lodgings and were greeted by a moustached, dark-eyed 'Rhodesian' wearing blue jeans and a white freshly pressed shirt that promised the likelihood of chest hair beneath. His curly hairdo was slightly overgrown and a little on the 'large' side. He leaned against the reception counter with his arms folded and one leg crossed nonchalantly over the other in what appeared to be a well-rehearsed pose. I surmised he was hoping to appear 'casual'.

'Hkello and welcome,' he declaimed with practised insincerity. 'You must be Mr Giamoreyos? May I show you your room?'

He shook Dion's hand and flashed a smile my way.

Dion and I followed the man down a cool, dank, concrete corridor and exchanged bemused looks as he wrestled with a stubborn lock and key. He gave the door a swift, unabashed kick and with a shuddering protest, it flung open. He flicked on a dull, naked light. The smell of mould assaulted us. The room was painted *Amityville Horror* red, with a toss and tumble double bed shoved in a corner. The only things otherwise adorning the room were a small wooden bedside bureau and a green plastic bucket with a soiled towel flung over its edge. Dion and I came to a unanimous verdict. The room sucked.

'We don't want to stay here,' I blurted.

'*Whut?* You no wunt room? But why? Come . . .'

We followed the hotelier back down the corridor to the reception area. He walked behind the reception desk and folded his arms.

'You wunt coffee?' he asked.

'No thank you.'

'Okhay, then tell me why you no wunt room?'

'We were really just hoping for something . . . um . . . a bit nicer,' Dion replied tactfully.

'*Nicer?* You tell me whut room nicer?'

There was a pause.

'Tell me!' he demanded softly, lowering his eyes and nodding and smiling.

We hesitated. We weren't entirely sure what the question was.

'Whut room nicer? Whut you wunt?' He continued smiling.

'A nicer room?' I sheepishly offered.

He turned to face Dion.

'Tell me. Whut you wunt?'

His tone remained even, dripping with fairness. I slinked away from what may or may not have been a rhetorical question. Out on the darkened street, I searched for an escape vehicle. Three drunk Italian men staggered past, arguing violently. Remarkably, the taxi that had dropped us off was parked a little further up the road, our driver apparently taking a power nap. I rapped on his window, startled him awake, raced back inside and announced to Dion that I'd found a ride.

'*Whut?!!*'

We fled to the taxi with the hotelier in hot pursuit, his even expression switching to desperation.

'But *whut you wunt?*'

Exasperation rang through the night. The receptionist shouted a final word into the cab before the door slammed.

'WHUT?'

The driver sped off. He told us he had anticipated such an eventuality. He described more suitable accommodation run by a cousin, which came as no surprise in a world where nepotism prevails. I turned to peer out the back window. The receptionist was standing in the middle of the road, his arms raised, his moustache-framed lips mouthing one word only:

'*WHUT?*'

Rhodes is the largest of the Dodecanese islands. Having only a weekend to explore the place, we concentrated our efforts on the medieval district that had impressed then terrorised us the night before. We walked the perimeter of the fortress, feeling much more at ease with the brilliant sunshine beating down on us rather than a moustached hotelier.

Dion – exhausted by the walk – dawdled and stopped for coffees and cigarettes while I strolled around souvenir and carpet shops sandwiched between impressive old buildings. Many had been built in the fourteenth and fifteenth centuries, among them the Palace of the Knights. The Turks had almost completely demolished this palace during their period of occupation in the mid-1800s. Thankfully the Italians, who had also claimed a stake in this little piece of Greek territory, restored it in the 1930s.

Dion and I decided to have a special lunch in celebration of our anniversary at a taverna overlooking a large section of the quarter. The usual menu was provided, the usual foods ordered. The usual orderer placed the order. The usual observer sat silent.

'Ktapodi, tzatziki, taramosalata, feta, salata, saganaki, patates tiganites kai spanaki.'

Although we were here to celebrate our anniversary, there remained something fundamentally different about Dion. He was distracted and distant. He hadn't felt so unfamiliar to me since we'd begun dating. Something just wasn't right. We chatted awkwardly. Breaking every commandment in *Men Are from Mars, Women Are from Venus*, I cut straight to the chase.

'Dion, I don't mean to freak you out. But can I ask you something?'

I watched my husband squirm, pick up a fork from the table and clutch it tightly.

'Yeah?'

'What's going on? Is everything okay with you? You seem . . .
I don't know . . . different. Is everything okay at work?'

'Nothing's wrong.' Dion stabbed randomly at his plate, the sun
glinting off the well-worn cutlery.

'Okay. Well, happy anniversary to us. Remember why you married me?'

I tried to sound cute, disguising the sense of dread that began
swirling in my belly. I hoped my question might evoke memories
of the beautiful love that Dion was perhaps taking for granted.
Instead, my husband's face became pale and, to my absolute horror,
he offered no response at all. I quickly ascertained I was facing the
silence of a man who'd been deliberating the very same question
himself. It was an ambush that came from beyond the periphery,
a reaction I never could have imagined in my wildest nightmares.

What's happening?

My stomach tightened. My heart sank. In spite of my panic,
I kept my voice calm, offering my own reasons for our marriage
and hoping to elicit reciprocated sentiments.

'I married you because you were the kindest, most dependable
man I'd ever met.' I smiled weakly and shrugged, my shoulders
rising to my ears.

Silence reigned. The clanging of cutlery against plates at surrounding tables sounded sharp and irritating. Although the table
before us groaned with food we barely ate. We wandered back to
our hotel, exchanging hardly a word.

What the hell is going on here?

When we arrived, Dion called his mother from his cell phone
and stood on the balcony so that I couldn't overhear his conversation in Greek. Not that I could ever hope to understand it. I knew
then and there that we were headed for troubled waters.

After Rhodes, it was as though an earthquake had shaken my world to its very foundations. Nothing was the way it had been. Things had shifted and cracked. Dion became a different man almost overnight and I felt the grip of his formerly supportive hand begin to loosen.

What the hell is happening?

The bottom line is the guy had everything he had ever dreamed of, except for one thing. His wife did not share the sense of belonging he felt in Greece – a country he now considered home. And now his wife was discussing children, a decision that would surely spell a return to Australian shores. It seemed that Greece wasn't content with the many attempts she'd made on my spirit and sanity; she was now making a play for my husband as well.

Dion no longer particularly cared for my company, but I was now more desperate than ever for his. A creepy woman had once told me that Greek men brought up in other countries change once they returned to the motherland. At the time, I scoffed.

You don't know my Dion.

Was I now witnessing this very transition in the person I treasured more than life itself?

killing me softly

The following Saturday morning Dion dashed into the city for coffee with Yianni, saying he desperately needed to talk to a friend. He explained that over the last three years he'd not made any real mates because he'd spent all his spare time with me.

With me AND your laptop? I thought drily.

I tried to put myself in his position as I stood at our sliding door, watching him disappear down our winding driveway, leaving me alone, yet again. Tim and Shane had darted off to visit another part of the globe, so once more I was at a loose end. When Dion eventually returned later that afternoon, I made polite enquiries into Yianni's health before ploughing into a well-rehearsed rant about how desperately I needed him. He nodded, but his flitting eyes gave away his discomfort. I worried that my distress had the potential to exacerbate matters. And maybe it did, because the next weekend, he pulled a repeat performance, fleeing the house solo.

The way I saw it, Dion was perfectly justified in wanting to cultivate external relationships in the same way I did. But wasn't I also right in wanting to spend time with him? This change had come from out of nowhere and I was fraught. However, I decided to ride it out. He was only going for coffee. What was the big deal? I amused myself by visiting Eleni the sad hairdresser, who may or may not have been taking out her sexual frustrations on my hair. Back home with it curled, teased and stupid, however, my patience began to wane. By 5 p.m., there was still no sign of my husband for the second weekend in a row. My blood began to boil.

What the fuck's he trying to do to me?

So I made a bold move. I packed my bags, jumped into my car and began driving. There was just one small problem. I had nowhere to go.

I soon found myself in – guess where? – Glyfada, walking aimlessly around the shops I'd walked around for years. There was nothing that I hadn't seen before. Same shops, same clothes, same people, same beggars, same Africans selling pirated CDs, same chaos, same dogs. I did what I always did: I bought myself a hkkamburger and sat alone in silence in a fast-food restaurant as life teemed around me.

I decided the only thing that would take up a substantial chunk of time was a film. The feel-good movie at the time was *Kill Bill*, and I queued for a ticket behind a bunch of laughing back-slapping teens. I looked on hatefully, adopting the expression I'd learned from my feral cat. As the cinema lights dimmed and my brain began to absorb the twistedness of Quentin Tarantino's psyche, I tried to come to terms with what was happening between my husband and me. The screen filled with blood and gore. I saw it as a metaphor for our current situation. Overcome by nausea, I left the cinema feeling much, much worse than when I'd entered.

Around 7.30 p.m., my mobile started to ring. I didn't answer. I was making a statement, though I wasn't sure what that statement was. I had to bide my time and think of something else to do.

I wanted Dion to see how it felt to be on the receiving end. I drove to the suburb of Vouliagmeni and parked my car by a cliff overlooking the water in which Dion and I had snorkelled together when we first arrived. I recalled the day gentle waves washed over us and we'd held hands tightly underwater. The tears began to flow slowly at first. I turned up the radio to amplify a song by Monaco, listening wearily to lyrics about a life being taken away and ruined.

A few weeks earlier, my life had been quite different. A few hours earlier, I'd had every intention of spending the night at a hotel. I now couldn't do it. I felt pathetic. I began the slow drive back to Lagonisi. Some statement! Parked outside the sliding gate that protected our compound from the world beyond, I sat in the dark listening to songs on the radio that seemed way too poignant. I switched off Evanescence's 'Going Under' and sat in silence watching tiny black waves lap against the shore of the small public beach. My mind flashed back to the Glyfada gypsy woman of years earlier. Had I been cursed? *Cursed?* What the hell was I thinking?

Eventually I pressed the magic button that opened the gate and drove up our winding driveway. As I entered the house, Dion came to the door.

'Where have you been?'

I struggled to decode his tone. It wasn't anger. It wasn't confusion. It seemed more like resignation.

'As usual, Dion, I've killed time going nowhere. Are you having an affair?'

Dion looked at me, shocked, and replied with sincerity.

'Of *course* I'm not!'

'Well if you're not, you need to understand something. You need to understand how much your actions are hurting me. Our life as a couple isn't the same as "ordinary" couples. As much as I wish I wasn't, I'm extremely reliant upon you. I have been since the day we arrived. Your latest freak actions aren't exactly conducive to us both living happy lives.'

'Don't you think you're over-reacting slightly?' came his unsympathetic response. He looked at me with intense eyes, his permanent smile nowhere to be seen.

Was I or wasn't I over-reacting? The only thing I knew for sure was that I felt as though I were going mad again. And in my mind's eye I saw the gypsy woman's face twisting into a saccharine grin.

In response to relationship pressures, my chin began to break out harder than Swing Out Sister. After a pimple epidemic had me resembling a nervous, pubescent McDonald's employee, I visited Tim's beautician, Artemis, the one who had indirectly caused him to be hosed down with tear gas. She was in Ambelokipi near central Athens.

Artemis was a slim beauty with flawless, porcelain skin, black eyes and shoulder-length, shiny brown hair. Her most endearing quality was her genuine friendliness, a characteristic that I embraced immediately.

Not only was she lovely, but very talented, and unlike other beauticians she offered unparalleled service that wasn't designed to rob me blind. Her spacious, light-filled salon was incongruously set within one of the many overbearing buildings that dominated Ambelokipi and was just off a fume-filled main road that would leave one collapsed and choking by the roadside on blinding summer days. I was determined not to let the location ruin therapy. This would *not* be like doing a poo right after taking a shower.

Artemis practised English on me that far outshone my Greek. I learned that she hailed from Crete and at the ripe old age of twenty-six was running her own successful business. It had been financed by her parents, as is often the Greek way. She also appeared every so often on a prominent morning television program commenting on the best way of maintaining skin elasticity and the importance of drinking large volumes of water, among other things.

Over the course of six facials, Artemis and I got to know one another quite well. The subject of love would invariably arise and as the relationship between Dion and I crumbled with each passing week, Artemis was incredulous. While I did my best to maintain composure, revealing only the barest details, I felt relieved to have an impartial 'girlfriend' to confide in in Tim's absence. Artemis took her role of confidante seriously. She began hatching an ingenious plan.

'*Oh, koukla mou!* I unbelieve it, but know whut we do.'

There was a pause as questions radiated from beneath the cool green goo that had been smeared across my face.

'We make hkim crraaazy!'

'What?'

'We make hkim crraaazy! Greek man, they go crraaazy! I know whut to do!'

'What do you mean?'

'Hkere! I call you phone. I hkang up . . . Hke go crraaazy!'

Artemis began cackling like a cunning crone. The expression hidden beneath my face mask was one of delight over the sheer absurdity of her logic.

Of course! This approach will solve EVERYTHING! Why hadn't I thought of it myself?

Before departing that afternoon, Artemis gave me final instructions.

'Remember. I call you phone. I hkang up. Hke go crraaazy.'

That evening, Dion and I struggled to make even stilted conversation. It was as though our words had passed their use-by date. All we could do was stare stupidly at Ginger who lay languorously by our feet and make the odd comment about the cat's god complex. Ginger became the 'child' that was the only binding element in our relationship. In a pained effort to encourage conversation, I revealed my beautician's infallible plan to try and make Dion jealous. He appeared as amused as he was confused. 'She sounds like a nut.' He reached down and scratched Ginger behind the ear.

Two hours later my mobile rang. I went to answer it. After two rings, it stopped. Dion and I looked at one another and for the first time in a while, laughed together.

Later that night, my husband revealed that he couldn't see us ever having children, that it just didn't seem 'right' any more. He was sorry but it was just something he'd 'decided' and he had little else to say on the matter. He may as well have punched me in the stomach. And ripped out my womanhood while he was at it. Standing at the kitchen bench, I fell silent and fought hard the urge to cry, pretending to wipe down a counter. With the option of having children suddenly taken away, I felt empty and rejected, not only as a companion, but as a woman. I spent that night in bed staring at the ceiling as Dion snored beside me.

I sat with Dion on the lounge on yet another brilliantly sunny Saturday afternoon, the view outside our doors as breathtaking as ever. Cleany glided by, throwing me a petulant glance, soon followed by Ginger prancing past like an extroverted show pony. It struck me that no matter how pretty the backdrop, it didn't always mean a beautiful story would play out before it. Dion stared intensely at the television watching the Discovery Wings channel. It was as though I wasn't there. A tear prodded the corner of my eye like a hot pinprick.

'Dion . . . what's happening to us? Please . . . can't you at least talk to me?'

'I don't know what's happening.' Dion's eyes remained fixed on a program on military aircraft.

'Is it this fucking country doing this to us? I can't take it any more. I really can't.'

I broke into sobs. Dion muted the television and reluctantly turned to face me.

'What do you mean you can't take it any more? What do you want me to do?'

His face grimaced. I saw the look of a man who on some level wanted to show compassion, but had none left to offer.

'I need you to promise me one thing. I don't want to be in this country any more.'

A look of dread spread across Dion's face.

'You've signed your contract but . . .'

'But what?'

'I want you to promise me that at the end of this term, we'll definitely go back to Australia. *Definitely.* Living in this place has almost killed me. I've put up with it, but mainly for you. For you and your career. Since we've arrived, it's been a constant battle not to lose my mind. So, September next year . . . I say we go home.'

Dion stared at me. His mouth moved, but no sound came out. Finally, the words I'd never wanted to hear made their assault.

'I'm sorry. But I can't promise you that.' He spoke softly and his tone was deep and regretful.

Time stood still. My vision blurred. This was not the response that the husband formerly known as Dion would have given. The deal had always been that when I'd finally had enough, when I finally said the word, when I couldn't take another second, we'd return home. I looked at him, stupefied.

'What do you mean?'

'Sorry, but I just can't.' His voice was flat and devoid of emotion.

I ran to the bathroom, fleeing my assailant.

From the tiny transistor in our bathroom, No Doubt's cover of 'It's My Life' could be heard faintly above my sobbing.

My mobile telephone rang three times and stopped abruptly.

This was my life, all right. A life that had made the leap from occasional joke to ongoing nightmare.

Tim and Shane returned to Greece and I met my closest friends for lunch. Shane conspiratorially revealed that he'd begun arranging a transfer out of the country and looked remarkably pleased with the idea. On the back of everything that was happening, I wasn't exactly jumping for joy at the news. However, I kept what was going on with Dion to myself, praying the turbulence would pass.

I proceeded to get uncontrollably drunk with my Kiwi comrades and in the early hours of the morning passed out like a starfish on the couple's living-room floor. Tim dragged my unconscious form along the hallway towards the bedroom like a murderer disposing of a body. I sprang to life and bolted for the bathroom, mistaking their bathtub for a toilet.

Rock on

Johnnie Jackie Holliday was an announcer on an Athenian radio station. Staples of his playlist included Judas Priest, Alice Cooper, Ratt, Black Sabbath, New York Dolls and T Rex with bursts of Garbage and Smashing Pumpkins. The guy was Rock with a capital 'R' emphasised with a sky-thrust two-fingered devil salute.

As an announcer, one thing in particular stood out about Johnnie. Like me, the guy seemed barely able to speak Greek. The difference between us, though, was that he was on the *radio* happily broadcasting his substandard linguistic abilities to anybody who cared to listen. His talk breaks, delivered in Greek via a New York accent, were therefore extraordinarily brief and to the point.

'Okay, afto eine to Motley Crrrrue me to Live Wirrrre.'

Or translated, simply:

'Okay, this is Motley Crue with "Live Wire".'

And that would be it.

His voice sounded camp, albeit creepy, as though it were more than plausible that his 'real job' was that of a hunchback working as a lab assistant in a castle atop a Romanian mountain range. Dion and I, during better times, had tuned in religiously not only because the music he played was such a relief from the banality of Greek commercial radio, but also because it afforded us the opportunity to perfect our imitation of him like a couple of fifteen-year-old hormonally imbalanced schoolgirls. By now, however, Dion had stopped listening.

I decided that Johnnie Holliday and I should become firm friends. It made perfect sense – he played rock music that I loved like a guilty pleasure. And he spoke English. Sure he may have also been an axe-murdering, salamander-breeding, gun-toting maniac, but what could be more important than rock and English? On my 'To Do' list, under a heading marked 'Potential Friends', his name was therefore carefully added and underlined twice.

One Saturday morning, as an arctic silence encircled Dion at his laptop, I daringly called the number Johnnie encouraged listeners to call with a view to making it so. I found myself on hold, listening to Axl Rose welcoming me to a jungle that got worse every day.

How apt!

A whiney, American voice eventually came on the line.

'Hallo?'

'Hi, is that Johnnie?'

'Surrrre. This is he.'

He sounded friendly yet somehow professional as though fresh from the American service industry.

'Oh, hi! My name's Lana. I'm an Australian who's been living in Athens for three years and two of my closest friends have just told me they're about to desert me,' I babbled. Only static hissed down the telephone line in response.

Why am I telling him this? Stop!

They say first impressions last and I was doing a shithouse job of coming across as mentally stable, but I nevertheless continued ranting.

'Anyway. I really love your show! My husband and I were wondering if you knew of any clubs that play the same kind of music you play?'

I left out the part that Dion would rather skewer his head with a chopstick than attend an Athenian rock club with me if, in fact, one existed.

'No, not rrrreally, man. I've been settling for goth clubs lately, 'cause everything's dead right now. I came straight from one to the show today. Man, I'm so burnt. Wanna hearrrr a song, dude?'

The concept of a Greek gothic club was something I'd never contemplated before. I found the very idea unnerving. The only Greeks I'd ever encountered wore co-ordinated, conservative garb and listened to Greek folk music or Eurotrash beats. The idea of a Greek dripping in black clothing and matching lipstick with a penchant for dead things, spiders and The Sisters of Mercy didn't seem to wash.

'Oh! A song? Okay, can you play The Cure's "Primary"? And can I have your email address?' I added boldly, hastily.

'Surrrre, man.'

He provided his email address. It contained the word *fucker*. He didn't play The Cure.

Shortly thereafter I began email-stalking Johnnie Holliday while insisting I was *not* a stalker, thus making me seem all the more stalkeresque. Why he humoured me with occasional responses, I'll never fully understand, but they only served to encourage me to force myself into his life. Via electronic mail, I explained my plight in detail. I shared how Tim had become like a brother to me, how I sometimes lurked around his Skoufa Street corridors, how my friends were about to abandon ship and how I couldn't bear to live in Athens without them.

With Tim and Shane's threats of desertion becoming more and

more frequent, and my husband continuing his 'this ain't really working out for me any more' trip, Johnnie was the most obvious candidate for New Best Friend.

Dion had passed out on the sofa when my telephone began ringing. Its shrill peal bounced off the walls and marble floor of our concert-hall-sized living room. Dion didn't stir. I hesitated before answering it, expecting it to be Artemis exercising her unique marriage counselling technique. It continued ringing. I answered it to hear drunken Kiwi slurs.

'Lana! He-eyyy! Et's Tim! Whatchya up ta?'

'Nothing. I'm bored. Dion's asleep. And, may I add, it's a Saturday night!'

'Come and meet Shane and me for a drink in the cintre then. Now!'

Two hours later, I was there, Jack Daniel's in hand, talking inanely about consciously willing away a sty on my eye using only the power of positive thought. We'd met in a cool Kolonaki hangout known as the Three Pigs. It was the kind of chic establishment that university students frequented by day to drink coffee, and by night to pash one another on plush sofa chairs.

Tim and Shane were well and truly tanked, Shane's angel face flushed, Tim's lids lowered to form mirth-filled slits. They'd been chug-a-lugging since late afternoon and as it neared midnight I did my best to catch up. Post-complimentary shot, Tim shrieked a suggestion.

'Let's go to Sodade!'

'So-*what*?'

'Sodade.'

'What's that?'

'Et's a club. Et's great. You'll love et!'

Tim and Shane swapped quick glances.

Sodade was located in Gazi, a fashionable district with a vast selection of funky restaurants and bars. It had much to offer if you knew where to look, which, obviously, I didn't. Fortunately, Tim and Shane did. We staggered arm in arm down a Gazi street lit by a single streetlight and entered the bar.

Sodade was a moderate-sized establishment pulsing with lithe, sweating bodies. Three walls were exposed brick, the other glass revealing a small outdoor area where only a handful of people congregated. Chandeliers adorned the ceiling. We squeezed our way through to the far end of the dance floor. Scrutinizing the clientele, I made a startling observation.

'Hey! How come there are only men in here?'

My question was naïve and stupid. Tim and Shane looked at each other and sniggered.

'Is this a *gay* bar?'

Their faces broke into wide smiles.

'What-do-*you*-thenk?' Shane asked delightedly, his familiar rapid-fire speech wrapped in a laugh.

And so it was that I'd entered my first Greek gay club. The music was good, the patrons a writhing mass of muscle, hair product and co-ordinated clothing and dance moves. Eyes darted in every direction. Everyone looked beautiful. I looked out of place. Not only was I wearing a skirt, I apparently possessed the wrong genitalia. There was no other woman in sight.

Almost as suddenly as we'd arrived, Shane decided to call it a night. He was drunk and tired. Stupidly, he left Tim and me to it. As soon as he left, the entire club made for us like flies to shit. I felt exceedingly heterosexual and a little bit old. Everyone was in awe of Tim's good looks and the fact that he was being chaperoned by one of his aunties.

Muscular men grappled for a spot within our view and began dancing seductively. A well-groomed tanned Adonis found himself in prime position by Tim's side as his friend distracted me with meaningless chit chat. But from the corner of my eye, I noticed a fuzzy pink tongue had been unfurled and was headed in Tim's general direction. As the tongue honed in on its target, Tim ducked and backed away. I protectively moved towards Adonis, Wielder of All Things Saliva-coated, as though I was a member of Tim's security personnel.

To my surprise, this did nothing to deter Adonis from getting his tongue into any orifice, irrespective of its owner's gender. Shocked, I watched in slow motion as his tongue inched closer, its sights set on doing the lambada with my larynx. I squealed and turned my head, only to find a tongue was also attacking from the opposite direction, extended from the mouth of Adonis' friend. With both tongues on a collision course with my head, I unwittingly became the meat in a proverbial tongue sandwich. I ducked out of the way and pointed to my wedding ring. Both men stopped and smiled politely.

'I'm married!' I squealed.

'We too are marry,' came the cheerful reply.

Lurking in the shadows, Tim chuckled heartily.

I was approached by more men in one night than in my entire pre-Dion life. I'd become quite the novelty. Some lifted me into the air. Some even extracted my telephone number so that we could nurture Hellenic *Will & Grace*–style friendships. By the early morning, I felt more of a gay icon than Madonna, Kylie and Dannii Minogue combined. It took a few days to realise that eliciting my telephone number was merely an elaborate ploy to get to Tim via his married, fag-hag friend.

A new restaurant had opened on Lykavittos, the hill from which Dion and I had overlooked the city of Athens in the first week of our arrival. So much had happened since then, it felt as though I'd lived a thousand lifetimes in the space of three years. I had grown older, more bruised, and in some ways more reckless. Dion too had grown older. The playfulness he'd arrived with had retreated.

The refurbished Lykavittos restaurant was the venue for Dion's work Christmas party. Of the eighty or so staff members in attendance, I knew six. I floated into a sea of strangers with hidden smiles, dark eyes watching me walk across the room. After we were seated at the grown-ups' table, the table of upper management, Dion said he'd be back momentarily. Like an amiable politician he then proceeded to visit every table to give personal holiday wishes to each staff member. I wasn't invited to tag along for the royal greeting. Dion had always maintained that the less his staff knew about us, the better. I was so tired of being anonymous, but sat obediently conversing with a sales manager about sofa cushions.

Soon meals were served and everyone at our table of ten was seated. I sat between Dion and Anna, Yianni beside her, his wide eyes bouncing from person to person. Conversation was in Greek. Two women from the marketing department chatted excitedly. Everyone erupted in laughter. I laughed along, but at what I didn't know. Someone retorted, and the laughter again rang through the room. And so the cycle continued: Greek garble. A second's pause. Vocalised hilarity. Fake laughter inserted by the boss's foreign wife.

After half an hour, I stopped laughing. No one was taking into consideration my linguistic retardation. Why should they have? It wasn't up to them to compromise their native tongue purely for my sake. I excused myself with a plastic smile and headed for the bathroom, laughter trailing behind me, an ocean of eyes from other tables staring after me.

I stood at the mirror and stared at the reflection of someone who didn't belong.

I can't take much more of this.

Just then, the bathroom door swung open and in breezed Anna. She'd come to see if I was okay. For the first time I saw her as a real friend.

'You okay?' she asked, compassion in her eyes.

'Anna, I can't follow the conversation out there. I don't belong here. And I don't just mean here tonight. I mean I don't belong here in Greece.'

'Is okay.' Anna smiled, her arm floating to mine reassuringly. 'You know . . .' She faltered, then continued. 'You know, I think Dion wunts to stay in Ellada. Forever. Thees ees something you must accept.'

I was taken aback.

How did she know that?

'NO! *Forever?* We can't stay forever. We were *never* gonna stay forever. That wasn't the deal. Oh dear God!' A tiny tear broke free from the corner of my eye, diluting black eyeliner.

Anna began laughing, not unkindly. She handed me some tissue and embraced me. I was clumsy in her arms.

'Ees okay!' she cooed reassuringly, stepping back from me. 'Eef you stay stin Ellada, maybe you take a lowver and be better!'

WHAT?

❧ 30 ❧

Promised you a miracle

'Dion, are you having an affair?'

'I swear to you I'm not.'

'Why was that marketing chick sitting at the management table at the Christmas party?'

'What?'

'That twenty-something idiot with the brown hair. She's not management. So why was she sitting at the management table?'

'What is *wrong* with you?'

'WHAT'S WRONG WITH ME? In case you hadn't noticed, Dion, we're facing a little bit of a problem here and I seem to be the only one trying to get to the fucking bottom of it.'

'Well, I'm not having an affair, okay?'

'Okay. But I hate that chick anyway.'

'I'm going upstairs to see Tasos.'

'Bye bye then. Be sure to send him my best. He'll probably think you're referring to an imaginary friend. I'm pretty sure he still hasn't realised I exist.'

As Dion bonded further with Tasos, I turned to Tim and Shane, eventually breaking my silence and conceding that there was indeed something very wrong. Things between Dion and me were slipping and sliding down the s-bend fast.

Thankfully, I had two wonderful and supportive people at my aid. After delicately discerning the severity of the situation, usually the morning after the night before, and usually after playing Kiwi Sharon O'Neil's 'Maxine' on repeat for hours at a time in their living room and singing along at the top of our lungs, the couple invited me to see the New Year in with them in Goa. It sounded like a good idea. I would go to Australia via India, giving Dion some space and the opportunity to miss the hell out of me. We would both have time to get our heads together. Dion was more than happy for me to go. It was an unspoken trial separation of sorts.

At the airport, I told my husband to have a good think about us while I was gone. As I attempted to hug him goodbye, he pulled away and walked out of the terminal.

I was soon in Goa breathing in the hot and spicy scents of vindaloo which did little for my hangover. On New Year's Eve we'd listened to Punjabi MC's smash hit approximately 473 times at an outdoor club-bar-Indian restaurant. Each time the pounding tabla kicked in, holidaying Indians flipped out, their bodies responding with an explosion of limbs. And each time, my in-depth discussions with Shane concerning matters of the heart were interrupted by a nearby body spasm that saw me christened with the contents of my plastic cup. Free-range beach cows, yoga, an ayurvedic consultation, deep conversations with my friends and an Indian full-body massage that incorporated breast manipulation did nothing to alleviate the suffering I felt as a result of my stalling marriage. A week later, crying alone in an airline seat after watching the Black Eyed Peas' 'Shut Up' video on an Air India flight, I was screaming through the air headed for Australia.

Once home, I reflected on the impact that living in Greece had

had on Dion and me. Despite being back on familiar shores, I felt weird and disassociated from those around me and told no one of the strange transition I'd been witnessing in my husband. I visited Katerina and Kostas and listened to Katerina regale me with tales of when she first moved to Australia. Back then, Australia was a developing country, barely aware of the newfangled technology known as 'electricity'. Mail would take months to reach Greece and vice versa. At fifteen, she'd left her mother behind and never saw her again. Her mother had since passed away. I sympathised with her. She told me I had it easy. I shuddered.

My parents and brothers too had no idea that there was trouble in paradise. That is, up until the day my heart was extracted and unceremoniously fed through a meat grinder.

Sitting in my parents' house overlooking my father's tenderly mani-cured garden, I leisurely checked my Hotmail account. My mother sat on a cane sofa behind me. A ceiling fan whirled overhead, barely alleviating the heat of a sultry Sydney afternoon. I saw there was an email from Dion and began reading. As I read through the first paragraph, my heart slam danced into my oesophagus.

Behind me, my mother gabbled.

'You know Nana went shopping for shoes yesterday. You really should visit her soon. She's been asking after you.' Her voice sounded faint, as though coming from another dimension.

'Hold on, Mum. I'm just reading something.' My throat went arid dry. Dion's opening paragraph read thus:

I need you to understand that despite the fact that I would do anything to make you happy, I just don't think I can leave all this behind and come back to Australia any time in the future. In fact I am willing to live here for another ten years.

The email continued:

> *I know what our original plans were and I understand what sacrifices you've made, but I just know that I won't be happy if I go back to Australia. It's also not fair for you to think any more that I will leave Greece if you are no longer able to handle living here. It's a promise that I think I cannot keep. I am sorry, but I don't want to leave.*
>
> *Today I was watching a video you filmed of this little turtle that you found in the yard. You said on the tape something like 'It seems I've made a new friend' in a beautiful sweet voice. It made me realise how lonely you really are here. I started saying to myself, 'I can't believe I have made her go through all this.' If I knew this is how you would be when we left Australia I would have ended our relationship back then. It would have been easier.*
>
> *It's just so hard here for you, not speaking Greek. Living in a place with a different mentality and generally hating being here is all putting a toll on me as well and I don't know how long I will be able to handle it. You've already gone through enough and I can't see you hurt any more. I just want you to be happy.*

My head spun. Ignoring my mother, I walked to the adjoining bathroom and clung desperately to the sink. I thought I was about to collapse or vomit. Or both.

If he'd known how I'd feel about Greece before we left Australia, he'd have ENDED our relationship? What the fuck was THAT supposed to mean?

Dion was breaking up with me. As far as I was concerned, he was choosing that bitch of a country over me. This could *not* be happening.

I gripped the basin, attempting to steady myself. Nobody needed to know about this. I could fix it. I walked around the house doing my best to appear normal. My father approached, his expression questioning.

'What's wrong?'

I doubled over. Shock consumed me. This time I was certain. I was going to be sick.

'Lana?'

'I think Dion's trying to break up with me,' was all I could manage. The look on my father's face shifted to one of horror. My mother entered the room.

'What on earth's going on?'

'I just got an email. Go and take . . .' my voice trailed off as I weakly pointed towards the computer.

My parents assumed the look that only parents can when one of their children is suffering, a mixture of deep concern and unfathomable sorrow. They disappeared into the back room, re-emerging a minute or two later. I sat staring at nothing, motionless.

This surely can't be happening.

We sat together in silence for a while, my father eventually breaking it.

'But at your wedding, he told me he'd look after you . . .'

He looked genuinely confused and beaten. My mother started crying. I started crying. My father soon joined in too. It was the first time I'd ever seen my Dad shed a tear.

I called Dion. I asked him if he was trying to end our marriage. He said maybe . . . he wasn't sure. I asked again if he was having an affair. He promised he absolutely wasn't. I asked him if he was experiencing an early midlife crisis. He said he didn't think so. I asked him if he was gay. He laughed, taken aback and embarrassed. Of *course* he wasn't. So if it wasn't any of the above, then what the hell was it? He said he didn't really know.

The days that followed were a blur. I locked myself in the same bedroom I had awoken in on the morning of our wedding and sat in the dark crying forever. This was *not* happening. My wedding day, so fresh in my mind, replayed over and over.

My brother Andrew visited to try and pacify me. I could barely speak through pain-wracked tears. Nothing anybody could say or do made any difference at all.

I jumped into my mother's car and began driving aimlessly. I turned on the radio. Right on cue, Pete Murray's 'So Beautiful' added to the soundtrack of my life, lamenting a former love so sweet and a sudden change of heart.

I felt bitter and defeated. But then, slowly, I became determined. We'd nut things out, face to face, and get to the bottom of whatever the heck was going on. I'd make every effort possible to assimilate. We'd try counselling, even though it would be weird to attempt conflict resolution when there'd been little conflict between us until now. Had we been a pair of passive aggressive monsters all along? I didn't know. But I did know I was going back to do whatever it took to make our relationship work, even if it ultimately meant seeing out the remainder of my days in Athens. Never before had I left Australia with such determination. And such desperation.

Act III

It would be better for me, should I lose you, to lie dead and buried, for I shall have nothing left to comfort me when you are gone, save only sorrow.

Homer, *The Iliad*

31

Don't give up

Touching down in Athens, I trembled at the prospect of reuniting with my spouse. Spying him frantically smoking beyond the exit gate, it seemed Dion didn't exactly look elated either. I dragged my luggage towards him and stopped for an embrace. It was like hugging a tree stump. Dion was rigid in my arms and there was no reciprocated affection.

'Hi, baby,' I offered feebly, taking his shoulders and searching his eyes.

'Hi.'

He finally smiled sheepishly, like a self-conscious schoolboy. I knew that the situation was as surreal for him as it was for me. As I forced mundane chatter in the car on the way home, the disconnection between us prevailed. And I wondered how someone I'd known so intimately for seven years could suddenly seem so distant. I sensed Dion didn't want to discuss what needed discussing. Regardless, I swan-dived into forbidden waters, experiencing the seconds of panic one feels before breaking the surface.

'Dion, this is tough right now, okay, but our lives are about to change again. But in a good way. We just have to try a little and if we do, everything will be okay.'

'Will they?' Dion stared dead ahead and I understood through his stiff response that he didn't believe it. Not even for one goddamned second. I felt sick to the stomach.

However, the determination I'd gained in Australia stayed strongly with me. I wrote out adaptation plans point by point. I reasoned that if I just made more of an effort to fit in, if I could just pick up this cryptic language, if I could just make more friends, if I could just find volunteer work, if I could just be happier, if I could just try harder, then coupled with Dion clearing his head, everything would be all right.

I'd bought a book on time management in Australia and spent my days typing out passages to help Dion be more constructive at work, thus allowing more free time for us and his male bonding. It was a strange attempt to demonstrate my worth and dedication. As I handed over a small stack of typed-up pages, I explained the method behind my madness.

'I've been thinking work has probably had a lot to do with what's going on right now. So this might help take a bit of pressure off and give you some room to breathe.' With my arms behind my back, I stood and watched him throw a glance over the first page. He shoved the pages into his briefcase.

'Thanks. I'll try and read them later.'

I had a sneaking suspicion they'd never see the light of day again. Over the next week, Dion threw himself so hard into work I feared he'd give himself a concussion. Predictably, reviving our relationship wasn't going to be easy.

For the sake of our marriage, I amplified every effort I'd ever made in the preceding three-and-a-bit years, forcing myself to adjust to a life that didn't exactly resonate with me, accepting a *lifetime* in

Greece if necessary. I found another language teacher and began private lessons again. I also ordered a language CD online and practised Greek in my spare time.

Pou eine to tiri? Where is the cheese? Pou eine to tiri? Where is the cheese? Pou eine to tiri? Where is the cheese? Pou eine to . . .

As my birthday approached, Dion called from work to say he'd organised a surprise trip away. I took this as a wonderful sign! We were soon in cold, grey and rainy Geneva holed up in our hotel room. We spoke about our relationship. Dion said he was having 'serious doubts'. As rain lashed against our window, the words *serious doubts* repeated ad infinitum.

Whatever happened to being sent to look after me?

Whatever happened to walking over hot coals?

Apparently these sentiments had been replaced by *serious doubts*. As I got myself ready to have dinner at an impressive restaurant by the French border, I wondered why Dion had brought me to Geneva in the first place. Was it to try and patch things up, or was it another attempt to dump me? I looked at my reflection in the mirror as I applied my make-up, carefully masking the circles beneath my eyes. The person looking back at me wasn't me at all. The woman who stared back looked positively terrified.

At the restaurant, the activity around us swam in my vision as I tried everything in my power to maintain my composure. But I wasn't feeling right. *Nothing* felt right. The flocked wallpaper seemed sickening, the spatchcock as vile an idea as chewing on a raw, damp pigeon.

'Is everything okay here, madam?' enquired an overly attentive waiter as I played with my food.

Oh dear God. If only you knew how NOT okay everything was.

'Everything's fine, thanks,' Dion replied on my behalf.

My eyes welled with tears.

Serious Doubts.

Another waiter brought wine to the table as another set something alight upon a tray. As hard as I tried to stay strong, I felt myself begin to buckle. How could I be expected to hold it together after Dion's latest proclamation? My focus on his waning smile lost out to a constant re-visitation of those two words. Suddenly my whole body went weak at the same time as the restaurant walls closed in on me.

'I have to get out of here,' I managed breathlessly.

'But we haven't even got through the first course yet,' Dion whispered, alarmed.

'No. You don't understand. I have to leave, like, *right now.*' I threw my napkin on the table and raced for the door, careful not to make eye contact with anyone on the way out. As I stood in the gravel car park in the freezing rain, an unrestrained anxiety now clawed its way through me. Ten minutes later, Dion stood by my side.

'Oh God! Dion, this is embarrassing. I'm so sorry. It's just that this is all so overwhelming . . .'

He put an arm around me and I smelt the leather of his jacket.

'I know. This is hard for both of us.'

'Please don't give up on me, Dion. Don't give up on us. Please! We can make this work. I *know* we can.'

'Do you think so? I'm so confused. Come on. Let's get you out of the cold.'

Geneva didn't turn out to be the place we would come to any kind of resolution. On the contrary, it was in Geneva that I learned that the situation was even more dire than I first thought.

As a symbol of my determination to remain in Greece for all eternity, I decided once and for all to dive headfirst into the Greek way of life. While Dion and I had been invited to countless weddings and christenings over time – elaborate invitations slipping daily from Dion's briefcase – the 'Old Lana' had usually declined, choosing instead to focus on updating her stamp collection. Dion, on the other hand, had often accepted, an arrangement that wasn't exactly in the spirit of togetherness. So when the next christening inevitably rolled around, in light of my determination to become the greatest faux-Greek there ever was, the 'New Improved Lana' agreed to attend. Dion's eyes almost fell out of his head.

'Are you *sure?* You don't have to, you know.' Dion anticipated that I'd find the spectacle tedious and braced himself for my usual insightful observations.

The christening took place in a beautiful church in the suburb of Paleo Faliro. Inside were over a hundred people dressed in their finery. As a priest chanted, parents and godparents, known as *nonos* and *nona,* looked respectful. Clearly, I was playing witness to something important. A naked baby was submerged in a font, re-emerging with a shocked scream. During the ritual, guests chatted above the racket. They walked around, mingled and laughed. This was obviously one of a thousand christenings they'd attended. I was suitably impressed by the casual nature of the affair. As we filed out of the church at the end of the short ceremony, each guest was presented a gift in the form of a small picture frame.

Outside the church, a crowd gathered around the newly christened child who was held firmly in the arms of her beaming, tired mother. A large, elderly woman in a navy blue dress hobbled over for closer inspection. She released a series of obligatory 'aahhhs' from her sagging face, her neck wobbling like the flopping comb on an epileptic rooster's head.

And then out it came: a shower of spray from her mouth that irrigated the gorgeous face of the little creature in question. That's right, she *spat* at the baby. Right in its face. I was outraged.

'Hey! *Did you see that?*

Did *ANYBODY* just see that?

SHE JUST SPAT RIGHT IN THAT BABY'S FACE!!!!'

I pointed a finger accusingly at the startled culprit, convinced I'd just witnessed an open display of child abuse. I could scarcely believe my eyes as everybody averted theirs and backed away from me. The old woman shot me a curious look. As it turned out, I was coming across as an ignorant git. You see, many people from the Middle East to the Mediterranean believe in the evil eye. Apparently, despite its connotations, the evil eye has as much to do with *admiration* as it does the conscious willing of harm. Should somebody admire or envy another, it is safely assumed that the evil eye has been cast, unintentionally or otherwise. Whichever way, the evil eye can bring with it misfortune in the form of physical illness or a particularly unenviable fava bean harvest. Thankfully, a little blue stone that resembles an eye acts as a repellent to such dire consequences. These stones are usually found hanging from rear-view mirrors, or in necklaces and bracelets in handy, easy-to-transport amulet form.

Although prevention is better than cure, if afflicted, human intervention can remove its ill-effects via a secret combination of water, oil, incantations and a series of tricky hand gestures passed down from generation to generation. However, there is another antidote that seems to work particularly well for babies, who are obviously more susceptible to ill-fated admiration than most.

It comes in the form of *spit*!

An admirer who inadvertently casts the evil eye can delicately atomise a baby's face with saliva in order to quash the negative effects of misguided positive thoughts. If the evil eye hasn't been cast via admiration, saliva still generally acts as a force-field against evil. Although I found the very idea to be quite absurd – me, the one who conjured cats – others take such matters much more seriously, not least being elderly, spit-hacking women. I soon bought a cheap evil eye bracelet to ward off any bad vibes headed in my direction. Just in case.

Another step in my Make Greece Work at Any Cost campaign saw me shelve my dignity and take out a personal ad in the *Athens News*, a paper widely read by the expat community. I was determined to increase my circle of friends.

The ad read:

Surely not every expat in Athens
is a boring, beige pant-wearing
septuagenarian? Where are all
the fun, music-loving people?
I'm looking for cool friends.
Weirdos, sickos and bores
need not apply.

I provided an email address for 'applicants'.

Then I waited.

And waited.

Then, slowly but surely, responses from weirdos, sickos and bores began trickling in.

One guy attempted to pass himself off as a woman. He signed off his emails as 'Nicole' despite his email address containing the name 'Nikos'. He wanted us to meet at a nightclub that I suspected might turn out to be a deserted alleyway. He was out.

A 63-year-old divorced American man also made contact. He had nobody to talk to except his daughter, who worked throughout the day. While I felt deep sympathy for him, I couldn't quite picture us discussing The White Stripes at any great length. Hell, call me cliquey, but he was out too.

Another person wrote to me in code. Another in a language I'd never seen before. Others replied in a style that they hoped appeared 'cool': 'I'm hip to the vibe on the slide. Music is life. Crazy!'

They were all out.

Thankfully a sane, potentially fun person finally surfaced – Maria. She was a thirty-year-old Greek Australian from Sydney. She too had almost lost her mind over the course of her seven years in Greece and had taken out a similar ad to mine a year or two before. She now had a little posse that met once a week for coffee. We arranged a meeting.

I arrived right on time, 10 a.m., at Glyfada Starbucks to find a woman in the corner bouncing a baby upon her knee. I prayed that she wasn't Maria. Despite my resolve to create a dazzling new life riddled with acceptance, I reminded myself that I'd still rather French kiss a rattlesnake than join a mothers' group.

Predictably, the woman picked up the baby, approached and introduced herself. She was indeed Maria. Seeing the expression on my face as I looked at the child who was either about to burp or cry, Maria quickly explained that the baby wasn't hers; she was minding her for a friend. I was selfishly relieved.

Maria was of slim build and had glowing olive skin. Her face was framed by a blonde bob haircut. She was friendly, but behind her hazel eyes I sensed there was sadness. Before the others arrived, we got down to the business of getting to know one another.

'When I met my husband, I thought he was a Greek god. Then I married him and discovered he was just a *goddamned Greek*!'

These weren't my words. They were Maria's. She was being

funny and I liked her. Although of Greek parents, Maria was born and had grown up in Australia. She first became formally acquainted with Greece at age twenty-one. Like me, she badly missed our country and explained her feelings by way of the following analogy:

'It's almost like I was an adopted child of a wonderful, loving, affluent couple. I always knew I was adopted, but didn't meet my birth parents until I reached twenty-one. I knew theirs was the blood that coursed through my veins, I saw myself in their faces, but who did I love more? Who were my "real" parents? They were the ones who raised me, loved me and offered me everything my birth parents couldn't.'

'So . . . you're adopted?'

I was a little slow on the uptake.

'No, you wally! *Australia* to me is the loving, adoptive parents that I know and love. I might be Greek, but sometimes I feel a lot more Australian . . .'

As Maria talked on, I learned that transition wasn't always easy for every repatriating Greek. While she'd been labelled a 'wog' growing up in the harshness of Sydney suburbia, in Greece she was still regarded as an outsider. In Australia she was Greek and in Greece she was Australian.

Added to this, Maria had grown up on a strict diet of Greek language, culture and history. Her bedtime stories were romantic tales of her parents' and grandparents' lives. The music piped through her living room was music from postwar Greece. So when she moved to Greece after marrying her Greek-born husband, she discovered an entirely different country from the one she was brought up to believe in, a country riddled with disorganisation and distrust. She began to wonder if her parents and grandparents had embellished things somewhat.

Maria had experienced many hardships in Greece. Her story was not dissimilar to mine. She'd also had a breakdown, and undergone counselling to get back on track. And she had also married a man who didn't recognise the appeal of re-settling in Australia. I started to see that for every few repatriating Greeks who adored Greece, such as Dion, there was one sadly lamenting that fate had returned them to the land of their ancestors.

As I listened to Maria, other women – all in similar situations – joined our table. The coven included Beth, a quick-witted and hilarious American screenplay writer; Tiffany, a British beauty who'd married a hip Greek film director; and Sarah, another Brit, and mother of two. We had all married Greek men. Also, regardless of our religion, we had all married in the Greek Orthodox Church.

We shared stories and discussed the implications of our cross-cultural relationships. It seemed that in one morning, through one silly newspaper advert, I'd gained an instant circle of friends. My spirits soared. We planned to meet sporadically at cafés for coffees, chats and English-written book swaps.

Dion seemed pleased that I'd made some new friends, although the chasm between us remained.

32

Jesus Christ pose

On every calendar in any Greek household, you'll usually find a fat red circle marking the Easter period. It's way bigger than Christmas, bigger than 'name days' that celebrate names shared with saints – heck, it's almost bigger than Jesus Himself. Everything stops as the entire country celebrates harder than at any other time of year.

Our landlords, Tasos and Despina, invited us to spend Easter 2004 with them at their family holiday residence in the Peloponnese, not far from Nafplio. My first impulse was to decline and sashay to safety, but that wasn't the way the new me operated. No, Dion wanted to go and, hey, so did I. We would soon discover that the 'holiday house' the couple mentioned was not the usual fibro shack on a small plot of land used as a weekender. Instead, it was a multi-bedroom construction set on an enormous block of prime coastal real estate, complete with tennis courts, jetty and a landing strip for aircraft. It was amazing. And there we were in such a setting, all mixed up, our marriage crumbling.

We were joined by two of Despina's friends visiting from Germany who were down to earth and quick to laugh. The six of us headed to the island of Spetses on the night of Good Friday, courtesy of a fifteen-minute zip across the sea in a late-night water taxi. En route we inhaled several lungfuls of toxic fumes from the outboard motor and quietly suffocated in the cabin, three of us unsure of what lay ahead.

Alighting, we ambled sheep-like along narrow stone-paved streets caught in a current of people making their way to church. The island was packed. Our goal was to get as close to a church as possible, which turned out to be about a mile away. We stood with the throngs who lined the streets and waited patiently. After a time, a gang of proud, strong Greek men solemnly passed us, carrying an enormous coffin smothered in flowers. This was to symbolise the death of Christ. The men made their way to the sea, where the coffin was lowered into the ocean. A brass band followed playing something slow and funereal. A respectful buzz erupted through the crowd, which then dispersed. This was a night of reflection. On the ride back we sat staring at one another as the outboard motor droned loudly behind us. That night, I slept deeply.

The following day was Megalo Savato, literally 'Big Saturday', and we again made the silent trip over to the island. It was late Saturday night and, according to Despina, we would be celebrating well into Easter Sunday.

The Greek Orthodox amongst us – except for maybe one – were nearing the completion of forty days of fasting, similar to the Catholic Lent period. There would soon be an eating frenzy, considering that most Greeks are very strict in adhering to the restraints leading up to this time, particularly elders. They abstain from dairy products, olive oil, eggs, wine, meat and, for that matter, any food with blood in it. This is said to keep carnal desires at bay and humble the mind. Likewise, the youth of Greece adhere to such practises, perhaps also happy to benefit from a spiritually enforced weight loss program. The Germans, Dion and I had adhered to nothing.

Once again Spetses was at risk of sinking beneath the weight of the thousands of people who packed the streets. I convinced myself I could hear abstainers thinking carnivorous thoughts concerning gnawing on animal carcasses. The atmosphere was positively electric, fizzling with expectancy. Again, we attempted to make our way to the church and again we found ourselves almost on the other side of the island. This time around, we were heading for something known as the candle-lighting ceremony. We wedged ourselves between milling hordes and at the stroke of midnight excitement crackled through the crowd as everyone began fiercely celebrating the resurrection of Christ.

People began double-cheek kissing with all their might. 'Christos Anesti! CHRISTOS ANESTI!' they all cried.

'What's that mean?' I asked our German friends. They both looked at me, eyebrows raised.

'Oh, sorry! Dion . . . what's Christo Zanetti mean?'

'It's Christos Anesti! Christ is risen. It's like saying Happy Easter,' he replied. 'Christos Anesti! . . . Now, you say in return "Alithos Anesti!" or "Alithos O Kyrios!" He is indeed risen!'

'Christo Zanetti!' I exclaimed like a first-grader with learning disabilities.

Tasos pushed his way closer to Dion and gently handed him two unlit candles. Dion passed one to me as Tasos, his not-so-secret admirer, began tenderly lighting Dion's from another. What I was witnessing was the lighting of candles from what is known as the Eternal Flame, which may or may not have been the inspiration behind The Bangles' hit of the same name back in 1988. It is said that all Orthodox Easter candles are lit by the one flame that originates in Jerusalem. Each year, the flame is transported from Jerusalem to Athens by aircraft. Orthodox priests converge on the airport en masse on Easter Saturday armed with lanterns that are lit by the flame in preparation for illuminating the entire country, an incredible concept. So as we stood lighting our candles, the same ritual was being carried out on every island and in every Greek province. As I looked around Spetses, I could see hundreds of tiny flames flickering and dancing in what appeared to be a fairy wonderland.

Despina told me that once my candle was lit, the objective was to get it home without it going out. Tradition says that upon re-entering the family home with candle in hand, the smoke from the candle leaves its mark on the doorframe, thus bringing the spirit of the Resurrection into the home. Mine, of course, snuffed out within microseconds.

'What's it mean if it goes out?' I whispered, concerned.

'Don't worry. You light again,' offered Despina before briskly removing her person from the presence of the anti-Christ.

I re-lit mine from Dion's candle. It went out again despite the unwavering concentration that I now devoted to it. I looked around to see if anybody else was having the same problem. They weren't. I obviously wasn't 'down' with the technique.

We inched towards a restaurant, passing two children cracking the tips of red-dyed boiled eggs in a type of competition similar to breaking a wishbone. Whoever did the most damage to the other's egg 'won'. Fireworks erupted, along with what sounded like shotgun fire. Everyone was definitely stoked that the Lord had risen.

At the restaurant, the six of us sat together to eat octopus with macaroni and sip on *mageiritsa* soup traditionally made from lambs' tongue, lungs, liver and intestines. I tried to force my unique personality upon the unsuspecting Germans and, to my surprise, they reacted favourably.

'You know, I could really do with some lamb's intestine right about now.'

God help them, the silly buggers laughed. So of course I was unstoppable.

'Food! Food! Food!' I began chanting, banging my cutlery against the table. They joined in less boisterously while I turned it up a notch.

'Lung! Lung! Lung! TONGUE! TONGUE! TONGUE!'

I couldn't shut up. I grabbed Dion's candle and waved it in the air with one hand, while pointing to it with the other and singing: 'Is this burn-in', an eternal FLAAAME?' I warbled through quivering lips, swaying even more enthusiastically than a *Young Talent Time* contestant.

Tasos cocked his head as a dog might upon registering a sound undetectable to human ears. He knew he was hearing *something*, but clearly didn't know what it was. Dion looked around, pretending my disrespect and cultural inaptitude weren't making themselves so obvious. But, to my surprise, it was Despina who cut me short. She simply talked over me. Naturally, she wanted me to shut the fuck up. She wanted her friends to enjoy a Greek Easter, not an idiot Australian's dubious stand-up comedy routine. So I shut up, and digested lambs' innards in sulky silence.

On our way back to the house, I was distracted every step of the way by a lighter that refused to work as I tried to cheat my way back into the Eternal Flame's favour. Five candles flickered gaily in our water-taxi cabin, illuminating happy faces. I sat brooding in silence.

The following day, the hills were alive. Right on cue, the landscape around us abounded with the saturated colour of wildflowers that had erupted everywhere, blanketing hillsides and complementing a brilliant blue sky. It really looked as though Greece was reawakening after a long, cold winter. I contemplated this as I silently ate spit-roasted lamb and sipped on heavy red wine supplied by the Germans. In the true spirit of Easter, I continued to have the shits after being smacked the night before. Dion left me to it.

As we drove from Tasos' luxury holiday paradise, I began reflecting on my situation. It was obvious that Dion felt more at home with Greek tradition than I did and that this continued to be a part of our problem. And it was beyond obvious that I still didn't exactly click with Tasos and Despina. I remained a fish out of water. I was away from my own. And this was *hard*. I choked on an unexpected sob. Dion couldn't offer any consolation – he simply didn't understand me and had seen me cry too many times. I was doing very little for our cause, and Dion was growing very, very tired.

I hated myself for the outburst and tried to pull myself together, quietly hoping that Greece coming to life around me might also symbolise the resurrection of a certain marriage.

As a further step in creating an Exciting New Life in Greece – a campaign that came complete with its ten-year plan – I began discussing with my Kiwi counterpart, Tim, the possibility of exploring more of Greece together during the week. He was more than up for it. After throwing a dart at the map, we chose to visit a place called Delphi, 180 kilometres from Athens.

Driving in Shane's big, fat four-wheel drive, we left Athens in pursuit of rolling hills and crisp, fresh air. The car transported three explorers in total: the brave and robust 22-year-old New Zealander Tim; an adventurous 21-year-old Australian acquaintance of Tim's, Nikki; and myself, playing the role of judicious, thirty-something chaperone.

The catchphrase of our journey north quickly became:
'SPRING BREAK! WOO-HOO!'

This was shrieked in fake American accents at sheep, passing trucks, startled birds, flower-blanketed hillsides and at nothing in particular. It was destined to be an amazingly cultural experience. After a couple of hours discussing *Golden Girls* re-runs and cosmetic tattooing, we arrived at a town called Arachova, a popular winter destination just before Delphi. It was a lovely place set at a high altitude overlooking a rocky landscape. Shops along the main drag sold huge sheepskin rugs, cowhide, locally made cheeses, honey, deli meats and ouzo. We found a room high above an Arachova precipice with three single beds, a tiny balcony with enough room to fit one third of a small child, and an even tinier bathroom. It was basic, but had a grand view. After checking in and dumping our bags, we drove on to Delphi, a few kilometres further along a winding, mountainside road.

Delphi is renowned for playing host to an ancient oracle. Primordial Greeks with questions pertaining to life direction and matters of spiritual consequence would bow before high priestesses who channelled wisdom from the gods themselves. Whether this was achieved through clever bullshit, divine intervention, vapours from the ground inducing trance-like states or hallucinogenic drugs remains debatable.

Delphi was not the only place in Greece where such phenomena occurred in ancient times, but the reason behind its particular significance is that Delphi was considered to be the very centre of the world. A rubble of ancient ruins nests beautifully against the southern slopes of Mount Parnassos, a perfect setting to pose questions to the divine. We posed questions of our own.

'What should we do tonight, oh ancient ones?'

We heard the unmistakable whispers of the early oracles. 'Get pissed? SPRING BREAK! WOO-HOO!'

And so with the blessings of the gods themselves, we proceeded to appease the ancient ones.

That night we hit the bars of Arachova. Being a seasoned profes-sional in the ways of Greek alcohol consumption, I warned Nikki of the dangers of getting shit-faced in Greece.

'They make drinks *extremely* strong in this country. I've seen non-Greeks come undone in my time. Not Tim or me, of course.'

Tim nodded in agreement, catching his reflection for a split sec-ond in the floor-to-ceiling windows. In that moment I could tell he was thinking more about whether Catherine Zeta Jones really loved Michael Douglas. I continued, 'I mean, I've *never* passed out on a pineapple or been dragged across Tim's living room unconscious before. But you really have to be careful, okay?'

With this wisdom safely imparted, I felt sage-like. Nikki, pale, thin and with long red hair, looked wide-eyed and respectful, but said nothing. Instead, she began sharing tales of her new job work-ing in a London sex shop.

We later found ourselves in a nightclub with a stupid name like 'Jokers' or 'Mysteries'. On a Tuesday night, it was packed with thirteen-year-old Greek kids visiting Delphi on a school excursion. Little boys were propped up on bar stools like old men, sensibly sipping beers with hands on hips. Cut to the same situation in Australia and you'd have drinking competitions, brawling, spewing, crying, and kids passed out in locked toilet cubicles. The nightclub would be shut down and the bar owners imprisoned. But not so in Greece.

I watched Nikki zigzag back from the bar with a tray, precari-ously balancing a variety of drinks.

'LOOK! THEY JUST GAVE US FREE SHOTS! THEY'RE SO *NICE* HERE. WOO-HOO! BRING-SPRAKE! WHO WANTS TO DANCE?'

She set the drinks down, spilling most of them, threw down a shot and began wobbling around the table. I gathered she was trying to dance. I glanced at the young, sober adolescents at the bar and then back at Nikki. Something wasn't right. Seconds later, her stomach contents introduced themselves to the floor.

The next morning, Nikki wasn't feeling so good. In fact, she confessed it was the worst she'd ever felt in her entire life. Lying on the backseat of the 4x4, her forearm draped sorrowfully across her forehead, she apologised several times a minute before eventually passing out.

'Sorry . . . Sorry . . . Sorry . . . Sorr—'

Tim eventually broke the news.

'I didn't wanna tell you this unless et was a certainty.'

He sounded different, less comical. I knew something ominous was coming. I held tightly to the steering wheel.

'Um . . . I'm not quite sure how to break this to you, but . . . Shane's been offered a job in Paris.'

The car engine roared beneath the sounds of New Zealand's Bic Runga on the CD player.

I tried to sound pleased.

'Wow! Really? That's great! Is he going to take it?'

'Yis. He's accepting today.'

I felt sick.

'Oh. Right. When will you leave? Six months? A year? In ten years like us?' I joked.

'More like a month.'

Tim looked out of the passenger window. I bit the inside of my mouth.

Spring Break. Woo-hoo.

When I told Dion of Tim and Shane's imminent departure, he scoffed.

'They won't go!'

'What are you talking about? Shane's already sorted things out with his company. They're going!'

'No they're not.'

'I love your optimism, but some might be forgiven for calling it denial, Dion. Look, can I ask you something? Can we go away, just for a weekend? I really think we need to take ourselves out of the picture for a while and think.'

I thought Dion's grip on the city that Tim and Shane were flee-ing could do with some loosening. Just a fraction. Perhaps if he viewed the place from a different perspective, we could both begin to relax a little. I suggested a long weekend in Malta. Despite my prodding over the years, Dion had shown no interest in visiting my mother's country of origin. On this occasion, though, he surprised me by agreeing.

I telephoned my mother to tell her the good news and gave her a progress report on our relationship, which I optimistically rated as 'hopeful'. My parents remained steadfast in their belief that our marriage was salvageable. Mum asked if we intended to drop in on our relatives. I wasn't sure, but once we'd landed in Malta I shared the idea with Dion. In view of current circumstances, he was reluctant. I asked him if he thought such an attitude was fair considering the hours I'd put in with Nota and Nikos. He said it was different. I asked him how. He said he didn't want to get into it. But I did. So I provoked an argument for the hell of it.

Later that afternoon, as Dion slept, I took a walk to Sliema to find the Church of St Gregory where my mother and her siblings used to giggle behind hands held in prayer. Attempting to retrace the steps I'd taken with my parents, I became hopelessly lost and asked locals for directions, eventually bumping into a friendly old woman who offered to walk me all the way to the church. As she hobbled alongside me, it turned out she knew my grandmother. I felt safe with her and as though I somehow belonged, walking the same pathways as those who shared my blood. As I watched passing people's mannerisms, expressions and features, again more pieces of the puzzle fell into place. A part of this culture made up a part of me.

This must be how it feels for Dion in Greece.

I entered the church and sensed the ghosts of ancestors surrounding me. And I prayed as hard as I could. I prayed to the Holy Trinity, my guides, angels, saints and my deceased relatives. I'd never prayed so hard before in my life.

Please, please, PLEASE help me save my marriage and get my husband back.

I entered what felt like an altered state.

It's time to let go.

NO!

I walked back to the hotel, distraught.

Back in our room, Dion confessed that he didn't love me any more.

In Athens, despite enormous protestation from Dion, we eventually began seeing a counsellor. We turned to Kristie, the woman who had helped bring me back to life a couple of years before. As always, she was empathic and, being a Greek–Brit, she had an understanding of Dion's cultural affinity for Greece as well as an understanding of my fragile make-up.

One afternoon she ended a session with startling honesty. She said that sometimes people simply had to prepare themselves for an ultimate break-up. I didn't want to hear it. Dion was glad to have an excuse to stop seeing her. So our sessions ended then and there.

Welcome to my nightmare

Johnnie Jackie Holliday – he of all things rock – grew up in both Athens and New York. His Greek parents had emigrated to the United States before he was born and he'd spent much of his life alternating between the two countries. For a large chunk of his childhood in Greece, a kindly uncle and aunt – and presumably a pack of she-wolves – raised little Johnnie while his parents remained in the States to earn their fortunes. Returning to the USA for most of his adolescence, Johnnie spent his teens running around the Big Apple while tattooed versions of rock album sleeves gradually materialised on his upper arms.

Haunting places like New York City's Waverly and Eighth Street Playhouse, the Mudd Club, Max's Kansas City and Studio 54, a disenchanted Johnnie felt it essential to dress up and parade around town like a queen, despite his staunch heterosexuality. Like every freak in New York at the time, he wore high heels and celebrated the era of glam. His natural evolution was to become a rock star in his own right.

By the mid-eighties, Johnnie was flitting between New York and LA fronting a rocking outfit known as Star Star. They wrote songs about go-go sleaze, whores and Johnnie's penis. Star Star had some success and, despite settling in Athens at thirty-four, Johnnie wasn't about to lose momentum. At forty-two, he rocked harder than Megadeth. He lived for his music. He lived for his band. And he lived for the moment. His band occasionally played around Athens and Johnnie was more than content with his lot in life.

After several months of intermittent email correspondence, an electronic flyer appeared in my inbox advertising a club where Johnnie was soon to DJ. I called Tim. I decided it was his responsibility to ensure a friendship-handover took place before he departed for Paris and that he was obliged to accompany me to the club. He agreed to join me – not that he had a choice.

Dion opted to stay home and rearrange his sock drawer.

Tim and I met at his Skoufa Street apartment to quaff a few well-placed drinks before venturing into the night. We were headed for a club called Texas in the bohemian suburb of Exarhia. Numbed by absinthe, we wandered in the chilled night air through mostly deserted streets, which reminded us that it was pushing midnight on a Sunday.

I was nervous, Tim was relaxed. I hoped I was about to meet my New Best Friend. Tim didn't give a shit. He was thirsty.

My pointless banter echoed off the surrounding buildings as we made our way down the darkened street of Ippokratous. The empty road was lined with cracked pavements, a few dumpsters, dull retail façades and an empty late-night café. The only sign of life came in the form of a moulting stray dog that trotted past. I counted down the numbers on each building until we reached our destination: a tiny little club with two amber lights glowing outside. Only a couple of subtly placed event posters hinted that we were not about to enter a swingers' club or an establishment in which people engaged in ancient pagan sacrifice.

I entered with enormous trepidation. Tim simply entered.

Three paces inside, we collided with the bar. The place was minuscule, with a capacity for around eighty punters. Ten people were already in attendance. They were all rockers. The lighting was low. The air was thick with cigarette smoke and the acrid odour of a thousand spilled drinks. The sound of wailing guitars rattled the bottles and glasses that lined the bar.

I turned to face a large wooden DJ booth opposite a never-used square-metre 'dance floor'. Housed within the booth was someone who I could only presume was either Johnnie Holliday or an extra from the *Rocky Horror Picture Show* lost on his way to a T-Rex concert after being crash tackled by Beavis and Butt-Head.

The guy wore a purple crushed-velvet shirt with rolled-up sleeves. His ears, nose, throat and wrists dripped with silver jewellery, each piece ultimately twisting to depict a skull or some other vague representation of horror. Beneath his wrist jewellery were homemade elbow-length black fingerless gloves fashioned out of women's pantyhose. Perched atop his head was an oversized tartan Oliver Twist cap. Strangely, I was bothered only by the hat. My time in Athens had become so eye-clawingly sterile that seeing such an open display of individualism was thoroughly refreshing.

Judas Priest's 'Sentinel' began pulsing through throbbing speakers. In between sips of beer from a dark green Mythos beer bottle, the DJ peered through dark, kohl-lined eyes. He took in all he presided over, his eyes glinting like those of a bird of prey. For a split second, our eyes met. Priest continued to assault our senses, the music shifting from haunting bridge to high-gear heavy-metal overdrive, and the DJ began writhing from side to side, laughing a little to himself. I turned back to Tim, my expression confused.

Tim by this point had ordered drinks that were more than likely manufactured in a moonshine distillery.

'Do you reckon that's Johnnie?' I asked, excited by the prospect of meeting a rock'n'roll cohort, disappointed by the hat.

'Yeah, maybe.'

Tim turned back to face the bar staff. He didn't care if it was Johnnie or not. His only concerns were having a drink and moving to Paris.

The Cult's 'Fire Woman' kicked off as I took in our fellow patrons. There were two small groups of long-haired males gathered at tiny tables, all clad in scruffy black T-shirts and jeans. As I scrutinised one group, a guy began playing air guitar. I inwardly smirked. Just beyond the air guitarist, I noticed two girls wearing matching black leather miniskirts, fishnet tops and black CFM boots. Modelled on a Lita Ford prototype, they looked like metal wenches, albeit Greek versions of same.

'What do you thenk of Anna Nicole Smeth's recent weight loss?' interrupted Tim. In this setting, tabloid gossip seemed slightly out of place. I was going to miss this guy more than he'd ever understand.

'Don't you thenk she looks great? I mean, honestly, she looks a mellion bucks.'

'Yeah, she does. Hey should I find out if that's Johnnie?'

'Maybe. But what do you thenk of Botox? I love et. Would you ever get et done? I heard you can get et done to stop perspiration . . . I can't *wait* to get plastic surgery!'

'Tim! You're twenty-two and *flawless*.'

I turned to notice the DJ had writhed all the way out of his booth. His eyes were fixed on the toilets in the far corner. Like every other male on the premises – except Tim who wore olive pants and a bright purple T-shirt – the DJ wore tight black jeans. On his feet were a pair of Herman Munster stack-heeled boots.

I saw my chance. Deserting Tim mid-sentence, on the words, 'beauty perfection', I made for the creature lurching across the floor. Catching up to him, I softly tugged at his crushed-velvet sleeve. Like an animal tranquillised, he turned slowly, his eyes rolling back in his head.

'Johnnie Holliday? Is that you?' I asked.

'Yeah, man. I'm Johnnie.'

'I'm Lana. Lana Penrose. The girl that hasn't been email stalking you!'

At once, the expression of the beast softened, his mouth curling into a smile. His skin was clear, his dark eyes bright and happy.

'No frickin' *way*, man! Lana Penrose! Is that really you? I can't believe it. How cool. I can't believe you came! How are you? I'm *so* drunk!'

And so the deed was done. I'd scored myself a new friend. Just like that.

Dion gave little outward signs of what he was feeling. He'd become cold. I'd become petrified.

Only once did I catch a glimpse of the old Dion. He arrived home one night and told me he'd heard Queen's 'Under Pressure' on the radio and that it had moved him to tears. He left it at that. So I studied the lyrics in earnest, scouring for a clue. The very title of the song spoke volumes. Under Pressure. Weren't we just. However, my fast-evaporating husband remained adamant that we wouldn't return to Kristie for counselling. I'd pre-empted such reluctance and, cunningly, Plan B was already in place. I'd heard of an exceptional Dutch psychologist who, unbelievably, lived only a minute up the road from us in remote Lagonisi. She was already on standby. I suggested to Dion that we give her a try. Foiled, Dion caved. Our new therapist's name was Michella.

Therapy with Michella took place in a spare room of her Lagonisi home, with an enormous, damp half dog/half horse panting in the corner. We were high up on a hill that provided a view of the ocean – a lovely setting to expose our hearts and have them shredded with the psychological equivalent of a cheese grater.

Michella went to great pains to learn our story from start to finish, from every perspective. She saw Dion alone, me alone and then brought us together. We got to the heart of how Dion's actions had affected me and vice versa, and we delved headfirst into analysing our own behaviour. Unfortunately, through no fault of Michella's there were to be no great revelations.

To underscore just how much of a breakthrough we *weren't* making, Dion disappeared one afternoon only to return a couple of hours later with a kayak under his arm. As in a kayak for one. In between helicopter lessons, he took to disappearing for hours on end, floating about the Aegean like a jubilant beetle upon a bright yellow leaf as I floated about our Lagonisi home like a lost soul.

In Vouliagmeni, which neighbours Voula, lies a beautiful natural wonder known as Vouliagmeni Limni, or Lake Vouliagmeni. Across the main road from a beach, the mineral-enriched lake is replenished by hot springs and is set at the bottom of a small cliff face. It is known for its healing properties for the skin, bones and muscles, and even for gynaecological problems. In light of the former, it was the perfect location to see off our Shane.

Dion and I met Tim and Shane on a Sunday afternoon in June. We lay upon beach chairs, our tanned bodies shaded by umbrellas as we gobbled on toasted cheese sandwiches. Tubby pensioners bobbed about in the water joyfully yelling to one another as they rejuvenated. Later that day, Shane would be jetting off to Paris to begin a new job and a new life. Despite being stabbed in the arse a week earlier by two thieves in the National Gardens, he was in high spirits. The stabbing marked the end of an era.

Tim would be hanging around for a little longer. But this was to be our last get together – all four of us – possibly forever. As I hugged Shane goodbye, my heart felt heavy. The departure of my friends was becoming a reality. It hit me with all the force of a juggernaut.

Of course, my sadness wasn't only about my friends fading away. All traces of the old Dion had practically vanished and he would not feel the loss of these people as I would. I wondered if he'd even feel the loss of me. I began hinting that this was a possibility while continuing a resuscitation program on our relationship.

'You know if you keep pushing me away, you could very well succeed. Have you stopped to think about that?'

From his lack of response, I got the distinct impression that that was the general idea.

So I tried kindness, anger, love, reminiscing, cooking, talking, reasoning and seduction, all in the hope of getting through to him. But nothing worked. As he slept at night, I'd lie beside him in bed, my head propped up by my hand, and stare at him. I'd whisper, 'What's happening to you? Don't you know I love you?' And at times the pain would prove unbearable. I'd creep outside in my nightwear and step up to the edge of the Aegean. As small waves smacked against the rocks, I'd wail at the sea like a tormented banshee, wracked by melancholy. I'd be lying if I said the thought of throwing myself in didn't cross my mind.

My ally was gone. In his place was a man I no longer recognised, a man who had become a stranger to me. After almost a year of trying everything to make our relationship work, I knew something had to give. I couldn't hold on for much longer.

Another Saturday rolled around and Dion disappeared with

Tasos to have coffee in a nearby café. I took the kayak down to the water and pushed my physicality to its limits, paddling until every muscle in my arms and stomach ached, pushing forward, trying to escape the pain. Tears streamed down my face, tears of grief and frustration. Sliding fast across the deep blue, I aimed for an uninhabited island towards the horizon. It was one I'd often gazed upon from our living room. If only I could row to it, beyond it. My muscles burned. As the kayak inched closer, my mouth became dry and the sun baked salt on my face and body. With each painful stroke, a decision became clearer. I had to escape.

34

It's raining men

I needed to get away from Lagonisi, away from Athens and away from Dion. I wanted to be close to Tim. He was my fast-disappearing wisp of support and it was only a matter of days until he moved to France. He'd hung back to finish packing up the Skoufa Street apartment – and to end his time in Greece with a bang, we were off to visit the infamous party island of Mykonos.

Waiting at Athens airport we grazed on a variety of salads, Tim estimating our caloric intake and revealing in profound detail what effect each piece of vegetation would have on our respective complexions and internal organs. Suddenly we were being paged over the public address system. We looked at one another, our mouths forming o's. *Shit!* We'd completely missed our boarding call.

We made a mad dash for our gate, dodging backpacks and travellers, all the while laughing at our own sweet stupidity. As we rounded a corner, women in sky-blue airline uniforms flapped their arms at us while barking urgently into walkie-talkies. A small car screeched to a halt on the tarmac outside the terminal building. We scrambled inside and found ourselves being chauffeured to our aircraft. Rather pleased with the arrangement, we relaxed into the leather upholstery feeling supremely smug. As we boarded the plane, however, our self-satisfaction was quickly overtaken by remorse. Our fellow passengers glared at us for delaying their flight. Sheepishly, we slunk to our seats with heads hung low, exchanging quick, guilty smirks.

Behind us, we listened to an older American woman quack away at her husband, 'Where are we going? Mike-a-nos? What's Mike-a-nos? What's Mike-a-nos all about, Claude?'

Thanks to her the half-hour flight seemed like an eternity. She was our karma.

Mykonos is the smallest, yet most famous island of the Cyclades group. Some would like to say it's renowned for its rich history and natural beauty, but if we're all honest, it's really famous for being an irresistible magnet to Italians, German nudists and homosexuals.

According to Greek mythology, Mykonos was created when Hercules hurled a bunch of giants into the sea. As Tim and I entered the town, Hora, taking in landmark windmills, we were pleased to see that Mykonos continued to crawl with those of Herculean proportions. We sat by the port watching buff bodies wander by and ate gloriously disgusting chocolate-filled crepes, our bellies napping lazily on our laps. Once again Tim agonised over every calorie, this time fraught with dismay.

As night fell, we scurried around whitewashed streets passing various *plateias*, modern restaurants, cafés, upmarket tourist shops and funky bars. The place had so much more to offer than I'd expected, and once again I marvelled over the diversity of Greece. We became lost in labyrinths, retracing steps, discovering new things at every turn. Eventually we stumbled upon Little Venice at the southwestern end of the port and settled into a stylish bar. Colourful lanterns decorated each table, creating beautiful reflections in the water as we discussed Tim's sleep paralysis disorder. Was he suffering a psychic, astral attack (as I believed) or was there a logical scientific explanation for it all (as he believed)? We didn't quite reach a conclusion, but that night, back in our humble room overlooking the town, I lay frozen with fear as Tim, unconscious, described in great detail a man dressed in a lime-green suit grinning at us from the corner of the room.

The following morning we hired a moped. Doubled by Tim, I played biker's moll, passing kilometre after kilometre of aridness on our way to one of the island's world-famous beaches. The occasional cluster of modest, box-like concrete houses glossed with white was the only interruption to the sparse scenery. After collecting a variety of deceased insects in the corners of my eyes, we eventually reached Paradise Beach or Kalamopodi. We made for a couple of sun beds and an umbrella as I marvelled over what appeared to be sand, but was actually ground pebble that was slightly painful to walk on. However, the water was crystal clear and soothing. I tiptoed over, relieved my feet, turned, gasped, squealed, then laughed, for we were surrounded by . . . wall-to-wall *exposed penises*. There were old penises, youthful penises; small, fat and large penises; tanned penises and lily-white ones. I was in penis paradise and I wasn't at all prepared for it.

'Tim!! Ohmygod! We're surrounded by *cocks*!!'

Tim retorted with a laugh. 'I know, Pinrose. But not iveryone's gitting ento the speret of thengs. Check her out. And I'm not gittin' my kit off around you either, you dirty perve.'

Tim made a covert gesture towards a couple directly across from us. An aging German man lounged all over his sun-bed, his penis limply sunning itself on his upper thigh, while his wife sat beside him neatly dressed in a safari suit.

'I'm with her. I'm not getting my flesh out with you around either, sicko.'

Our giggles were drowned out by over-powering beats. I looked over my shoulder to spy two Scandinavian girls dancing on a wall behind us dressed in what appeared to be tinfoil mini dresses. They shook and shimmied in their high-heeled boots under a blazing sun like a couple of oven-baked street whores. It was their job to go through this daily ritual in an attempt to entice patrons into the nearby bar that had a swimming pool at its nucleus. It kind of worked. As the sun began to set, people flocked to it, mostly of the Italian tanned-cock variety.

We headed back to town like a couple of uneasy riders on our silly little moped and got ourselves tarted up for a night on the town. By midnight we were in a club throwing back drinks in our usual style and I was back to being the gay magnet I'd always been. Practically every gay man on the island felt compelled to dance with the fascinating fag hag. Even a heterosexual Greek male resembling a bulldog spent a large proportion of the evening dancing hard in my face.

As the sun began to rise, Tim and I painfully ascended the stairs to our room. Drunk, I lay in bed wondering why it was that strangers appeared to have more admiration for me than my own husband. Tim, asleep, displayed yet another aspect of his sleeping disorder by attempting to climb the walls, slurp on bottles of water, and scream and point at things that weren't actually there.

In my inbox one day I discovered another electronic flyer sent by Johnnie Holliday. I hadn't seen him since our first meeting a couple of months earlier, but we'd emailed one another occasionally and spoken on the telephone twice. Reading the flyer, I saw that legendary shock rocker Alice Cooper was playing a one-off performance in Athens. Star Star was the support act. I almost wet myself, not only because I was a closet Alice Cooper fan, 'Cold Ethyl' – a necrophiliac love song – being the first single I'd owned as a child, but because a live rock act was passing through town. After a flurry of emails filled with exclamation marks, Johnnie invited me to tag along with a posse of his friends. I was *so* there.

The gig was just after Tim was due to depart for Paris. I used every type of enticement to try to persuade him to stay just a couple of days longer, including emotional blackmail and bribery, but he flatly declined. It seemed that the 22-year-old Kiwi pop and dance prince preferred a new life in Paris – or even permanent facial disfigurement – to watching an old man in make-up snake around the stage with a top hat and cane.

I also invited Dion. He was even less interested than Tim.

I was on my own.

The day I'd been dreading finally dawned – my Best Friend's last day in Athens. It was sunny and warm and we hurled friendly abuse at one another as though it were just another day.

'Hey, Tim? It must suck being a New Zealander. Do you want to talk about it at all?'

'Pinrose, if I were an Australian, I'd dunk my head in a bucket of water three times and breng et up twice. And while we're on heads, you really shouldn't rule out Botox.'

We splashed about in the ocean for the last time, Tim discussing the pros and cons of breast enlargement in between disappearing beneath the water's glassy surface. I couldn't believe he was leaving. He'd become like another brother to me, or, rather, the sister I never had.

As the day wore on, I handed him a CD compilation I'd made commemorating our time together. It closed with Jeff Buckley's 'Last Goodbye', the most poignant line concerning giving another person more to live for than they'd ever know. It was true. Tim had given me more to live for than he ever knew. Before him, I was essentially alone, my soul half-dead. But we laughed at other lyrics that suggested an end to a relationship. Of course our friendship wasn't over . . . was it?

We jumped into my dusty grey Hyundai Accent for the last time and headed to the airport through sparsely populated neighbourhoods, sparring verbally all the way. At the airport terminal, we embraced awkwardly, just as we'd done at our very first meeting. We didn't really know what to say.

'I'll miss you, you know.'

'I'll mess you too.'

Tim headed for the gate. I headed towards my car, blinded by tears he'd never see.

On the drive back to an empty house, I wailed like a child plunged into a font of chilly water at a Greek christening, reminiscing over the hours dedicated to discussing physical aesthetics, alcohol and matters of the heart, remembering the hilarity and, most of all, the greatest companionship I could ever have hoped for.

How could I possibly be expected to survive Athens for the next decade without my Best Friend Tim?

For those about to rock

I stared into the mirror at great length, observing myself from a variety of angles.

My foundation isn't pale enough, godammit.

If I just lightly dust my face with talcum powder . . .

If I just go another round with the eyeliner . . .

I sniffed beneath an armpit and made a mental note to purchase a stronger antiperspirant.

The day of the Alice Cooper concert had arrived, and by midafternoon I'd already commenced the drawn-out process of vamping myself up. With Tim gone, I was grateful for the distraction. I shaded the lids of my eyes with black eye shadow and threw on a pair of black jeans, a black top and black pointy boots. I was mourning my Ex-Best Friend and back in black for Alice.

Following instructions, I made my way to Syngrou Avenue and gave Johnnie a call from my mobile. He directed me to wait for him outside a Goody's burger restaurant. It was to be only our second meeting. I wasn't exactly nervous, but certainly had reservations about fraternising with a relative stranger. The fact that I was transitioning from a homo friendship with Tim to a hetero one with Johnnie wasn't lost on me. What if this particular Holliday gave me just one day out of life that I'd live to regret? It was a risk I decided to take.

It was an extraordinarily hot day. People plodded about the streets in humidity-induced slow motion. Sweat beads formed above my upper lip. My black clothing absorbed the heat, my blood simmered; it was pushing 40 degrees Celsius.

I knew I'd spot Johnnie well before he spotted me. For a start, he'd admitted he'd forgotten what I looked like. I took this as a great compliment and told him to look out for a woman in all-white. I could barely contain the delight over my trickery, desperate to witness a tattooed freak approaching overheated women in white, asking them if they were ready to rock. But, alas, my plan failed. Before I could duck behind the sweltering living dead, Johnnie appeared, his dark eyes at once upon me. Unperturbed, he laboriously made his way over, my joke evaporating unacknowledged. As he neared, I made two observations. Firstly, Johnnie was limping. Secondly, in the blazing heat he wore a long-sleeved shirt, a heavy denim jacket, a pair of jeans, platform boots and – there it was again – that fucking hat. Sweat trickled from every pore, absorbed by thick denim. I'd never before contemplated how difficult it must be for Athenian rockers to survive a Greek summer.

'Heyyyy!' he greeted, squelching a path towards me.

'Hey, Johnnie. Are you ready to rock?' I made a quick succession of devil signals with both hands.

We hailed a taxi and were on our way to the outdoor venue of Theatro Petras. On the way, I tactfully broached the subject of Johnnie's limp.

'Hey, how come you limp?' I asked.

Johnnie began telling his story.

One of Athens' main roads into the city centre and famous for its *bouzoukia* nightclubs, hookers and strip clubs, Syngrou Avenue is dangerous territory for pedestrians. Three lanes run in each direction, with cars, buses and motorbikes careering down it at breakneck speeds, swinging in and out of lanes and overtaking recklessly. A decade earlier, just as he'd done a thousand times before, Johnnie stood patiently on the sidewalk awaiting safe passage. Imagining a break in the traffic, he took a brisk jog, unfortunately coinciding his crossing with the untimely approach of a hurtling car. It hit him at such speed that Johnnie, in full rock regalia, was sent flying 15 metres into a street kiosk, sending crisps, pornographic magazines and packets of chewing gum flying all over the road. He spent the next month in hospital.

At this point, I should share what I'd heard it's like to do time in an Athenian public hospital. Private rooms are a dream, smoke-filled shared ones are not. Squeezing in as many visiting relatives as possible is compulsory. Families are sometimes expected to provide full-time care on site and supplement the small meals that are provided. And then there's the whole *fakelaki* system to contend with. *Fakelaki* literally means 'little envelope' and represents a kind of palm-greaser to subsidise doctors' government salaries. If *fakelaki* is refused, so, too, is first-class treatment. It's virtually compulsory. It's far preferable to stay out of harm's way and out of hospital.

Johnnie checked himself out of hospital as quickly as possible, but remained bedridden at home for months nursing a broken shoulder, leg and head. His leg was broken in sixteen places, the bone shattered to the consistency of breadcrumbs. To this day Johnnie has enough metal in his leg – and in his soul – to construct a light aircraft. So Johnnie was left with an Athenian battle wound in the form of a permanent limp. As he recounted the story, I visualised him in a hospital gown with a tartan cap adorning the ensemble.

My heart filled with pity. And not just because of the hat.

As his story concluded, we arrived at Theatro Petras in the suburb of Petroupoli. It was a rocky natural amphitheatre that wouldn't have looked out of place in the middle of the Nevada Desert. As we exited the cab, a squadron of Greek rockers advanced towards us like a swarm of flies. They recognised Johnnie Jackie Holliday, who apparently was well known on 'the scene'.

'Hki Tzonnie.'

'Tzonnie!'

'Yia Tzonnie, man!' ·

Johnnie took it all in his limping stride.

'Hey, maan!'

He doled out random high fives, looking cool and secretly wallowing in the attention. He was, after all, a rock star. I was shocked to hear him speak Greek fluently to a security guard.

Why does he speak such rudimentary Greek on the radio?

I tactfully broached the subject with the man himself.

'Why do you speak such fucked-up Greek on the radio?'

He didn't know what I was talking about.

'What, maan?'

With Star Star being the support act, we were able to mill about backstage. We made our way to the band area and began a torturous five-hour wait for live proceedings. Thankfully, I had plenty to busy myself with. A stream of people paraded before me, all known to Johnnie. The first person I met was Star Star's bass player, Weeds.

Weeds was a lanky New York Italian who peered at me from a slim, olive-tanned face framed by braids. Post-introduction he retreated fast in a pair of tight black leather pants in which I was certain an intricate irrigation system had sprung to life. Unlike Johnnie, he seemed dismissive and elusive.

Next up were two bottle-blonde Greek girls in their early thirties who exhibited something I'd never before encountered in a Greek person – an appreciation of *sarcasm*. In dialogue laced with it, we bagged out Johnnie, a guy I barely knew. I was loving it! They told me that Johnnie was the best friend a person could ever hope for. As I watched him limp around, his hat casting a cumulus-like shadow on the ground, I prayed like hell they were right. And *not* being sarcastic.

We chatted for hours, watching Alice Cooper's daughter, Calico, and the road crew play football in the dirt with a screwed-up piece of paper. Alice was nowhere to be seen.

With an audience of 8000 growing expectant, Johnnie took this as his cue to change outfits. He disappeared into the Green Room and quickly re-emerged all frocked up in a voluminous cotton housedress and buckled black boots. There were no traces of bashfulness or nervousness. According to him, he'd done this hundreds of times before. So as the scalding sun set, Star Star finally took to the stage with a ring-in session drummer. Onstage, Johnnie alternated between subtle aggression and unrestrained campishness. If nothing else, I was impressed that he could switch so effortlessly between the two. Notwithstanding, I giggled uncontrollably. The band exited to thunderous applause.

Later, Alice Cooper was chauffeured the 10 metres from his dressing room to the stage in a mammoth tour bus to avoid any interaction with backstage liggers. I found this almost as hilarious as Johnnie's dress. Cooper pulled off a superbly professional show, chock-full of classic rock theatrics, just the way I liked it. Surrounded by live music and colourful personalities, this was the closest I'd come to my old life in Australia in almost four years.

It would soon become apparent that Johnnie Jackie Holliday was the sum of many parts. There was Compassionate Johnnie, Bitchy Johnnie, Homely Johnnie and Childish Johnnie. While most people have similar aspects to their personality, Johnnie's would often emerge in exaggerated or even grotesque form. Thankfully, one of the more common contenders was Homely Johnnie. With a fetish for cooking and an incredibly generous nature, Homely Johnnie espoused the values usually held by elderly Greek women. He would invite friends to his tiny apartment and customarily begin serving. His black buckled boots would be replaced by house slippers and his mascara-smudged eyes would dart from condiment to condiment as he fished through crammed cupboards. Like a prancing rock'n'roll pixie governed by a Greek sense of providing, he'd bounce from wall to wall, clanging pots and pans while cooking up generous, oil-based feasts, driven by the old Greek woman within.

36

Last night a DJ saved my life

When pain becomes unbearable, the human psyche has an amazing capacity for all manner of weird and wonderful tricks. So how did mine respond to a failing marriage? By regressing, becoming a rebellious teen driven by the conviction that there can never be enough rock coursing through one's veins, of course. I proceeded directly to studded leather. And there was absolutely no way I *couldn't* see Judas Priest when they visited Athens. Being around music and people was the only thing that made me feel alive during this very confusing time.

I called Johnnie to find out how we could acquire tickets. To my utter disgust, Johnnie Jackie Holliday and Weeds, allegedly the biggest Priest fans this side of Turkey, needed convincing.

'No way, maan. I've seen them eighteen times already,' yelled Johnnie into the telephone receiver. I'd apparently been patched through to Bitchy Johnnie. In the background I could hear Weeds playing a Judas Priest bass line that demonstrated he could just as easily entertain himself.

'Eighteen times?'

'Yeah. *So?*' he yelled. He wasn't giving an inch.

'And they come to Athens and you don't want to see them? Are you *mad*? You call yourself a Priest fan? What would Rob Halford say? What would the Metal Gods make of someone so goddamned lame?'

'NO! I'm not going, Lana.'

'Oh, come on, Johnnie. Please?'

'Go with Dion, you crazy Australian freak!' he shouted, then half-covered the mouthpiece. 'Wow, this chick's burnt, man.'

Johnnie and Weeds were well aware that I was married, but they knew nothing of the associated turmoil. So I chose my response carefully. Bitchy Johnnie was somebody who certainly didn't need to hear about my relationship woes.

'I can't ask Dion. You don't understand how busy he is at the moment. Plus he doesn't like Priest. Not like we do. *Come on!*'

A few weeks later, Johnnie, Weeds and I were off to see Priest and all was as it should have been. Well . . . almost. Dion had fled the mainland, making a pilgrimage to his family island of Lesbos, by now both of us seeing to our own extracurricular activities. Before leaving, he'd revealed he wasn't completely comfortable with the idea of me fraternising with a man he'd never even met.

'So meet him then.'

'No, I don't want to.'

'See, that makes no sense to me.'

'In any event, the idea of you hanging out with him just doesn't sit right with me.'

'Doesn't sit right? So now that Tim's left, what do you expect me to do? Float about, friendless, while you do whatever the hell you want? Until I have another nervous breakdown?'

Dion thought for a moment, and then nodded.

'It's okay, I read you loud and clear. We both need friends. I get it.'

I was relieved.

'Thanks. I know it might seem strange, but since when have our lives ever been normal here?'

Dion nodded again. God, I still loved him so much. We'd been through so much together. In my heart of hearts, I knew we could still make it if we didn't give up. But one of us had given up more than the other.

Johnnie, Weeds and I arrived at a field in Malakasa, 45 kilometres from the centre of Athens. Nobody did bag searches upon entry, which was a good thing. I'd brought a plastic water bottle filled with Jack Daniel's and Coke to anaesthetise any deeper feelings that threatened to ruin my allegiance to rock'n'roll and my newfound friends. Deep within I felt dead, rejected and, more than anything, unlovable, but on the outside I appeared ecstatic. And I drank diligently. Johnnie, not so big on drinking, probably thought I was a bit of a loser.

Judas Priest was playing to a crowd of 50 000 as part of the annual Rockwave Festival. Unlike the metal crowd I anticipated, they were subdued, sober, well behaved and definitely nonviolent. I felt safer there than I did walking through Bankstown Shopping Centre in Sydney on a Saturday morning. Small pockets of long-haired males banged their heads, and that was as wild and crazy as things got.

The gig itself was amazing as we were far enough back not to notice that the studded leather jackets ambling across the stage were filled by mature-aged rockers. From our vantage point, vocalist Rob Halford looked as though riding onto the stage on a Harley Davidson rather than a pensioner's Shoprider was the most natural thing in the world to do. As Johnnie pre-empted each song on the set-list, having seen the band eighteen times and all, Weeds and I rocked along, laughing, having the time of our lives.

We celebrated afterwards by visiting the rock bar Texas back in Athens.

'Why does it feel like we've known each other forever, maan?' asked Johnnie, his puzzled black eyes widening. Owing to the J.D., the more I looked at him, the more he resembled a buzzard.

'Don't ask me. But it's a good thing, isn't it?'

'I guess so.'

Johnnie invited Dion and me to attend a *rembetika* night that offered an 'underground' Greek equivalent to the blues. He wanted to get to know Dion, having heard so much about him. He was completely oblivious to the trouble brewing in Lagonisi.

Since the turn of the twentieth century, *rembetika* has been hiding in Greece's shadowy underground scene. When 1.5 million Greek refugees came to re-settle in Greece from Asia Minor in the early 1900s, shantytowns began springing up around Athens. The working class and refugee communities melded. Musicians from the two groups met in hash dens where they threw back coffees and sucked on water pipes sizzling with the best hash Ellada had to offer. Ideas were exchanged. They were soon singing about opium, hashish and the woes of the world, and then later about gaol. It was the music of the poor and displaced. The music would often inspire the solitary dance of the stoned male that came to be known as the *zembekiko*. Featuring arms outstretched to the sides, downcast head and slow dramatic leg crosses and finger clicks, it's strangely comparable to the moves of the stoned Woodstock hippy.

Today *rembetika* is more highbrow than it was originally, and while the hash pipes and heroin aren't quite so prevalent, the lamenting remains.

When Dion returned from Lesbos, I told him that Johnnie had

invited us out with him to experience *rembetika* for ourselves. He refused the invitation.

'But *why* don't you want to meet him?'

'I just *don't*, okay?'

It widened the gap between us even further. I now understood how it felt for Dion when I'd refused to attend the countless christenings of his colleagues' children and the coffee evenings with Tasos and Despina, whom he now regarded as dear friends. I kept this understanding to myself, stifling the guilt I felt for the grand contribution I'd made to the mess we were now in.

Johnnie Jackie Holliday was such a rock'n'roll cliché at times that it would have been easy to misjudge him as a shallow deadhead, but I soon learned that he had a rare sensitivity, unusual for a man who didn't obsess over Judy Garland. If the situation demanded, he was open-minded, deeply compassionate and happy to share his store of hard-won wisdom.

As we became closer, I finally revealed the difficulties in my relationship with Dion and discovered how fortunate I was in my new choice of friend. Compassionate Johnnie would patiently listen to me for hours at a time and boy, did I ever need the support. He'd stop whatever rock activity he was indulging in and calmly listen like a gentle brother. With his trashy exterior, he was a living conundrum.

As I began shedding kilos faster than an Olsen Twin on the Atkins Diet, owing to an ongoing state of high anxiety, Johnnie took it upon himself to supervise my eating habits, force-feeding me home-cooked meals and supplying me with pieces of raw fish wrapped in paper, like a fussing Greek aunt. I was incredibly grateful, especially since I'd phased Aunty Nota out of my life due to the embarrassing state of my marital affairs. When I wasn't under

Johnnie's personal supervision, which was more often than not, he would regularly call to make enquiries about my weight and health, ensuring I didn't waste away to nothing. In the meantime, Dion arrived home late at night armed with takeaway food containers, fending for himself. Although Bitchy Johnnie was sure to highlight that he mostly saw me as a 'conservative square', Compassionate Johnnie took me under his wing. Like my parents, Kristie and Tim before him, Johnnie saw to my survival.

By now my alienation from Dion was reaching critical point, yet I continued to dangle spider-like from a thread of hope. We could still make it, I just knew it! But by now we had separate bedrooms. One day, I'd simply moved all my things into the spare room and gone into hiding. As far as I was concerned, it made no sense for us to be sharing the same bed, and Dion ran with the idea. In fact, he didn't even mention the new arrangement. The silence within the walls of my new bedroom was oppressive and I spent a great deal of time locked away in darkness, staring at nothing and wondering why the hell this all had to happen. My evil eye bracelet soon broke into a thousand pieces, its ocean-blue miniature eyeballs bouncing and skittling over the cool marble tiles of a lonely room.

While I had no Tim to party with, I did have Johnnie and Weeds. I drove into Athens one night to meet them, relieved to be escaping the heavy atmosphere of Lagonisi. From my driver's seat, I saw them waiting for me on a street corner, as always looking out of the ordinary: Johnnie with his jet-black eyes, jet-black hair, Herman Munster boots and one of his many silly hats; Weeds skinny and tall, with braided hair resting placidly on taut shoulders. They had no idea how important their company had become. I looked at them with immense fondness and admiration. Kemopetrol came on the radio, singing about angels dressed as junkies. The lyrics seemed oddly apt. These guys had become my personal seraphim and, as startling as they looked, the unlikely duo made me feel remarkably safe. Safe enough even to attend an Athenian goth club.

Rebound is tucked away on Plateia Amerikis (America Square) in the centre of Athens, its exact location available only to those indoctrinated into a dark sect with its own version of the Satanic Bible written in goat's blood, or so I hypothesised. At midnight, we descended a steep staircase into the depths of a large, cavernous club. The final sounds we heard on the street were yowls from a pair of feral cats in the throes of passion.

Although I'd worn all black, I had no real hope of passing myself off as a goth and felt a little conspicuous. I knew I looked more like a mother poised for tuckshop duty than I did 'underground'. I felt old and silly. Johnnie, who apparently didn't, worked the room. Weeds and I made our way across the club, our shoes sticking to the floor as we walked. We propped ourselves at the end of a large oval bar and ordered fake Johnnie Walkers.

The place was obligingly dark. A bass-heavy Siouxsie and The Banshees track droned in the background. Black-clad Greek teenagers with big, teased hair lined the walls in small booths smoking and looking despondent. But as they greeted Johnnie with smiles and friendly pats on the back, they betrayed their true natures.

As Xmal Deutschland took over where Siouxsie left off, a goth girl, all of fifteen years, suddenly sprang to life. She wore monster boots that rivalled Johnnie's, fishnet stockings, a short black skirt, a bondage-style patent-leather top and a choker. Her lips were ruby red, her eyes pots of black oil, her skin pale, but her beautiful flowing blonde hair gave her away – she hadn't yet graduated to fully fledged goth. But right then and there, she was hoping to go up a grade.

She took to the small dance floor, the only person daring to display any real signs of life. Holding an invisible whip, she proceeded
to mime the act of lashing an unseen carcass that lay somewhere
around her feet, her face contorted in an expression of gritted,
sadistic determination. Everyone in the club ignored her except
me. I was mesmerised. I turned to Weeds with an amused smile.
He was ignoring her too.

Even before the Xmal track had concluded, Johnnie came limping back towards us, breaking my concentration.

'Let's get outta herre! This place sucks! It's dead, maaan. Let's
go to Revenge.'

Apparently, in the space of five minutes, Johnnie and one of
his personalities had had an argument.

'Revenge? What's that? Another goth club?' My fingers were
crossed.

'Revenge of ROCK. It's a rock club, Lana. Derrrrrr!'

I would have protested, not just at the 'derrrrrr' punctuating the
latter sentence, but at leaving a club that was so intriguing to me.
However, checking out a place called Revenge of Rock sounded
equally appealing. Before I knew it, Johnnie, Weeds and I had
resurfaced at street level and were hailing a taxi. The cat, copping
it sweet in some alley, continued to wail.

Revenge of Rock is one of the biggest treats that Athens has to
offer . . . if you happen to have an undying passion for studded
wristbands, long knotted hair and old-school heavy rock, and if your
testosterone levels exceed those of the Italian World Cup soccer
team combined. Three times the size of Texas, the club is located
on Leoforos Alexandras (Alexandra Boulevard). Despite it having
a 99 to 1 male to female ratio, Johnnie entered the premises as
though entering the Playboy Mansions.

'Where are all the chicks, maaan?'

His reaction made no sense. According to Weeds, there were *never* any 'chicks' at Revenge of Rock. The place was packed to the rafters with metal dudes obstructing an enormous screen that covered the far wall. A Van Halen live clip played. In between hedges of hair, I could just make out a pair of legs in pink spandex tights attempting mid-air splits. Then David Lee Roth's sweating brow filled the screen. Most looked up in worship, their long hair moving rhythmically.

Aside from the big, blonde, metal babe working behind the bar and myself, there were no other women in sight. I scanned the perimeters, searching for anyone else of my gender, but was not prepared for what I saw next. Propped up on top of the bar was an older man with long, dark hair falling past his shoulders. Part biker, part aging crone, he wore a large black cowboy hat shadowing a weathered, moustached face covered with protruding moles. It was as though he'd been accused of witchery, tied to a stake and pummelled with soggy Coco Pops. Upon closer inspection, my eyes bulged as I identified him as Lemmy Kilmister, demented bass-playing frontman of seminal British metal band Motörhead. I got the impression that Lemmy, too, was scanning the room for anyone, anyone *at all*, who could pass for female.

'Ohmygod! Guys – Weeds! Johnnie! Look who's sitting on the bar. It's *Lemmy*! What the hell's *he* doing here?'

'Yeah, Motörhead are playing Athens this week, maan. Don't you chicks know anything?' Johnnie looked at Weeds and rolled his eyes.

'They're playing at the beach near Paleo Faliro. But don't you start, Lana! There's no freakin' way I'm goin', maan,' he added. 'No way.' He held up a finger to ward off what he knew would come next.

'Are you shitting me?'

'I'll go, maan,' Weeds piped in, making a lot more sense than his tartan-capped friend. Johnnie shot him a dirty look.

I looked back up at Lemmy, still stunned that he was in Athens, let alone within spitting distance. At the same moment, Lemmy looked in our direction and his eyes stopped on me. *Me*. The solitary woman. In a rock club. A rock club with its very foundations creaking beneath the weight of compounded male hormones. I broke eye contact and focused intensely on the wooden floor.

'Guys, can we go now? I've gotta get home.'

We did end up seeing Motörhead – kind of. We really only *heard* them and that was only if the wind was blowing in the right direction. The concert was set on a long, extremely narrow stretch of beach. It was quite possibly the most poorly organised event I'd ever attended. In the brain-baking Athenian heat, support bands begged the crowd to supply them with water since the promoters had failed to do so. From what I could determine, there were two toilets provided for the entire audience of a couple of thousand. Still, we did have the ocean at our disposal.

We heard later that the promoter skipped town as the gig played out. The windows of his home were smashed – the revenge of rock actualised.

(This is) the end

I awoke one morning with a knot in my stomach. My marriage was over. Despite more than a year of trying to fix it, and praying for Dion to come around, things would never be the same again. I telephoned Dion at work and asked him to come home. We needed to talk. We needed to talk *now*, face to face. He obliged.

We sat on deckchairs facing one another, the ocean behind us rough and uninviting. I explained that I'd arrived at a decision. From that day forward, we would officially be separated, continuing to live separate lives under the same roof until I made my next move.

'Okay,' Dion replied, his face drawn.

'I thought we could get things on track, but look at us. We've evolved into two completely different people so . . . ' There was silence as my words evaporated.

' . . . so it's probably for the best,' Dion finished. 'I'm sorry.'

'I'm sorry too, Dion. So, so sorry.' My eyes stung and I could barely swallow. Dion couldn't stand to see me disintegrate into tears. He walked back into the house. I walked in the opposite direction, and threw myself into the sea, fully clothed. I needed to feel alive. I felt anything but. I began hyperventilating, thrashing about in the water, sinking beneath the surface, waves slapping me in the face when I finally re-emerged, gasping for breath. As I fought for air, my new reality hurricaned through my mind. A marriage that was meant to last forever was dead. This was *not* the way things were supposed to happen.

I'm surrounded by people who offer no love or understanding. A faceless figure is being particularly cruel to me. I remain friendly, pretending not to notice until it takes my left hand and wordlessly points at my engagement ring. It laughs a tight, malicious laugh. I look down to see that two of the prongs that hold my diamond in place have been loosened. Mockingly, the figure produces a diamond from its pocket and shows it to me. It's identical to the one in my engagement ring. I don't know which diamond is real and which is fake.

I begin screaming for my brother, a desperate sadness filling my heart. I know that the diamonds represent my marriage, that they represent me and Dion. But I don't know him any more. I don't know myself any more. I can't trust anybody.

My brother floats into the picture as I'm consumed by grief. I hold out my ring finger and, sobbing with all the innocence and pain of a child, I wail:

'Why did I ever come to this place? WHY? It has fucked up my life. Greece has completely fucked up my life.'

I cry so deeply that I wake from the dream in agonising grief. The pain is indescribable.

A fortnight later, driving along the jaw-droppingly amazing coastline from Glyfada to Lagonisi, I came to an irrevocable decision – to make the separation permanent. Over the past two weeks, Dion had shown no sign of wishing to reverse the arrangement. He was no longer in love. My life with him was over. My life in Greece was over. I wasn't unhappy about the leaving Greece part, but was devastated about leaving Dion. I thought of him every second of that drive home, oblivious to the brilliant blue sea below, the blinding sunshine, the silk-blue sky. The stunning scenery could not inspire happiness. It never had. I thought of Dion's patience and sweetness in earlier times. Despite all the shit we'd been through, I still looked upon him lovingly and without a sense of blame. As one of Dion's radio stations saturated Athens with Coldplay melancholy, I understood my husband's transition was the result of a lifetime of passive cultural conditioning that sprang to life in the perfect environment. I knew his change in character and inability to tear himself away from Greece was never intentional and that my resistance had also played its part. But I also knew we'd have to let go of one another. As I listened to the song, I heard the old Dion speaking through the voice of Coldplay frontman Chris Martin about never meaning to cause me trouble, never meaning to do me wrong.

I broke the news to Dion that night. We sat stiffly opposite each other in our lounge room, our conversation almost business-like.

'I'm leaving Greece in a month's time. My tickets have been booked and I'll be moving temporarily to London and then back to Australia. Is it okay if I pack my things and have you send them once I'm settled?'

'Sure, that won't be a problem. What work will you be doing?' he asked softly.

'I'm going to work for a music management company. Leonie told me about a small job that's going.'

'Oh. That will be good for you, to finally be working again.'

As I looked at Dion, he seemed more than ever like a small boy. And my heart ached.

We civilly discussed the logistics of separation, but underneath, an unfathomable, painful regret lurked. I certainly felt it, and I'm sure I saw it in Dion's eyes, too. Mostly, however, I watched him carefully restrain his emotions, something he'd mastered over time. What he wanted me to see was that he was happy for me, and he demonstrated a surety that this was 'for the best'.

'It's gonna be okay,' he soothed as my face creased in anguish. Hadn't I heard that somewhere before?

We'd arrived in Greece during the 2000 Olympic Games, clinging to one another, all set for an adventure. Now, during the 2004 Games in Athens, here we were separating and making pained attempts to avoid one another. The bitter irony of the Olympic Games neatly book-ending our relationship was duly noted.

Still, the Games were a welcome disruption. Maria – my short-lived friend acquired through a newspaper advertisement – decided at the last minute to go Olympics crazy, and bought multiple tickets to multiple events. Unfortunately, she had ended up playing only a bit part in my life, our relationship lost in the craziness of a marriage demise and me running wildly from my pain via a rekindled fascination for rock'n'roll. Once she'd become aware of our situation, however, she sought to ensure that I wasn't left alone in the house surrounded by sharp objects and invited me along to every event going. In an effort to remain neutral, she asked both Dion and me if we'd like to attend the Opening Ceremony. It would be Maria, her husband Themis, Dion and myself. The idea of stepping out as a couple and celebrating Greek culture wasn't exactly something I was gagging for. Being a historic occasion, however, I relented. Dion accepted too.

In the years leading up to the Games, Dion and I had often speculated about what the opening ceremony might be like. Laughing, we decided it would either be dismal, with folk dancers holding makeshift olive branches made out of papier mâché, or over-the-top, with acrobats dressed in electric blue spandex flying through the air above pyrotechnic displays. In our wildest dreams, we never thought it would mark the end of our relationship.

In the end it was a classy and – for us – bittersweet affair. Maria was so moved by the ceremony she burst into tears, which nearly made me do likewise, but mainly because I felt like a war widow *and* because I was embarrassed by her unexpected patriotic outburst. Despite the awkwardness it was an unforgettable evening. The hideousness of our situation became lost in an artistic demonstration of Greek history backed by ancillary Mexican waves, whistle blowing, fireworks, Olympic spirit, solidarity and friendship. The only thing that brought me crashing back to Earth was the sight of the Australian team marching past in the most preposterous uniforms I'd ever seen, a murky trail of brown, green and yellow that reminded me of the dolmades I'd attempted to make many years earlier. To my dismay, I couldn't spot swimming genius Ian Thorpe anywhere. I could only assume he'd refused to be seen in public wearing such regalia.

During the Olympics, I stared at the walls of my room for hours at a time. I'd taken up smoking and now chained away as heavily as Dion, willing the excruciating hours to pass. How Dion and I held onto our sanity during this time, I'll never know.

In the meantime, Greece positively relished in proving the world wrong. Despite extreme disorganisation leading up to the Games, everything was ready on time. Although the Elgin Marbles were never returned, the city of Athens had been transformed. We now had a much tidier city with a vastly improved infrastructure, due to the introduction of light rail, a brand-new airport and a new city freeway. And the population now smiled acceptingly as they welcomed visitors from all over the world. With our marital relations being what they were, Dion and I could only take this in with heavy hearts.

And by this point, an improved Athens? Like I gave a shit.

Epilogue

So today's my final day in Greece. Alone in Lagonisi for the last time, I pack another cardboard box full of bits and pieces that only serve to convince me that my roller-coaster ride was taken in vain. I pack away my study pack for a counselling diploma I never completed. I pack away literature on hypnotherapy, a 'hobby' I never mastered. I leave the iron behind.

I flick through a notebook I find on our office desk. A page headed *Who Am I?* opens to mock me. Beneath the heading, paragraph after paragraph scribed in crazed handwriting reveals a personality struggling to define itself, but with more questions than answers. I tear pages out and screw them up, throwing paper missiles across the room. Another page reveals itself, full of notes following my commitment to stay in Greece for the next decade with headings such as *Make More Friends* and *Find Things To Do* underlined, and methods of achieving such goals listed below in bullet-point form. Again I feel mocked.

Worse, I see memorabilia at every turn, on every shelf, around every corner – reminders of a deep love shared between two inno-cents that vanished in the blink of an eye. Sadly I see the last four years of my life wasted. I cry out loud because today Greece is the bitchiest I've ever known her to be . . . and to make matters worse, I'm convinced she thinks she's won.

I return to our lounge room, passing Valentine's Day cards, anniversary cards and a framed wedding photo. I sit on the sofa with my head in my hands, trying to collect my thoughts. I refuse to be defeated. I run through the reasons why I could still win this game, if only on a technicality. I tell myself that living in Greece afforded me the opportunity to live a different kind of life: a life of travel, a life of privilege. I remind myself of friendships with immortal angels like Tim and Johnnie, and the host of other people who picked me up and re-ignited my spirit when the flame of my soul had all but extinguished. People who showed me that individuals not only need a sense of purpose, but one another. I recall Tim's mock vanity, Johnnie's outrageous hats. And in spite of my situation, I catch myself in a half-smile.

While doing time in Greece may have ended a marriage, it didn't end a friendship. Dion and I remain friends. In fact, as friends, we love one another dearly and always will. I'm one of the few who understands his transition, if only for having been on the same path at the same time. Well, I kind of understand, anyway. I will forever be indebted to Dion for attempting to play the roles of husband, breadwinner, parent, brother, friend, lover and counsellor all rolled into one. Let's face it: I was high maintenance. I'm the first to admit that the peculiarities I experienced in Greece were, for the most part, exaggerated by a mind that felt as though it had been chucked into a high-speed blender. I was a victim of culture shock. It was never easy for Dion, just as it was never easy for me. Neither of us could have predicted a lifetime's worth of dormant culture springing to life in him. And who knew I didn't possess the coping mechanisms required for integration?

My time in Greece also forced me to look at the idea of tolerance more closely. 'Tolerance' is not my favourite word. To begin with, it suggests a need to tolerate that which is intolerable – usually something or some*one* different. I often felt I was that someone. I was also guilty of thinking the same way about others. As I see-sawed between being tolerant and tolerated, I was tested in a thousand different ways. And I gained an understanding of what people face all over the world as they attempt to begin new lives in foreign countries. The day-to-day challenges are so often over-looked. Obviously, this book was never intended as a critical analysis of Greece. And for the record, the innocent guidebook being shaped by my extremely limited experiences eventually mutated into what you now hold in your hands.

Now I'm smiling. I've won because I'm regaining the independence I had relinquished for four long years. I'm moving to a place where I can express myself, be understood and once again feel like a normal part of society. No matter how privileged I once was, from this day forward I will be free from a familiar yet nagging sense of compromise.

I sit on the couch, and Cleany creeps silently through our glass sliding doors, daringly sitting just inside the house. Facing me square on, his wide yellow eyes observe mine filling with tears. Too many have spilled in this country. Through blurred vision, the cat's face appears less aggressive, almost compassionate. He lets out a soft, soothing *meow*. I've never heard a sound from him before beyond an ominous hiss. It's the tamest act he's demonstrated over the past two years. I move towards him and for the first time ever, he remains still as I approach. My sobs dissipating, I reach out a hand and, miraculously, he allows me to stroke his filthy, gritted coat. As with Greece, it seems that an unspoken acceptance has finally been reached between us, an acceptance that arrives just that little bit too late.

Author's note

In August 2006, long before any publishing interest in this book, I returned to Athens. I'd completed the first draft of *To Hellas and Back* a year earlier and the plan was to do some research on some of the places I'd written about, to re-experience Athens, to *feel* it once again so I could double check the authenticity of all I had written.

As my plane descended, I found myself once again mesmerised by the beauty of Greece. Through a tiny plane window, I gazed down upon the shimmering expanse of blue, the islands and the varied landscape, a utopian, dream-like portrait. Of course, this didn't stop me from hyperventilating. Like you didn't see *that one* coming! Yeah, I pretty much lost it and cried like a big, fat baby while a million memories jackhammered my consciousness. Fidgeting uncomfortably in my seat, I felt like hightailing it straight back to London before I'd even landed.

But land I did, and one of the first places I visited was Labrou Katsoni. Standing outside that innocent-looking building, I couldn't quite believe it had been the place where I'd experienced all that I'd experienced. As I wilted on the pavement outside, I realised this visit was going to be less about closure and more about traumatising myself half to death! Whose bright idea was it to come back to Athens anyway? Oh, that's right. It was mine. Couldn't I just forget about this stinking book? Then I caught up with Johnnie Jackie Holliday and all was right with the world. Of course he wore his trademark tartan cap, of course I sniggered to myself at the sight of it, and of course he was as complex and beautiful as ever.

I also found myself cavorting with a certain Greek guy who felt more than a little familiar. Over the course of a couple of weeks, we visited some of the most beautiful places just outside the city that I hadn't known existed – Mati, Loutsa and Skinias. I met some of the most incredible, funny and warm-hearted people who welcomed me without question. I chatted to people in taxis, in shops and on beaches. And I noticed something striking – everyone who crossed my path was friendly and, well, nothing short of wonderful! And I'm talking *everyone!* Within the circles I was mixing and out on the streets, I watched in awe as people looked out for one another and shared an uninhibited sense of camaraderie. And they were beautiful enough to include me. *Me!* The girl who'd just written an entire book about not understanding the country and culture in which they belonged! God, there was so much to this place. I'd barely scratched the surface.

This again highlighted an earlier realisation of mine that what you expect is indeed what you get. Generous, sociable people gravitated towards me on this visit because – in a positive, holiday frame of mind – that's precisely what I expected. In the good ol' days I was always bracing myself for quite the opposite and nine times out of ten the opposite was forthcoming. It also struck me just how much Athens had changed since Dion and I had first moved there. Post-Olympics, the place had maintained and worn its facelift well in the true spirit of Anna Vissi!

Though it was only a fleeting visit, something clicked and, unbelievably, I even found myself open to the idea of a new romance. And there you were thinking I'd never be mad enough to tempt history to repeat itself. Today I wonder if a happy ending isn't completely out of the question after all.